Cryptocu

CH01457404

+
NFT for Beginners
+
Metaverse Investing

The Complete Guide to Boost your
Portfolio and create a Passive Income
on Web 3.0

Easy Blockchain Academy

Tables of Contents

The purpose of this document is to provide accurate and reliable information about the topic and subject at hand. The book is sold to understand that the publisher is not obligated to provide accounting, legally allowed, or otherwise qualifying services. If legal or professional counsel is required, a well-versed specialist should be consulted. A Committee of the American Bar Association and a Committee of Publishers and Associations recognized and approved the Declaration of Principles. No portion of this publication may be reproduced, duplicated, or transmitted in any form, whether electronic or printed. It is strictly forbidden to record this publication, and any storing of this material is only permitted with the publisher's prior consent. All intellectual property rights are reserved.

The data shown here is said to be accurate and consistent. Any liability arising from the use or misuse of any policies, processes, or directions included here, whether due to inattention or otherwise, is solely and completely the responsibility of the receiving reader. Under no circumstances will the publisher be held liable for any compensation, damages, or monetary loss incurred due to the material included herein, whether directly or indirectly. All copyrights not held by the publisher belong to the authors. The material provided here is solely for educational purposes and is therefore universal. The information is presented without any type of contract or guarantee assurance.

The trademarks are utilized without the trademark owner's permission or backing, and the trademark is published without the trademark owner's permission or backing. All trademarks and brands mentioned in this book are the property of their respective owners and are not linked with this publication.

CRYPTOCURRENCY FOR BEGINNERS

How to Master Blockchain, Defi and start Investing in Bitcoin & Altcoins

Easy Blockchain Academy

Chapter 1:

Cryptocurrency Basics and

Blockchain components

The term "cryptocurrency" refers to a digital currency developed via encryption techniques. Cryptocurrencies are both money and virtual accounting systems, thanks to encryption technology. You'll need a cryptocurrency wallet if you want to start using cryptocurrencies. These wallets might be software kept on your computer or mobile device, or they can be cloud-based services. Your encryption keys, which verify your identity and connect you to your bitcoin, are stored in your wallets.

Basic Knowledge to Know
It is a store of value, a medium of trade, and a unit of measurement all rolled into one. Cryptocurrencies are used to price other assets, notwithstanding their low intrinsic worth. A cryptocurrency, Bitcoin may also be seen as a speculative commodity (how much is it trading for) since it was established in 2009 and is primarily regarded as the first digital asset in existence. Blockchain and encryption have made it feasible for digital assets, often known as crypto assets, to exist. Their initial purpose was to act as a medium to transfer value without a bank or other third-party trustworthy party, and they succeeded in that goal. Digital assets (crypto assets) may be divided into cryptocurrency, commodity, and token categories. Cryptocurrencies linked to solid assets like the U.S. dollar may become an essential part of decentralized finance in the future (Defi).
To comprehend cryptocurrencies, you need also grasp the following technologies and principles:

Cryptography

Users' data and transactions are protected using cryptography, the science of scrambling and decrypting digitally signed bits of information. The term "crypto" is a euphemism for hidden or secret in the Greek language. Personal writing, or "cryptography," is the capacity to send messages that their intended recipients can only read. Cryptographic technology may provide pseudo- or true anonymity when configured correctly, depending on the settings. Encryption is used in cryptocurrency to ensure the safety of transactions and participants and the independence of operations from a central authority.

Sending encrypted communications is the most straightforward kind of cryptography, it is a method in which communication is encrypted or hidden by the sender and then decrypted by the recipient using a specified key and algorithm. In the most basic cryptography, the sender encrypts a message using a specified key and algorithm and sends the encrypted message to the receiver. Then the receiver decrypts it to decode it.

Blockchain

Bitcoin and other cryptocurrencies are built on blockchain technology. All transactions are recorded on a public ledger that is updated in real-time. The revolutionary aspect of blockchain is that it eliminates the need for a central authority, such as a bank, government, or payments business, to handle transactions. There's no need for a trusted third-party intermediary since the contracting parties interact directly. As a result, companies and services may operate independently and without expensive intermediaries.

For one thing, blockchain technology is accessible to all parties involved. Like Google Docs, the ledger may be accessed simultaneously and in real-time by various parties. When you write a check to a buddy, the cheque is deposited in the modern world, and both of you balance your checkbooks simultaneously. If your buddy forgets to update their checkbook ledger, or Things might go awry if you don't have enough cash on hand to cover the cheque. (when there is no way for the bank to foresee).

You and your partner would see the same transaction log if you use blockchain. Both of you must approve and validate the transaction before it can be put into the chain since the ledger is not under your control. Even more importantly, no one can alter the chain after the fact because of cryptography.

Distributed Ledger Technology (DLT) encompasses blockchain, a database shared by several parties (computers, servers, nodes, etc.) **Distributed Ledger Technology (DLT)**This technique powers a whole coin. Accounts, balances, and transactions are all recorded in a digital ledger. Other than financial transactions, blockchain may be used to manage supply chains, monitor ownership of art, and even create digital treasures.

Node In addition to the phrase "blockchain," we'll use the term "node" throughout this essay. A node is a piece of the broader blockchain data structure. The whole system would disintegrate if there were no nodes.

Digital currencies rely on cryptography and blockchain to generate new coins, verify transactions, and build a safe system.

De-Centralized

Blockchain's decentralized means transferring power and decision-making from a centralized entity (person, organization, or group) to a distributed network. The goal of decentralized networks is to lower the degree of confidence that users must invest in one another and dissuade their capacity to assert authority or control over one another in a manner that degrades the network's performance.

All authority is shared across the network's peers, and there is no single point of failure, as shown by Bitcoin's decentralization. To "hack" Bitcoin, someone would need access to at least 51% of the machines that make up the Bitcoin network, which is regarded unfeasible.

Peer-To-Peer

Cryptocurrencies have the advantage of not requiring the involvement of a financial institution as a middleman. Because there is no "middleman," transaction costs are reduced for merchants. Customers benefit greatly if the financial system is breached or the user has faith in the conventional method. For comparison, if a bank's database were compromised or corrupted, it would be forced to recover any lost data from its backups. Even if a piece of a cryptocurrency were to be hacked, the remaining components would still verify transactional information.

There is no requirement for a third-party intermediary to facilitate cryptocurrency transfer. Users may avoid the significant transaction costs associated with conventional money transfer services thanks to minimal processing fees paid to the network. No PayPal or bank account is required.

Bitcoin Story

Investors' excitement and unhappiness with Bitcoin's potential alternatively reflect on the currency's price swings. Anonymous Bitcoin creator Satoshi Nakamoto created the currency for everyday transactions and to avoid conventional banking systems after the 2008 financial meltdown. It has since acquired popularity as a medium of exchange and attracted traders who bet against the currency's price fluctuations. As a result, it has evolved into a new investment that serves as both a store of wealth and a hedge against inflation. Even while this new story may have more validity, the past price swings were driven mainly by individual investors and traders wagering against a rising price without many bases in reason or facts.

In recent years, though, Bitcoin's pricing narrative has evolved. The cryptocurrency markets are maturing, and regulatory bodies are developing regulations expressly for institutional investors. Even though the price of Bitcoin is still fluctuating, it is no longer a tool for speculators seeking quick riches.

The following is a brief history of Bitcoin:

2009 TO 2015

At its inception in 2009, Bitcoin had no value. This product's price went to $.09 on July 17, 2010. From $1 on April 13, 2011, to a high of $29.60 on June 7, 2021, Bitcoin's price increased by 2,960 percent in three months. Bitcoin's price fell to a low of $2.05 in mid-November after a substantial decline in cryptocurrency markets. The next year, it rose from $4.85 on May 9 to $13.50 on August 15 of the same year. For Bitcoin, 2012 was a relatively quiet year, but 2013 witnessed a significant increase in the currency's value. In January, it was trading at $13.28; on April 8th, it was trading at $230; on July 4th, it was trading at $68.50. It was selling at $123.00 in October, and by December, it had soared to $1,237.55 before falling to $687.02 three days later. The value of Bitcoin fell to $315.21 by the end of 2014.

2016 To 2020

Coins like Ethereum and Litecoin have emerged to challenge Bitcoin's dominance in the digital currency market. Over the year, prices gradually increased to over $900. At the beginning of the year, the cost of Bitcoin was approximately $1,000, but it rose to almost $19,000 on December 15 after breaking the $2,000 barrier. For the following two years, Bitcoin's price hovered in a narrow range with occasional spurts of activity. As an example, in June 2019, the cost of bitcoin surpassed $10,000, and the volume of trade surged. By the middle of December, it had dropped to $6,635.84. When the COIVD-19 epidemic struck in 2020, Bitcoin's price surged to new heights. Bitcoin was valued at $6,965.72 at the beginning of the year. Government policies during the epidemic closure added fuel to investors' anxieties about the global economy, which in turn fueled the ascent of Bitcoin. On November 23, the price of one bitcoin was $19,157.16. By the end of 2020, the cost of one bitcoin had risen by 416 percent, too little under $29,000.

2021-Present

By January 7, 2021, the bitcoin price had risen over $40,000, shattering the previous record set in the year 2020. A new all-time high in Bitcoin value of almost $60,000 was reached when cryptocurrency exchange Coinbase went public in mid-April. Thanks to this increased demand, institutional buying pushed Bitcoin's price to $63,000 on April 12, 2021. By the summer of 2021, prices had fallen by half to $29,795.55 on July 19. In September, prices hit $52,693.32 before plunging to $40,709.59 after a significant drop. On November 7, 2021, Bitcoin reached a new record high, reaching $67,549.14. In early December 2021, Bitcoin was trading at $49,243.39.

Decentralized Finance

Using distributed ledgers like those used by cryptocurrencies, Defi is an emerging financial technology. Banking and financial institutions are no longer in charge of the money, economic goods, and services.

Defi has several appealing features for users, including:

- Banks and other financial institutions no longer charge fees for utilizing their services.
- Instead of putting your money in a bank, you use a safe digital wallet.
- Anyone with an internet connection may use it without getting permission from a manager.
- In a matter of seconds or minutes, you can move money throughout the world.

Understanding Defi

Understanding how centralized finance differs from Defi is essential to comprehend how Defi operates.

Centralized Finance

Banks, for-profit businesses whose only purpose is to earn money, hold your cash under centralized finance. Several third parties enable money transfers between parties, each collecting a charge in the financial system. Suppose, for example, that you use your credit card to buy a gallon of milk. Credit card networks get the information from the acquiring bank, passing it to the merchant.

The network contacts your bank to collect payment for the cleared charge. After the acquiring bank has approved the bill, the network transmits the approval back to the merchant. For the most part, retailers must pay for the privilege of using your credit and debit cards. In addition to the high cost of other financial activities, loan applications might take days to be accepted, and you may not be allowed to utilize a bank's services while abroad.

Decentralized Finance(Defi)

Financial transactions may now be carried out directly between individuals, corporations, and merchants using new technologies. To do this, peer-to-peer networks require security protocols, connection, software, and hardware developments to make this possible. Using software that records and validates financial transactions in distributed financial databases, you may lend, trade, and borrow from wherever you have an internet connection. In a distributed database, all users may access the same information, and the database utilizes a consensus technique to verify that the data is correct.

Decentralized finance leverages modern technology to abolish centralized finance models by making financial services available to anybody, independent of their identity or location. Personal wallets and trade services tailored to the needs of people are available via Defi apps, giving consumers more control over their money. However, decentralized finance does not guarantee anonymity, even while taking external parties' authority away. The organizations that have access to your data can track your transactions even if you don't. This might be a government agency, a law enforcement agency, or any other entity that exists to defend the financial interests of individuals.

- Financial transactions may now be completed without the involvement of third parties, thanks to Defi, a kind of decentralized finance.
- Defi is made up of stable coins, software, and hardware that can build apps.
- Regulation and infrastructure for Defi are currently being developed and debated.
- Two of Devi's primary objectives are reducing transaction times and making financial services more widely available.

Working Of DeFi

The blockchain technology that cryptocurrencies use is used in decentralized finance. A distributed and secure database or ledger is known as a blockchain. Decentralized applications, or dApps, power the blockchain. Transactions are recorded in blocks on the blockchain and then cross-verified by other people. In this case, the block is closed and encrypted; a new block that contains information about the preceding one is produced.

The word "blockchain" refers to the fact that each block is linked to the previous one by the information contained in the preceding one. There is no method to edit a blockchain since information in prior blocks cannot be modified without impacting the succeeding ones. A blockchain is safe because of these and other security mechanisms.

Defi Crypto Trading

Another use of decentralized finance is the use of decentralized exchanges. Digital currencies are often held and moved through a system of titles or ownership via regular exchanges. Coins are not stored in a central location or function in a decentralized exchange. The exchange or organization enables, safeguards, and secures a peer-to-peer operation. Binance operates as a controlled exchange. The cryptocurrencies that are traded on Binance are held in a single location.

Founded by the Binance organization, Binance Dex is a decentralized exchange. The buyer and seller negotiate the transfer of cryptocurrency shares from one account to another. Binance Dex facilitates transactions and often charges a transaction fee for buyers and sellers.

One of Koinal's primary partners is Binance, a prominent cryptocurrency exchange that sells Defi goods (Binance Dex). You may use decentralized exchanges like Binance Dex and Koinal to buy cryptocurrencies that you can then trade or sell as you see fit.

Defi Financial Products

Defi is based on the idea of peer-to-peer (P2P) financial transactions. Two parties agree to trade cryptocurrencies for products or services, and a third party is engaged in a P2P Defi transaction. Consider the process of applying for a loan in centralized finance to grasp this properly. To get one, you'd need to apply at your bank or another lending institution. To use the lender's services, you'd have to pay interest and service fees if you were approved.

There are several ways to make a payment on your dApp, and they all go through a similar sequence of events. Using a dApp, you would submit your loan requirements, and an algorithm would match you up with other borrowers that fit your criteria. To get your money, you'd have to agree to one of the lender's conditions. It is recorded on the blockchain, and you will get your loan when the consensus process validates it. Finally, you may start making the agreed-upon repayments to your loan provider.

DeFi Currency

For transactions, DeFi is meant to work with bitcoin. It is impossible to predict how current cryptocurrencies will be applied, if at all, since technology is continuously evolving. A stable coin, a cryptocurrency backed by an institution or tied to a fiat currency like the dollar, is a crucial part of the idea.

The Future of Defi
The field of decentralized finance is still in its infancy. There are many infrastructure errors, hacks, and frauds to contend with in the uncontrolled cryptocurrency environment.

As a result of distinct financial jurisdictions, the regulations that now govern the financial industry were developed. The potential of Defi to conduct borderless transactions raises important issues for this form of code. For example, who is responsible for investigating a financial crime across international boundaries, protocols, and Defi apps?
Existing financial regulations may potentially be challenged by the open and dispersed character of the decentralized finance ecosystem. System stability, energy consumption, and carbon imprint are other issues to consider.
Before Defi can be safely used, there are still a lot of unanswered concerns and breakthroughs to be made. If Defi works, it's more than probable that banks and companies will find methods to get into the system; if not to control how you access your money, then at least to earn money from the system. Financial institutions will not give up one of their key sources of generating money.

Chapter 2:

Basic Trading Strategies

Other asset classes haven't been able to keep up with the advances. One technique for investing in Bitcoin is to purchase and hold. Holding cryptocurrencies like bitcoin has been a beneficial long-term strategy. This is particularly true during crypto bull markets when corrections tend to be brief. However, investors must keep in mind that Bitcoin and other cryptocurrencies are very speculative investments and should be treated.

The previous performance of an investment does not guarantee future success. There is a slew of options available to those who want to try their hand at day trading. Technical analysis may be one of the most popular trading tactics since it has spawned whole communities of traders. Short-term traders must have a trading strategy based on rules to succeed. The following are five methods for trading cryptocurrencies throughout the day.

Technical Analysis
Technical analysis (TA) uses mathematical indicators and chart patterns to anticipate the direction of prices. Humans are required to identify specific technical indicators, such as the RSI. In contrast, others may be created by a computer tool like Trading View (For example, the cup-and-handle design).
The relative strength index (RSI) is a well-liked technical indicator (RSI). Charts with a value between 0 and 100 will show this as a single line. The more the RSI approaches 100, the more overbought the market is considered to be, indicating that prices may fall. As the RSI approaches zero, oversold circumstances are believed to exist, which might lead to a surge in prices. When it comes to day-trading cryptocurrencies, TA may be a helpful tool.

Sentiment Analysis and the News
The cryptocurrency market may be moved swiftly by significant news events on occasion. Short-term traders may not utilize headlines and general market mood, but it may still be employed in day-trading Bitcoin. When this article was first published in mid-April 2021, Turkey declared that it would no longer accept Bitcoin and other cryptocurrencies as payment alternatives inside its borders.

An immediate 3.2 percent drop in Bitcoin's value was followed by more than a 10 percent drop afterward. The mood of the most popular cryptocurrencies may also be tracked by examining Twitter activity. According to this idea, more optimistic emotion is generated by tweets praising a cryptocurrency, whereas more bearish sentiment is generated by tweets criticizing it.

Speculative Trading
Assuming prices tend to stay inside a particular range, range trading works. A support or a resistance level may be used as a trigger for traders to purchase or sell. Candlestick charts with support and resistance levels are used in this method.

Or, if prices reach a point of resistance, they may decide to go short and then cover their short when prices return to a topic of support. In the context of range-bound trading, pivot points serve as an illustration. Calculating pivot points offer investors a sense of where price reversals are likely to occur.

Scalping
This method aims to make money from modest price changes over short time frames. Market inefficiencies like bid-ask spread or liquidity gaps are often to blame. To increase their profits, "scalpers" often employ leverage, such as margin or futures contracts, to profit from even the most minor price changes.

Scalping is best suited to experienced traders because of its fast-paced and high-risk nature. However, this also increases the likelihood of losses, making risk management more critical when using this technique. Scalpers may use a variety of technical indicators, such as volume heatmaps or order book analysis to discover the best times to enter and exit trades.

Bot Trading

Using bots or high-frequency trading (HFT) is a way to execute many deals using algorithms and trading bots swiftly. A solid grasp of complex trading methods and programming is required for this approach. High-frequency traders don't just sit back and let a computer program handle their cryptocurrency trading. Developing a trading strategy, creating a program to carry out that plan, and monitoring, backtesting, and upgrading the algorithms are all part of the process of building a trading bot.

Trading bots that have already been made and are ready to use may be purchased from specific merchants. Why aren't people utilizing the bot since it's lucrative and straightforward to use? If so, why aren't its developers doing so instead of using it themselves?

Long Position

When investors take a long (buy) position, they hope the price will go up. A rising cost is a good news for a long-term investor. Long stock asset purchases are the norm when it comes to stock purchases. An investor who acquires a call option has a long call position. Consequently, an increase in the underlying asset price favors a long call. The purchase of a put option is required for a long-put position. Puts and long calls both use the same rationale to justify their "long" aspects when the value of the underlying asset decreases, the value of a put option increases—the value of a long-put increase as the value of the underlying asset decreases.

- In a long-term asset transaction, the risk of losing money is limited to the purchase cost. Benefits are almost limitless.
- The dangers of holding long calls and puts are more nuanced. In our choices case study, we examine these issues in further detail.

Investments made to see its value grow are known as long positions (also known as long positions). The term "long position" is most often associated with derivatives and forex, although it may be used for just about any asset or market. It is possible to buy a purchase on the spot market to hold it for an extended period. It is the most typical investment method, particularly for just beginning individuals. It is assumed that the asset would rise in value in long-term trading methods like purchase and hold.

To put it another way, purchase and hold is just a long-term strategy. On the other hand, you are long doing not always imply that the trader intends to profit from a price increase. Take, for example, tokens that can be leveraged. Inversely connected to Bitcoin's price is BTCDOWN. When Bitcoin's value rises, so does the value of BTCDOWN. Whenever the price of Bitcoin drops, the cost of BTCDOWN increases as well. A decline in the price of Bitcoin is exactly what you'd expect if you had a long position on BTCDOWN.

When should a long position be taken?
Depending on the period you're working with, you could be interested in going long when the price of a cryptocurrency seems like it's set to move up. For example, on the daily chart, if you anticipate the price will rise in the days or weeks to come, you may go long.
The asset may be purchased on a spot market, or a long position can be opened via futures, options, or other derivatives contracts. Your selection must, of course, be supported by some fundamental or technical analysis. High-profile cooperation or a significant improvement to the platform may prompt you to consider going long on the native token of the blockchain project.
To get a clear picture of the market mood, it's a good idea to be active on social media and keep up with current events. An alternative or additional method is looking for patterns on the charts, such as whether or not the price has broken over a key resistance line, which might imply the continuation of an upward trend.
If you aim to go long, you should be sure that the price will rise no matter what form of research you use. If you don't, you'll be going against the grain of the market. Like corporate shares, cryptocurrencies are traded against fiat currencies, such as the US dollar, constantly aiming to raise. This is unlike foreign exchange pairings, which have no long-term goal. As a result, when it comes to Bitcoin, you'll see many investors opt for the "buy and hold" approach.

Short Position

The opposite of a long position is a short position. The investor and advantageous to him desire a decrease in the security's price. Executing or initiating a temporary position is more complicated than acquiring an asset. An investor with a temporary stock position expects to make money if the stock's price falls. When a stockbroker lends you a certain number of shares, you sell them at the current market price. There will be an open position in the investor's account that must be closed at some point in the future. If the price declines, the investor may buy X number of stock shares at a lower price than they paid for the same number of shares before. The extra money is theirs to keep. Many investors find it challenging to comprehend the notion of short selling, yet the method itself is relatively easy. Let's have a look at an example to see if it helps. Stock "A" presently trades at $50 per share. If you believe that the stock price will decrease shortly, you may benefit by selling short. The following is how a short sale might go:

Optimal time to enter a short position for traders?

If you think the price of a specific cryptocurrency will fall for some time, you may want to consider selling short. As previously said, you should rely on market research to support your conclusion. In general, short-sellers initiate positions when the market has reached an overbought level—i.e., the uptrend may have been oversaturated—and the demand has been rising for a lengthy duration. Going short is also an option when the price fails to break a resistance level and begins to deviate from it. It might be challenging to analyze Bitcoin (BTC) and altcoins since the market is still in its infancy, and there aren't any solid fundamentals to support the changes. Before making a long or short trade, you should, of course, consider all of the market's influences.

- To get a loan of 100 shares of stock from your brokerage business, you put up a margin deposit in the form of collateral.

- After receiving your broker's loan of 100 shares, you immediately sell them for $50 each. Your 100 shares are gone, but you've got $5,000 in your bank account thanks to the buyer ($50 multiplied by 100 equals $5,000). It is claimed that you are "short" the stock if you owe 100 shares to your broker. (Imagine if you told someone, "I'm short 100 shares of what I owe my broker.")
- The stock's price has started to plummet, as expected. After a few weeks, the stock price has fallen to $30 a share. You decide to complete the short sale because you don't think it will drop further.
- You now pay $3,000 for 100 shares of the stock ($30 x 100 = $3,000). To repay your broker for the 100 shares he gave you, you hand over those 100 shares of stock. By returning the 100 shares borrowed, you've ended your position as a "short" on the stock.
- Your short sell transaction brought in a profit of $2,000 for you. After selling 100 shares, your broker borrowed you for $5,000 and then purchasing 100 shares to repay him for just $3,000, you got $5,000. Figure your profit this way: Received $5,000 - $3,000 = $2,000 paid (profit).

Short stock positions are usually only provided to accredited investors because of the high confidence level required between investor and broker. It is common for investors to be asked to put up a margin deposit or other kind of collateral with their broker even if their short position is successful.

HODL Crypto

In the Bitcoin investing community, the phrase "HODL" is often heard. You may use it as an investing technique and a term of art. "Hold" is a "hold" type with an intriguing backstory. In addition, the word extended to other cryptocurrency groups.

- "HODL" is a type of "hold," referring to cryptocurrency investors' buy-and-hold strategy.
- Holding lets investors avoid short-term losses from cryptocurrency volatility and benefit from long-term value increases via the "holding" technique.
- While "holding" is less dangerous in theory than trading, investors must still consider the risk of changing regulations and the general public's viewpoint.

Cryptocurrency "HODLing"

Blockchain technology underpins cryptocurrency, a kind of digital cash. There are several uses for this currency, including trading, investing, and even as a means of exchange. Coins like Bitcoin, Litecoin, Ethereum, and Ripple are all examples of cryptocurrencies. Because a central bank does not issue bitcoin, it has a significant characteristic and advantage: decentralization. The great breakouts in 2017 and 2020 have led to a surge in interest in cryptocurrencies as an investment option. Digital currencies have the opportunity to expand as the trend toward financial decentralization and decentralization continues.

Investors are also holding cryptocurrencies as a value reserve in the post-COVID low-interest climate. It is a term used to describe the buy-and-hold investment approach. Long-term value appreciation is a primary motivation for buy-and-hold investors, who often hang on to their investments for at least five years.

On the other hand, traders are considerably more active in their transactions and look for profits by buying cheap and selling high. Traders may take advantage of the extreme volatility of cryptocurrencies by taking long and short bets, which can be liquidated at will. On the other hand, holding may provide more security to investors since it shields them from short-term volatility and the danger of overpaying for a stock.

"HODL 's" History

An investor's remark on the Bitcoin Forum, where they may voice their thoughts on Bitcoin and the economy, gave rise to the term "HODL." As "HOLDING" is the misspelling of "HOLDING," a forum user with the pseudonym "Game Kyuubi" created an article titled "I am hoarding!" in December 18, 2013. That the post's author made, the right choice has been shown. Bitcoin had a banner year in 2013. The price went from $15 in January to almost $1,100 at the beginning of December, which resulted in a 7,230 percent return. The price decreased from $716 to $438, a 39 percent drop. Possibly due to China's central bank's restriction on third-party payment businesses operating with Bitcoin exchanges, the price of Bitcoin fell. As opposed to engaging in more frequent trading, many who invest in cryptocurrencies do so over the long term, a strategy known as "buy-and-hold" investing. Midway through 2017, the price of Bitcoin launched a new boom that culminated in a record high of $19,167 for the year. A year later, in early 2021, it set a new all-time high of well over $58,000 after the COVID-19 pandemic.

Chapter 3:
How to buy a Crypto

Choose a Cryptocurrency Broker or Cryptocurrency Exchange

Before you can acquire cryptocurrencies, you'll need to find a broker or exchange. Both allow you to develop cryptocurrency, but there are a few essential distinctions to bear in mind.

Cryptocurrency Exchange

To trade cryptocurrencies, buyers and sellers must cooperate on a cryptocurrency exchange. For beginner crypto investors, deals might be scary because of their more complicated interfaces, including several trading kinds and detailed performance charts. Coinbase, Gemini, and Binance are a few well crypto exchanges. The US. Even though the standard trading interfaces of these organizations might be intimidating to novice investors, they also provide user-friendly and simple buying choices.

The Flexibility of use comes down to the fact: beginner-friendly choices charge much more than each platform's conventional trading interface to acquire the same coin. Before making your first crypto buy, or not long after, you may want to learn enough to use the traditional trading platforms to save money.

As a beginner to crypto, verify that the exchange or brokerage of your choice allows US dollar transfers and purchases. Many cryptocurrency exchanges can't buy cryptocurrency directly with another cryptocurrency; As a result, you'll have to go via a different exchange to get the tokens you need.

Cryptocurrency Broker

By communicating with exchanges on your behalf and providing clear user interfaces, brokers make the process of purchasing cryptocurrencies easier. Some levy costs are much greater than the fees charged by exchanges. Many "free" brokers make money by selling information about your transactions to major brokerages or funds or by not carrying out your business at the best available market pricing, both of which are deceptive trade practices. Two of the best-known cryptocurrency brokers are Robinhood and SoFi.

Digital wallets may not seem like a huge problem, but advanced crypto investors prefer to keep their currencies in them. Even though brokers are undeniably convenient, You need to be informed that transferring your bitcoin off the site may be difficult. You cannot withdraw any of your crypto assets while utilizing Robinhood or SoFi, for example. Some cryptocurrency users opt for offline, non-internet-connected hardware wallets for an extra layer of protection.

Create an account and verify it

Preventing fraud and complying with federal regulations necessitates taking this step. Signing up for an account with a cryptocurrency broker or exchange is easy after you've decided on one. You may have to prove your identification depending on the platform and the amount you want to purchase. When the verification procedure is complete, you may not be able to do so to buy or sell any cryptocurrency. Even a selfie may be required to verify that the papers you provide match your look on the site, which may need your driver's license or passport.

Make a cash deposit to invest.

You'll need to have money in your account before purchasing cryptocurrency. If you're using a debit or credit card, you may make a payment by connecting your account to your crypto wallet and requesting a wire transfer. You may have to wait a few days to use the money you deposit for certain exchanges and brokers to buy cryptocurrencies.

One word of caution before you buy: While you may deposit money with a credit card at certain exchanges or brokers, doing so is exceedingly risky—and costly. As cash advances, credit card issuers accept cryptocurrency transactions made with a credit card. As a result, you'll pay more excellent interest rates and extra cash advance costs than you would on everyday purchases. When you take out a cash advance, you may be charged a fee of 5% of the transaction amount. Assuming that your crypto exchange or brokerage charges costs of up to 5 percent, this means you might lose 10% of your crypto buy to fees.

Submit a Cryptocurrency Order

A bitcoin order may be placed as soon as the funds in your account are available. Cryptocurrencies like Bitcoin and Ethereum are well-known, but there are other less prominent coins like Theta Fuel and Holo.

You may enter the ticker symbol (Bitcoin is BTC, for example) and the number of coins you wish to purchase when picking which cryptocurrency to buy. A fractional share of high-priced tokens like Bitcoin or Ethereum may be bought on most cryptocurrency exchanges and brokers.

Cryptocurrencies with the highest market capitalization are listed below:

- The cryptocurrency is known as Bitcoin (BTC)
- The Ethereum virtual currency (ETH)
- Tethered (USDT)
- Bitcoin (BNB) (BNB)
- The city of Cardano (ADA)
- The Dogecoin cryptocurrency (DOGE)
- A cryptocurrency denoted by the symbol XRP (XRP)
- The currency of the United States (USDC)
- A polka-dot background (DOT)
- Uniswapping (UNI)

Choose a Storage Method
Money worth millions of dollars in Bitcoin is already gone because people forgot or lost the codes to their accounts. As a result, cryptocurrency exchanges are vulnerable to hacking and theft since they are not insured by the Federal Deposit Insurance Corporation (FDIC). That's why having a safe location to store your cryptocurrency is so crucial.

To reiterate, you may have little to no control over how your bitcoin is held if you acquire it via a broker. More possibilities are available if you buy cryptocurrencies on an exchange.

The crypto should remain in the exchange
As soon as you purchase a cryptocurrency, it is generally kept on the exchange in a "crypto wallet." A hot or cold wallet is a good alternative. If you don't trust the service, your exchange utilizes or wants to keep it out of the public eye. A minor charge may be required depending on the exchange and the amount of money you are transferring.

Hot wallets
These are online crypto wallets that can be accessed from any internet-enabled device, including smartphones, tablets, and laptops because they're still linked to the internet and pose a more significant theft risk.

Cold wallets
Because they are not linked to the internet, cold crypto wallets are the safest way to store your bitcoin. A USB flash drive or a hard disc is one example of an external storage device. If you misplace the device's keycode or it malfunctions, you may never be able to retrieve your bitcoin. If you are locked out of your hot wallet, custodians can assist you in getting back into your account.

Buying Cryptocurrency in Other Ways

At the moment, purchasing cryptocurrency seems like a good investment idea, but it comes with a lot of volatility and danger. Here are a few alternatives to using an exchange or a broker to invest in Bitcoin or other cryptocurrencies:

Anticipate the Crypto Exchange-Traded Funds (ETFs)

Exchange-traded funds (ETFs) are a popular investment vehicle (ETFs), which provide you access to hundreds of different assets at once. Because of this, they are less hazardous than investing in individual assets and offer rapid diversification.

Many people are eager for bitcoin ETFs, which enable investors to invest in many cryptocurrencies at once. There are currently no cryptocurrency ETFs accessible to the general public, but this might change soon. Kryptcoin, VanEck, and WisdomTree have applied for three cryptocurrencies ETFs to be reviewed by the US Securities and Exchange Commission (SEC) as of June 2021.

Invest in Companies Connected to Cryptocurrency

To get a taste of the cryptocurrency market, you may want to explore investing in firms that utilize or own cryptocurrency and the blockchain that supports it. Governed oversight is in place. As an example of a publicly listed corporation in which to invest, consider

Nvidia (NVDA)

Mining cryptocurrencies relies on graphics processing units (GPUs), which this technological business manufactures and sells.

PayPal (PYPL)

In addition to purchasing goods and services online or sending money to loved ones, this payment network just included the ability to buy and sell various cryptocurrencies using PayPal and Venmo accounts.

Square (SQ)

People may now purchase, trade, and store cryptocurrencies with Square's Cash App. More than $220 million has been spent by a small-business payment service provider since October 2020 on Bitcoin purchases. The company revealed in February 2021 that Bitcoin accounted for almost 5% of its total cash on hand.

It's essential to consider your long-term financial objectives and present financial condition before investing in cryptocurrencies or cryptocurrency-related firms. One tweet may send the price of cryptocurrency plunging, making it a hazardous investment. As a result, funding should be approached with prudence and caution.

Crypto wallets

Using a wallet is the most secure method of storing your Bitcoin. Hosted wallets, non-custodial wallets, and hardware wallets are the most common forms of crypto wallets. The appropriate cryptocurrency for you will depend on your goals and desired level of security.

Hosted Wallets

Hosted wallets are the most popular and easy-to-use crypto wallets. It's termed "hosted" because a third party manages your crypto assets on your behalf, just as a bank does with your cash. On Coinbase, for example, your cryptocurrency is stored in a hosted wallet. If you've ever heard of somebody "dropping their keys" or "missing their USB wallet," you don't have to worry about that with a hosted wallet.

Keeping your cryptocurrency in an online wallet means you won't lose it if you misplace your password. A downside to using a hosted wallet is that you can't use all of the features of crypto. When it comes to hosted wallets, though, this may alter.

Hosted wallets: How to get started

Pick a reliable platform.

You must focus on three things: security, usability, and adherence to legal and financial mandates.

Open an account.

Choose a strong password and enter your personal information. Using two-step verification provides an additional degree of security (2FA).

Purchase cryptocurrencies or make a transfer of them.

It is possible to acquire cryptocurrency using a bank account or credit card on most crypto platforms and exchanges. Hosted wallets may be used to store any cryptocurrency that you currently hold.

Self-custody wallets

An independent wallet like Coinbase Wallet or MetaMask gives you complete control over your coins. Non-custodial wallets don't depend on a third party to protect your coin. While they supply the software to store your crypto, you are alone responsible for remembering and protecting your password. You can't access your crypto if you lose or forget your password (also called a "private key" or "seed phrase"). Anyone with your private key may access your assets.

A non-custodial wallet You can access complex crypto activities like yield farming, staking, lending, borrowing, and more. A hosted wallet is the simplest way for buying, selling, sending, and receiving bitcoin.

Creating a non-custodial wallet:

Get a wallet app

Like Coinbase Wallet and Meta Mask.

Open an account

Unlike a hosted wallet, a non-custodial wallet requires no personal information. Not even an email.

Note your secret key

It's a 12-word sentence. Please keep it safe. You can't access your crypto if you lose or forget this 12-word phrase.

Wallet crypto transfer

Buying crypto using fiat currency (such as dollars or euros) isn't always available, so you'll need to move crypto into your non-custodial wallet from somewhere.

Customers of Coinbase may choose between a hosted and self-custody wallet. The Coinbase app is a hosted wallet. You may also use the Coinbase Wallet standalone app to benefit from a non-custodial wallet. It's simple to acquire crypto using regular cash and engage in sophisticated crypto activities for our consumers. Ether wallet setup is free.

Hardware wallets

Hardware wallets, which are more complicated and expensive, offer certain advantages, like the ability to keep your cryptocurrency safe even if your computer is compromised. Using a hardware wallet, the private keys to your cryptocurrency are saved on a device the size of a thumb drive. As a result, these devices are more challenging to use than software wallets, and they may cost as much as $100 to purchase.

Hardware wallet setup instructions:

Buy the hardware

It's hard to go wrong with either Ledger or Trezor.

Activate the software

Wallets may be set up with different software for each brand. Create your wallet by downloading the software from the company's website and following the instructions.

Transfer crypto to your wallet

To acquire crypto using conventional currencies (US dollars or euros), you'll need to transfer crypto into your hardware wallet, just like you would with a non-custodial wallet.

Cryptocurrency may be stored in various places, much like cash (in a bank account, a safe, or even beneath the mattress). When it comes to cryptocurrency, the choice is yours. You may use a hosted wallet to make things easy, or you can use a non-custodial wallet to have complete control over your crypto, or you can use a hardware wallet to be extra cautious.

Chapter 4:

Crypto Portfolio and Market Capitalization

Cryptocurrencies are no different from regular investments when managing your portfolio. You may significantly lower your investment risk with the right profile and approach. Investing in several cryptocurrencies is all that is required to get started. Both sides of the debate are good and bad aspects when diversifying your portfolio. On the other hand, diversification is widely acknowledged as advantageous in moderation. Investing in various cryptocurrencies (including stablecoins) and regularly rebalancing your portfolio will help decrease your risk exposure. Using a third-party portfolio tracker or manually recording your transactions on a spreadsheet might help you better manage your portfolio. It is possible to connect specific trackers to your wallets and bitcoin exchanges, making the procedure simpler. When you buy your first cryptocurrency (BTC, ETH, etc.), you're on your way to becoming a crypto investor. The more prominent cryptocurrencies are preferred by confident investors, while others prefer to explore with altcoins. But how do we go about it? A well-balanced crypto portfolio is more likely to succeed if you consider your asset allocation carefully and do so frequently. There are several methods to do this, depending on your risk tolerance. It's not difficult to keep your portfolio under check, and the benefits may be substantial.

Crypto Portfolio

A **crypto portfolio** is a collection of crypto held by an investor or trader in the cryptocurrency world. Altcoins and other crypto-related financial instruments are standard components of portfolios. Like a regular investment portfolio, except that you're only investing in one asset type. If you want to check up on your cryptocurrency investments, you may do it manually using a spreadsheet or using specialist tools and software. A decent portfolio tracker is useful. Day traders and other short-term traders must use trackers, but long-term investors and HODLers may also benefit.

A **cryptocurrency portfolio** keeps track of your various digital currency holdings. It gives you the ability to keep tabs on each coin's progress and run multiple analyses on that data. Cryptocurrency exchanges offer many portfolio management systems real-time data feeds and price updates. They may notify you of significant market developments.

While Bitcoin remains the most popular digital money, it should not be your only cryptocurrency investment. It's not uncommon for investors to invest in various cryptocurrencies to mitigate risk. But how can you pick which of the almost 3,000 cryptocurrencies to invest in? The ultimate objective is to have a diverse collection of cryptocurrencies.

According to cryptocurrency specialists, you should only invest in digital currencies you fully understand and have done significant research on. That is good advice. You do the same thing with traditional assets like stocks and bonds. In the words of Benjamin Franklin: "The highest return on an investment is knowledge."

Diversified and Concentrated Portfolio
There are both advantages and disadvantages to diversifying your investment portfolio. The consensus is that you need to have a well-diversified cryptocurrency portfolio. As we've previously established, a well-diversified portfolio lowers an investment's total risk and volatility. Gains may counterbalance losses, allowing you to maintain your position. With each coin in your collection, you have additional options to generate money. With correct asset allocation and diversification, you have a better chance of making money in the long term.

In order to achieve more profits, most traders and investors want to outperform the market. However, the closer your portfolio tracks the broader market, the more diversified it is. The average return from a well-diversified portfolio is higher than the average return from a concentrated one. Low-earning ones might offset High-earning assets. To correctly manage a diverse portfolio, you'll need to put in more time and effort. To make wise investments, you must know what you're getting into. Having a vast portfolio reduces one's ability to comprehend everything. You may need to utilize various wallets and exchanges to access your assets if they're spread across different blockchains. Whether or whether you choose to diversify is entirely up to you, but it's always a good idea.

Asset allocations and diversification
You should be conversant with asset allocation and diversification ideas while putting up an investment portfolio. Investing in various asset types is known as asset allocation (e.g., cryptocurrencies, stocks, bonds, precious metals, cash, etc.). In the context of investing, diversification refers to distributing your money across various investments or industries. There are several ways to vary your investments, such as by investing in a wide range of various sectors. Both of these methods will lower your total exposure to danger.

Cryptocurrencies may be considered a single asset class from a technical perspective. The advantage of diversification in a cryptocurrency portfolio is that it allows you to own various assets with varying objectives and use cases. According to this example: 40 percent Bitcoin, 30 percent Stablecoin and 15 percent NFT.

Types of Cryptocurrencies in your Portfolio
The new asset class of cryptocurrencies offers more significant profits and more significant risks. They are gaining traction throughout the globe and should be included in any future secure portfolio that you put up. When you first join, you may allocate up to 2% of your portfolio to crypto, and you can gradually grow that percentage over time. Fixed deposits, gold, real estate, and even free cash may all be used to offset these risks. It would be best if you conceived of as your crypto capital is the money you can afford to lose. When market volatility hits you hard on the downside, you won't be harmed as much since you've minimized your exposure to the risky asset.

Payment coins
New currencies that deal solely with payments are rare to come by these days. Historically, however, most cryptocurrency initiatives have been mechanisms for exchanging value. Ripple, Bitcoin Cash (BCH), and Litecoin (LTC) are a few additional examples of decentralized digital currencies worth noting. Before Ethereum and smart contracts, these coins were the initial generation of cryptocurrencies.

Stablecoins
Some stablecoins seek to mimic the value of tangible assets, such as gold and silver. BUSD, for example, uses a 1:1 reserve ratio to tie the U.S. dollar to the BUSD. Unlike PAX, which is based on the price of a single troy ounce of fine gold, PAX Gold (PAXG) employs a different methodology entirely. Stablecoins don't always bring in big profits, but they keep their value steady. Having a stable asset in your portfolio might be helpful in the turbulent cryptocurrency market. A drop in the crypto market shouldn't harm a stable coin if it is pegged to anything other than the crypto ecosystem. Using a dollar-backed stable coin like BUSD, you can quickly transfer tokens out of a coin or project to protect your profits. Transacting with money requires more time and effort than doing so in exchange for a stable coin.

Security Tokens

A security token, like conventional securities, may stand for a variety of things. Equity in a firm or a bond from a project might be a form of compensation. Essentially, guarantees have been digitized and placed on the blockchain, which means that the same set of rules governs them. Due to this, security tokens are subject to the authority of local authorities and must go through a legal procedure before issue.

Utility Tokens

If you want to get into a service or product, you'll need some kind of token. BNB and ETH, for example, are utility tokens. You may use them to pay transaction fees while using decentralized apps, among other things (DApps). Several projects create their utility tokens to raise money via a coin offering. The token's value should presumably be linked to the value of its usefulness.

Governance Tokens

Having a governance token enables you to vote on a project and even a portion of the profits generated by that project. PancakeSwap, Uniswap, and SushiSwap are decentralized finance (Defi) systems. When a project succeeds, so does the value of a governance token, much like utility tokens.

Crypto Market Capitalization

An individual **cryptocurrency's market capitalization** represents the entire worth of all of its circulating units. The crypto market capitalization is calculated by multiplying the price of the cryptocurrency by the number of coins in circulation instead of the stock market capitalization, which is calculated by multiplying the share price by the outstanding shares.

There are over 18 billion Bitcoins in existence, and their market value is calculated by multiplying the current price of Bitcoin by that amount. Market capitalization changes with Bitcoin's price, which is the case regularly. Bitcoin's price has fluctuated between $45,000 to $55,000 in the last several weeks, resulting in a significant shift in the cryptocurrency's market capitalization:

- Eight hundred and forty-six billion dollars
- $50,000 multiplied by 18,8 million is $940 billion.
- $55,000 divided by 18.8 million is $1.034 trillion.

Ethereum's market capitalization is compared to Bitcoin's in the following table: Ethereum has a market value of $351 billion, with a price of $3,000 per coin and an overall supply of about 117 million coins in circulation worldwide. Ethereum's market valuation is higher even though many more coins are in circulation.

Crypto Weighted Market Cap Strategy

A weighted market cap strategy entails investing a certain percentage of your money into each asset class based on market capitalization. Since Bitcoin and Ethereum each have different rates of the entire market capitalization, you'd get 71% for Bitcoin and 29% for Ethereum when dividing the total by the percentages held by each cryptocurrency.

You can figure out how much to invest in the two main cryptocurrencies, Bitcoin and Ethereum: On the Ethereum side, you'd support around $29. If you want to invest a certain percentage of your overall investment in each coin, divide the total by the market capitalization of each coin. If nothing else, this assures you're investing lesser amounts into other cryptos and more significant amounts into Bitcoin and Ethereum, both of which are secure. Despite what the experts say, the same idea can be applied to any asset you choose to include in your portfolio, even if it's not Bitcoin.

Furthermore, it's essential to keep in mind that the market capitalization of cryptocurrencies fluctuates continuously. Because of this volatility and the possibility of a market collapse, experts advise investors to restrict their investments to a minimum and only invest what they are willing to lose.

Crypto Market Cap for Investors

You may classify a firm into one of three investing categories: small, mid, or large-cap based on its market value. There are various reasons why an investor would decide to split their investment into multiple categories; therefore, understanding the market cap is critical. As measured by its market cap, maybe the valuation is a good indicator of how hazardous it is to invest in it. Investing in large-cap companies might be less risky, but the returns are longer to materialize.

However, Bitcoin is a relatively new phenomenon. It's so fresh that these kinds of categories have yet to be established. Using market cap in making investment choices is less necessary now that experts recommend sticking to Bitcoin and Ethereum and not allowing crypto to account for more than 5% of your whole portfolio. To better understand a token's potential, you may want to know its market cap, but it shouldn't play a significant role in your investment selections as it does on the stock market. With crypto, "It's crucial to know that it's different from the stock market," explains Jully Alma-Taveras, the personal finance expert behind "'Investing Latina'" on Instagram. This is an entirely new world. While market capitalization has a more restricted use with crypto trading, there is one method that might influence the way you invest in Bitcoin and Ethereum.

Market Cap Ratio

You can make better investing selections by comparing one cryptocurrency's market cap to another's. The market capitalization of cryptocurrencies may be divided into three categories:

- More than $10 billion worth of **large-cap cryptocurrencies**, including Bitcoin and Ethereum. As a result, investors see them as low-risk investments since they have a proven track record of growth and can survive a more significant number of individuals selling without significantly affecting the price.
- The market capitalization of **mid-cap cryptocurrencies** ranges from $1 billion to $10 billion, and they are often thought to have more upside potential and more significant risk than large-cap cryptocurrencies.
- Market mood may have a tremendous impact on **small-cap cryptocurrencies**, which have a market capitalization of less than $1 billion.

For comparison purposes, the market capitalization may be informative. Still, it's important to consider other factors such as market trends, a cryptocurrency's stability, and your financial status before making an investing decision.

Large Cap

If a cryptocurrency's market capitalization is more than $10 billion, it is considered a "large-cap." According to that estimation, there are now just four large-cap currencies in the market. Only Bitcoin, Ethereum, USDT (stable coin), and XRP are available in this writing. It's safe to say that these cryptocurrencies have a long track record of reliability and security, making them critical participants in the market.

Mid Cap

The market capitalization of mid-cap coins and tokens ranges from USD 1 billion to USD 10 billion. Already established, these initiatives are growing and may see considerable expansion shortly. Chain Link, Cardano, Litecoin, Tezos, Monero, and Binance Coin is among the most popular currencies and tokens in this category.

Small-Cap

These initiatives lack experience and funding compared to the most successful ones. Their age and size put them in greater danger than smaller coins. Moreover, $100 million in market value, but less than $1 billion, is considered a small-cap. However, when you do your research and check at low-cap currencies carefully, you may uncover one that has enormous growth potential.

High Liquidity, Low Volatility, and Low Risk Characterize Large-Cap Stocks

Large-cap cryptocurrencies are the least dangerous of the three. You won't see big returns in a short period by investing in significant companies, but you will see steady growth over time. Liquidity is strong for coins with significant market capitalization. It signifies that these currencies can be found on most cryptocurrency exchanges and have a large volume of activity. Investors may quickly enter and exit a market with a high level of liquidity. A multiple purchase or sell order may be placed, and the order will be completed instantly. Larger companies are less volatile, making it more challenging to influence the price in any way. In spite of this, they're still more volatile than more established investments, such as equities.

Mid-Caps: Medium Risk, Decent Liquidity, and Enormous Growth Potential

The risk and volatility of mid-cap cryptos are greater than those of large-cap cryptos. They aren't as well-known as the big ones. Many mid-cap currencies have yet to achieve their full potential since their usefulness is still expanding. In comparison to big-cap currencies, they thus have more significant growth potential. Mid-cap cryptocurrencies, on the whole, tend to do well over the long term, making them an excellent diversification tool. Even yet, keep in mind that not every coin has the potential to become a significant cap.

Small Caps: - High Risk, Volatile, and Lacking Liquidity

A cryptocurrency's volatility is a significant determinant of risk. Since smaller market caps tend to be more volatile than larger ones, a coin's price may fluctuate more often. Put another way, small market size companies are more vulnerable to price changes. An enormous purchase or sell order has the power to change the price quickly. Your investment in this instrument is hazardous because of the rapid increase and price fall. As a result, small-cap stocks are more susceptible to market sentiment. A single favorable or bad media report may easily make or destroy a coin since these coins are generally new and have little history.

Final Thoughts

Investing in cryptocurrencies isn't just about choosing coins based on their market capitalization. A cryptocurrency's market capitalization is a good indicator of its popularity and market domination. Not all metrics are created equal, though. In addition to the project's core team, fundamentals, technical, and value proposition, you should consider these additional aspects while making your cryptocurrency selection.

Then there is the number of coins and tokens, which significantly impacts the market valuation. To improve their position in the CMC rankings, the majority of centralized projects may burn coins and change the parameters of the currency supply. Before purchasing a cryptocurrency, an investor should do extensive due diligence on the project. Check out the project's history. ' The daily traded volume of most mid-and small-cap currencies is heavily controlled, so keep an eye on it as well. Do not be fooled by currency promotions that promise the moon in YouTube videos or Twitter profiles. Because this is a speculative asset class, you should only invest at your own risk and make your own investment choices.

Chapter 5:
Most Important Crypto Coins

Complex cryptography is used to create and handle digital currencies and their transactions over distributed networks, thus the term "crypto" in cryptocurrency. Decentralization is a frequent "crypto" trait, and cryptocurrencies are often produced as code by teams that include methods for issuance (usually, but not always, via a mining process) and other regulations. The core component of the cryptocurrency sector is that it is supposed to be free of government manipulation and control; however, this has come under scrutiny as the industry has risen in popularity. Altcoins, and even shitcoins, are a collective term for Bitcoin-inspired cryptocurrencies that have attempted to promote themselves as better or more advanced versions of Bitcoin. Even if they may boast capabilities that Bitcoin doesn't, Altcoins have yet to reach the degree of security achieved by Bitcoin's networks.

But first, a disclaimer: A list like this will never be complete. There are over 8,000 decentralized cryptocurrencies in regulation as of January 2022, which is one cause for this. 1 These cryptos, despite their lack of notoriety or trading volume, have a strong following and support among their supporters and investors. Furthermore, the area of cryptocurrencies is constantly evolving, and the next significant digital token might be created as soon as today. Analysts use various methods to assess tokens other than Bitcoin, even though it is often regarded as a pioneer in the realm of cryptocurrencies. Analysts, for example, tend to place a lot of emphasis on the relative market capitalization of different cryptocurrencies. This has been taken into account. However, a digital token might also be provided for other reasons.

Bitcoin

A decentralized digital currency known as Bitcoin may be purchased, sold, and exchanged without the need for a bank or other middleman. According to Bitcoin's initial developer Satoshi Nakamoto, a "cryptographic evidence instead of faith" payment method was needed.

BTC transactions are recorded in the public database that is open to the world, making them impossible to reverse or spoof. That's the goal: There is no central authority or issuing organization to support Bitcoins, which is a crucial characteristic of the currency's decentralized structure. Anton Mozgovoy is the co-founder and chief executive officer of the digital financial services business Holyhead and believes that the only reason anything has a monetary value is that we as a society have determined that it does. Bitcoin's value has increased considerably since first made public in 2009. Today, a single Bitcoin costs more than $62,000, even though it was formerly valued at less than $150 per coin. For this reason, many believe that its price will continue to rise as more major investment firms start treating it as a kind of virtual gold as a hedge against market volatility and inflation.

Why Purchase Bitcoin?

Cryptocurrency exchanges are the most common method of purchasing Bitcoin. As with creating a brokerage or bank account for buying, selling, and holding cryptocurrencies, you'll need to authenticate your identity and offer some form of money source to create a cryptocurrency exchange account. Coinbase, Kraken, and Gemini are all well-known exchanges. Online brokers like Robinhood allow you to acquire Bitcoin. A Bitcoin wallet is required regardless of where your Bitcoin is purchased. This is either a hot or a cold wallet depending on the temperature. It is possible to store cryptocurrency in a hot wallet (also known as an online wallet) hosted by an exchange or service provider in the cloud. Exodus, Electrum, and Mycelium are just a few of the many online wallet service providers. A mobile wallet is a device used to store Bitcoin offline and is not linked to the web.

Due to its near-synonymous status with cryptocurrency, Bitcoin can be purchased on practically any crypto exchange, whether you're using fiat money or another crypto asset. BTC trading is offered in several major markets, including:

- Binance
- OKEx
- Coinbase Pro
- Kraken
- Huobi Global
- Bitfinex

Alexandria, CoinMarketCap's educational site, is a great place to start learning about purchasing Bitcoin and other cryptocurrencies if you're new to the space.

The following are a few things to keep in mind while purchasing Bitcoin: You may be able to acquire fractions of Bitcoin from specific retailers, despite the high cost of Bitcoin. Bitcoin purchases mustn't be immediate as many other equities transactions seem to be. Miners must verify all Bitcoin transactions before they appear in your account, which may take anywhere from 10-20 minutes.

Investing Bitcoin

Investing in Bitcoin is similar to holding stock. Bitcoin IRAs, a new kind of retirement account, make it possible to do so now. People invest in different ways: some purchase and keep for the long term; others buy and hope to sell at a profit when the price rises; still others wager that the price will fall. The price of Bitcoin has fluctuated dramatically throughout the years, dropping as low as $5,165 in 2020 and as high as $28,990 in the same year.

However, "Bitcoin is an asset that appears like it will be gaining in value quite fast for some time," adds Marquez; in certain regions, people may use Bitcoin to pay for items. "So why would you sell something that will be valued so much more in a year than it is now??" The vast majority of those who retain it do so for the long haul. A Bitcoin mutual fund is also available to the general public, but only to accredited investors that earn at least $200,000 or have net worths of at least $1 million, which is presently the case with the Grayscale Bitcoin Trust (GBTC). To put it another way, the vast majority of Americans cannot afford it. However, Bitcoin diversification is becoming more accessible in Canada. Purpose Bitcoin ETF (BTCC) and Evolve Bitcoin ETF (EBIT) were authorized by the Ontario Securities Commission in February 2021 as the world's first Bitcoin ETFs. Investors in the United States who are hoping to get exposure to the technology behind cryptocurrencies may explore blockchain ETFs. Although crypto-based funds may help diversify cryptocurrency holdings and reduce risk significantly, they nevertheless do so at a considerably higher cost and with far more trouble than traditional index funds. Index-based mutual and exchange-traded funds may be a good choice for investors who want to build wealth over time (ETFs).

Bitcoin in Circulation

According to Bitcoin's software, there will never be more than 21,000,000 coins in circulation at any one time. The procedure known as "mining" is used to produce new coins. When transactions are sent over the network, miners pick them up and bundle them into blocks safeguarded by complicated cryptographic computations. For each block that is successfully added to the blockchain, the miners are rewarded for using their computer resources. With every 210,000 additional blocks mined — a process that takes the network around four years — the payout for mining, a bitcoin is half to only 25 bitcoins. There will be just 6.25 bitcoins in the block reward in 2020.

Premined Bitcoin does not indicate that the creators of Bitcoin had any coins mined and distributed before the public release of Bitcoin. Competition amongst miners was relatively low in the early years of BTC's existence, enabling early network players to amass large quantities of coins via frequent mining: Satoshi Nakamoto alone is estimated to control a million BTC moreover. If the current hash rate and the price of Bitcoin are favorable, mining Bitcoins may be a lucrative endeavor for miners. We examine how long it takes to mine one Bitcoin on CoinMarketCap, although mining Bitcoins is complicated. After the 2020 halving, the Bitcoin mining reward will be limited to 6.25 BTC, or $299,200 at today's pricing, by the middle of September 2021.

Ethereum
Ethereum is a decentralized and open-source blockchain. Ether (ETH) is the platform's native currency. The market capitalization of Ether is second only to that of Bitcoin. Gavin Wood, Charles Hoskinson, Anthony Di Iorio, and Joseph Lubin were Ethereum's co-founders. It's a platform that anybody can use to build and run permanent, decentralized apps that other users can interact with. There is no need for traditional financial intermediaries like brokerages, exchanges, or banks to offer a wide range of financial services in Defi apps, such as enabling cryptocurrency consumers to lend on their stocks or lend them out for interest. It is also viable to use Ethereum to create and trade non-transferable tokens (NFTs) linked to virtual pieces of art or other actual commodities and marketed as unique digital property. On top of Ethereum's blockchain, numerous other cryptocurrencies use ERC-20 tokens and have raised money via ICOs on Ethereum.
Ethereum 2.0, a set of enhancements that involves a switch to proof of stake and attempts to boost transaction throughput via sharding, has begun implementation.

Performance in 2020

Ethereum's revival was set for 2020. So even if 2020 didn't hit a new all-time high, its foundation should allow for a further price increase. More than $90 billion worth of total value was trapped in Ethereum or ERC20 tokens based on Ethereum since DeFi's first explosion. Ethereum-based Defi and NFTs are in great demand, driving up the price of ETH as a way to pay for the exorbitantly high gas costs. Scalability and investment success are two critical goals for the next Ethereum 2.0 version implemented in stages.

ETH has already reached an all-time high of $2,000 per ETH owing to exceptional demand to pay for gas expenses in 2021, positive for Ethereum. Ethereum's ecosystem has developed to such a size that it's unlikely to be overtaken by newcomers. The total value locked in Ethereum has surpassed $90 billion, and the demand for the cryptocurrency is only going to increase, and the supply will decrease as that continues. Most of the Ethereum in circulation is now held in smart contracts, with a large portion of it held at Ethereum 2.0's staking address. EIP 1559, a new upgrade, is expected to significantly influence the supply of Ethereum, making ETH increasingly rare over time. Ethereum may be a better investment than even Bitcoin because of all of these considerations, as well as Wall Street's conviction that Ethereum is here to stay. However, there is still the possibility that this bullish currency has run out of steam after such a significant increase in 2020 and 2021. The remainder of the year is up in the air.

Ethereum Investing

By purchasing Ethereum, you are making a long-term bet on the future of money. The smart contract platform has already started substituting shares and bonds with tokens connected to smart contracts in some corporate operations, displacing Wall Street's outdated, antiquated backend. Since Ethereum is a platform for developers to create and innovate on, its potential is maybe even more incredible than Bitcoin's. An excellent example of this is the current Defi craze. In finance, there is always a new and exciting initiative or addition that sets the sector on a new path. New buzzwords like "yield farming" and "liquidity pooling" have been coined as a result. Scams and projects with no real-world use are common, but there are also plenty of gems to be found. Traditional finance is being disrupted by promising Defi initiatives that enable permissionless lending and borrowing. Non-fungible tokens, or the NFT market, play a vital role in the evolution of the Ethereum price since most NFTs are developed using a different standard for Ethereum smart contracts. Ethereum-based blockchains, such as Defi, need those transactions to be paid for using ETH as gas.

Regardless of what these initiatives become or how they evolve, Ethereum and its investors will reap the benefits. Ethereum has recently outperformed Bitcoin and practically all other cryptocurrencies because of the Defi craze, making it an excellent investment for 2021. Even though Ethereum has already achieved a new all-time high, Ethereum's current upswing may be just getting started, which means that now is the best moment to buy in the cryptocurrency.

Crypto to invest in 2022

On Wednesday, the most popular cryptocurrencies sank sharply as a broad Nasdaq sell-off resumed for the third day in a row. Investors were scared away from riskier assets such as cryptocurrency when the Federal Reserve promised eight interest rate increases over three years, putting a damper on the flames of the financial crisis.

Avalanche (CRYPTO: AVAX), Terra (CRYPTO: LUNA), Solana (CRYPTO: SOL, CRYPTO: LUNA, and CRYPTO: SOL) were all down more than ten percent in the last 24 hours, according to statistics from CoinGecko.com when markets reopened on Thursday.

Solana

During the Asian-Pacific trading session on Tuesday, Solana's token was trading at $105.6 per token, a decrease of over 50 percent since January. Since January 28, the digital asset has gained 20 percent and has maintained a solid resistance-turned-support line of $86.6. There is a resistance trendline in SOL's recent bullish efforts, though. Solana might rise to at least $128.0 if it breaks through the support level. Solana-based coins were added to Coinbase, the biggest cryptocurrency exchange in the United States. Coinbase says the FIDA/ORCA pair will begin trading on February 1 at 9 a.m. Pacific Time.

Terra

It's still too early to predict a complete return to November's all-time highs after the January freefall. Terra's governance token, LUNA, has risen 15% in the last two days, suggesting a possible retest of the previous support level. TVL has a market capitalization of $13.7 billion as of the first trading day of February. While other Defi systems saw a significant drop in TVL, Terra's was not as affected. Since 2021, its market share has risen from 0.46 percent in March 2021 to a solid 7 percent in February 2022. With Terra's recent daily increase, Terra also surpassed Binance Smart Chain (BSC) in terms of market cap and moved silver to the level of gold held by Ethereum (ETH).

Avalanche

With a $17 billion market worth, Avalanche, another Ethereum killer, fell over 40% in January. Despite this, the digital asset has been steadily rising since January 22. Like SOL and LUNA, it is premature to expect a complete recovery before the end of the year. The token's setup might fuel a bullish bias.

A bullish reversal pattern is known as the "Falling Wedge," representing a bullish setup. AVAX might break the resistance trendline and reach the support bar at $80.0 to $85.0 by following the formation.

Crypto Staking

Many cryptocurrency exchanges have implemented incentive schemes to assist individuals in gaining more value out of their digital assets, even though these marketplaces have typically concentrated on offering a location to purchase and trade digital assets. In terms of their details, each of these initiatives is unique. "Staking" your cryptocurrency, or using it to help verify transactions on the blockchain network, might earn you money in some instances. Others allow users to earn income on their assets by storing them on a platform via lending programs. Below, you'll find information on each platform's reward scheme. NerdWallet-reviewed exchanges that will enable consumers to utilize their bitcoins to earn rewards are included in this list.

It's important to think about the rates at which rewards may be earned, how frequently they're given out, how simple it is to remove your holdings from the program, and how many qualifying cryptocurrencies there are when selecting an exchange for staking or rewards. In addition, we looked at important aspects of any exchange service, such as the quality of the website and the ratings of mobile apps.

Nexo Wallet

Nexo is an ERC20 security token that pays interest and is certified by the corporate marketplaces to be SEC-compliant. Developed by Credissmo, a Fintech business based in Europe, Nexo is a cryptocurrency-backed lending system. Instant cash in EUR or USD may be received by depositing the supported digital currencies into a Nexo wallet. Nexo was first given through airdrop before being made available for sale as a token. Clients may now deposit their NEXO dividend tokens into their Nexo wallets as of June 4th, 2018, making this a significant step toward creating the industry's first credit product of institution-grade.

Celsius Wallet

Although Celsius isn't regulated like a traditional bank, it functions. Weekly interest payments are made to those who deposit Bitcoin, Ethereum, or Tether. On the other hand, Celsius pays interest rates that are tens or hundreds of times greater than those offered by regular banks. To put it another way, it has doubled its assets to $25 billion in the past year. When Mashinsky informs his Celsius users that they can aid the poor and fight back against greedy banks via Celsius, they give him a standing ovation since he has helped them earn enough money to repay loans or even leave their employment. It is worth noting that Canadian pension fund Caisse de Dépôt and Placement du Québec invested another $750 million in Celsius last year. A $3 billion value of the investment round made Mashinsky a multi-billionaire.

Chapter 6:
The future of Crypto

In the future, we may guess about what value bitcoin may have for investors (and many wills), but the truth is that it is still a very new and speculative investment, and there isn't much history on which to make forecasts. Nothing an expert says or believes will change that no one knows for sure. So, it's crucial to stick to more traditional assets for long-term wealth creation rather than risking all you have. Would you be okay when the developed countries prohibit cryptocurrency and lose its value? Life water Wealth Management's CFP Frederick Stanfield recently spoke to Next Advisor on diversifying one's portfolio. Don't put your crypto investments ahead of anything else, including retirement savings or paying off high-interest debt. Instead, keep your assets modest.

Cryptocurrencies such as Bitcoin and others. Cryptocurrencies like Bitcoin and Ethereum are essentially trustless since they are not tied to any government or other institution. Because it is not tied to a single government, cryptocurrency advocates argue that it is better than traditional fiat currencies. Grundfest points out that this isn't correct, regardless of how you feel about it. In reality, cryptocurrencies aren't entirely trustworthy. For the time being, they are still heavily dependent on the backbone of cryptocurrencies like Bitcoin, most of it situated inside the Chinese government. It is theoretically possible for China's government to make significant changes to cryptocurrencies by forcing its will on the data miners who power them.

Many of the oddest news in 2021 was about cryptocurrency. It was said that digital currencies might revolutionize the globe and empower individuals who don't have bank accounts. Cryptocurrency's environmental impact and use in online crime were cited as points of contention by its detractors. It will be challenging to bridge the abyss between these two points of view. There is a lot of buzz in the bitcoin market because of all the weird dog and outer-space emoji jokes. On the same business, venture capitalists and individual enthusiasts have invested an incredible amount of money in actual technological advancements that might fundamentally transform the way we interact with money. We may not receive what we anticipate from new technology, as is so frequently the case.

Cryptocurrency to gain more traction in the mainstream.

Cryptocurrency is being examined by some of the world's largest corporations. This year, everyone from hedge fund managers to Starbucks CEOs makes decisions that might significantly influence how we utilize digital money. Cryptocurrency is often associated with Elon Musk's tweets, overnight billionaires, pricey digital art, and hacks when it appears in the news headlines. However, the more fundamental, long-term developments are typically overlooked in favor of the daily crypto-hype machine.

Denelle Dixon, CEO of Stellar Development Foundation, stated, "I think we're going to see a lot more attention on usefulness." "An increased emphasis on use cases that provide actual value will replace a narrow concentration on just a few popular use cases. There will also be increasing debate over financial inclusion."

Libra: It's not all that it seems to be

Facebook's foray into the cryptocurrency realm, Libra, has been heralded as the panacea to a slew of financial ills by some. Additionally, the platform was meant to simplify international payments and remove transaction fees. Professor Grundfest admits that the objective is noble, but he thinks the technique is faulty. He doesn't believe that launching a new cryptocurrency is the best way to reduce payment transactions, and he doesn't support Facebook's efforts to avoid altogether established banking institutions.

A preferable strategy for Facebook would have been to develop a significant financial institution for its users, according to Professor Grundfest. Better use of firm resources would have been to establish banking systems tailored to the needs of each country or area, meet regulatory requirements, and reduce expenses. To develop a global network, all that is needed is to connect each existing one and build public confidence.

Cryptocurrency: Stable Coin the Future

Like the gold standard, stable coins have become more popular to underpin bitcoin with real-world assets. There are a wide variety of investments that may be used as collateral. Grundfest has a few concerns with this strategy. For starters, it re-creates an existing system. Because it's difficult to audit and monitor, it might make it simpler for criminals to perpetrate fraud than conventional currencies.

On the last slide of his presentation, Professor Grundfest discussed some of the cryptocurrency's most robust use cases. Investors in nations with weak currencies, for example, may benefit more from putting their money in Bitcoin than in local equities or bonds. The future of cryptocurrency is still very much up in the air. On the other hand, critics perceive nothing but the danger in the idea of a new product or service. Although Professor Grundfest remains skeptical, he acknowledges that bitcoin can be used in certain situations.

Bitcoin and other cryptocurrencies have become a phenomenon in the media because of their volatility. In the blink of an eye, you may become a multimillionaire or lose all you've worked for. But if you attempt to purchase a coffee with bitcoin, things might become a little tricky quickly.

Stable coins are a solution to this problem. There's less volatility in this subgroup of cryptocurrency since it is linked to an asset. To make cryptocurrencies more accessible, stable coins might play an essential role in making it easier to perform our regular transactions.

"Stable coins, both as a payment method and as a digital currency pegged to the dollar, are something to keep an eye on. Stable coins have the potential to speed up the transfer of assets. This value is significant for businesses that need the rapid and efficient transfer of digital assets and cash. In 2021, cross-border payments, assistance relief, and prompt settlement payments will all experience an increase in popularity, "In an email, Circle vice president of product Rachel Mayer said.

Crypto Market Prediction for Future

Throughout 2021, cryptocurrency investors were on high alert because of the new year. Since the beginning of the year, Bitcoin (CRYPTO: BTC) and Ethereum (CRYPTO: ETH) were up 309% and 459%, respectively. 2020's bullish market momentum carried over into robust gains in 2021, according to the latest data. As a result of the rise of Bitcoin and Ethereum, tens of thousands of altcoins had their first taste of popular success. However, the broad market trend has been slowly rising, albeit a bumpy ride. Cryptocurrency and its investors' long-term trajectory will be decided by the 2022 calendar, which will resolve specific critical concerns that have remained unanswered in past years.

In 2022 and beyond, it's hard to predict what will happen in the bitcoin industry. There are a lot more questions than there are answers. As the crypto market continues to change, you will be able to make smarter investment choices if you keep an eye on a few underlying trends. The following three specifics must be adhered to:

- Regulating in the United States as well as elsewhere.
- Cryptocurrency payments are gaining traction in the mainstream.
- Bitcoin ETFs and other digital currency ETFs are traded on exchanges.

A clear picture of the cryptocurrency industry's long-term prospects will emerge when these problems are addressed and remedied over time. A constant stream of incremental development has been made since Bitcoin's inception. Our understanding of what's going on will improve by the end of 2022.

Cryptocurrency: The Currency of The Future

By 2022, authorities throughout the globe might come up with a worldwide framework for regulating cryptocurrencies. Treasury Secretary Janet Yellen and Securities and Exchange Commission Chairman Gary Gensler have been brought together by the Biden administration to lead the cryptocurrency regulatory process. Yellen has been keeping tabs on this industry for years, but with a cautious eye. In 2018, Gensler was a visiting professor at MIT, where he taught courses on bitcoin, blockchains, and other cryptocurrencies.

There is genuine optimism that a functional system can be built for investors, consumers, cryptocurrency firms, and conventional institutions if well-informed individuals set the tone for future laws. Regulators who are well-versed in these matters will distinguish between, for example, the differences between a value storage system like Bitcoin and an advanced ledger with smart contracts like Ethereum.

Once the federal government has established a legal framework and taxation system, a considerable number of cryptocurrencies may reach the digital wallets of American residents. However, despite El Salvador accepting Bitcoin as legal cash in 2021, the United States is unlikely to follow suit soon. Soon, however, many merchants are expected to accept payment in digital currencies similar to cash, such as Bitcoin, Ripple's XRP, or Litecoin (CRYPTO: LTC). The growing popularity of cryptocurrency should prompt regulation and political action, and blockchain systems should gain from this as well.

In 2022 and beyond, these procedures will permeate the crypto economy. So even an unduly tight regulatory framework would be welcomed by investors who are fed up with today's incoherent monitoring.

Future hacks and ransoms

In 2021, cryptocurrency was used to finance ransomware payments of millions of dollars. This is because digital currencies have qualities that make them appealing to thieves. Once payment has been made, it's practically hard to reverse a payment; tracking and tracing them is very tough once payment has been made. Gurvais Grigg, a senior tech officer at Chainalysis, stated in an email that "we should anticipate seeing more criminals flocking to cryptocurrencies and services that promise to conceal illegal cash owing to the misperception of ultimate anonymity." When used for lawful purposes, Bitcoin is attractive to criminals because it is cross-border, fast, and liquid.

In 2022, Grigg and others predict that cryptocurrency-based decentralized finance would be a favorite target for hackers due to its small but growing business. A single authority or organization that doesn't control financing is called Defi or decentralized finance. People may directly connect to Defi items over a dispersed network rather than depending on a bank or credit card network. Defi is a fast-moving, high-tech business with a lot of promise, even if it's still in its infancy. Consequently, it has garnered interest and money, making it an ideal target for criminals.

According to Grigg, for both hacking and money laundering purposes, criminals are likely to investigate Defi. "These systems are ideal targets for experienced criminals who have made similar attacks previously, due to how new Defi is and the boom in use in developed economies."

Cryptocurrency regulations are on the rise

Legislators in Olympia recognize the significance of cryptocurrencies. The difficulty in grasping it is, nonetheless, evident. The "series of tubes" moment for crypto may be just around the corner, courtesy of an unprepared representative. Whether it comes to cryptocurrency, lawmakers in the United States have indicated an interest in a wide variety of issues, including whether stable coin producers should be deemed banks and when to tax cryptocurrency. It's a thorny subject. It will take some time to have the correct standards in place.

American citizens may have to wait to see a complete framework for crypto-focused legislation before further milestones are reached. However, normal bitcoin users and investors may gain while business leaders and political authorities collaborate while environmental and security issues are addressed. Because of this, we should expect even more radical changes as the bitcoin market matures. There's no doubt about it: Cryptocurrency will play a role in our future.

Crypto: What the Future Holds

The volatility and component of cryptocurrencies, particularly Bitcoin, has been well-documented throughout the years. Volatility in Bitcoin is mainly determined by the choices made by financial authorities in the United States regarding its use. When everything is said and done, it may be summed like this: Users of Bitcoin believe that by 2024, roughly 94% of the many Bitcoin varieties will be revealed.

According to Snapchat's original investor, Jeremy Liew, Bitcoin might reach a whopping $500,000 by 2030. Because it is decentralized, secure, and anonymous, this kind of cash is projected to expand in popularity dramatically. Cryptocurrencies like Bitcoin have a bright future since many tech-savvy people and businesses choose to use alternative encrypted currency forms. Miners used to make a lot of money when they added new blocks to the blockchain, but that is expected to go away soon. Even though cryptocurrency is only getting started, it is too early to predict whether or not the next big thing is money or what impact it will have in the future. Suppose a computer crashes and wipes all the information, including the crypto wallets. In that case, the loss of all crypto portfolios might be prevented in the future, thanks to technological improvements. Other advantages include a possible defense against hackers who may wipe away your whole bank account within seconds. As more companies embrace crypto as a payment method, its adoption has grown.

To jump into the technology revolution, several governments have begun developing their cryptocurrencies, and legislation has been issued in many countries to restrict the usage of these currencies, giving them greater credibility as a form of cash for businesses and people to utilize. It is expected that the use of crypto would increase due to more restrictions. The safety of a currency is an important consideration, and bitcoin meets this need admirably. Because it is open source and has never been hacked, blockchain proves to be very secure. If a company in the ecosystem has a weakness in its website and links to information that can be used to hack wallets, Bitcoin may be hacked. However, cryptocurrency is broadly safe and can be used for a long time like money in the future.

Conclusion

Cryptocurrency's future is bright because of its widespread popularity and acceptance. As crypto grows, a lot of stability and a store of value will be achieved. It may be used more broadly by businesses, the government, and individuals in their everyday lives. In the early phases of its development, cryptocurrency is still a bit of a mystery, and some people are still hesitant about it. Still, it is here to stay, has been adopted into our daily lives, and will soon be utilized by everyone.

NFT INVESTING FOR BEGINNERS

Easy Guide to make Money with Digital Art

Easy Blockchain Academy

Chapter 1:

History of NFT

Who was the first person to develop an NFT?

Now, how did we get here with all of this new technology? On May 3rd, 2014, Kevin Mccoy, the guy who invented the NFT, started his narrative. In the crypto art market's burgeoning boom, Quantum coined its non-fungible currency.
A pixelated representation of an octagon filled with symbols signifying circles, arcs, or other forms that share a common center, with more prominent characters surrounding smaller ones, is known as Quantum. The one-of-a-kind "Quantum" artwork (2014-2021) is now for sale for $7 Million.

Mccoy stands head and shoulders above the others. He and his wife Jennifer have made a name for themselves as top-tier digital artists over many years. Indeed, "the NFT phenomena are intimately part of the art world," Mccoy claims. Artists have been using creative technologies for a long time. The Metropolitan Museum of Art is now showing their result, "Every Shot, Every Episode." ardent art collectors have purchased their work, but Mccoy prefers to sell in a gallery or one-on-one rather than participate in public bidding wars.

History OF NFTs

Initiated by CryptoKitties, Rare Pepe, and CryptoPunks, the CryptoArt category was born. Due to viral network effects and the willingness to spend significant amounts of money to obtain these pieces, these pieces of 'art' became famous.

2012-2013: Colored Coins

Let's get started on this adventure, with many individuals, artists, and projects involved. In 2012-2013, a "colored currency" was first released on the Bitcoin blockchain, and the concept of NFTs was born. It is possible to utilize colored coins to establish the ownership of any asset, from precious metals to real estate, even shares and bonds, on the blockchain. The initial concept was to utilize the Bitcoin blockchain to store assets such as digital collectibles, coupons, real estate, and stock in a corporation, among other things. As a cutting-edge innovation, they were hailed as a potential game-changer.

2014: Counterparty

Open-source internet protocol based on the Bitcoin blockchain was created in 2014 by Robert Dermody, Adam Krellenstein, and Evan Wagner as Counterparty by three cofounders. Users might develop their tradable currencies using Counterparty's asset creation and decentralized exchange features. Ideas and possibilities abound, including meme trading without counterfeit concerns.

2015: Spells of Genesis on Counterparty

Counterparty and the developers behind Spells of Genesis collaborated in April 2015. The Spells of Genesis video game developers were pioneers in launching an ICO and the first to issue in-game assets into a blockchain using Counterparty. BitCrystals, the in-game money introduced by Counterparty's designers, raised funds for the project.

2016: Trading Cards on Counterparty

New tendencies started to appear in August of this year. Counterparty and the famous trading card game Force of Will have partnered forces to provide their cards to Counterparty users. As measured by sales volume, Force of Will was the fourth most popular card game in North America. It showed the benefits of storing such assets on a distributed ledger despite having no previous blockchain or cryptocurrency knowledge.

2016: Rare Pepes on Counterparty

Memes made their way onto the blockchain in 2016. As of October of that year, memes were being shared on the Counterparty site. Rare Pepes became popular when people began to contribute assets to the meme. This frog meme has gained a large following throughout the years because of its unique nature. Pepe the Frog started as a comedic figure but has become one of the most famous memes on the internet. As the platform grew in popularity, rare Pepes began to be exchanged on Ethereum in early 2017. Live auctions were conducted during the first Rare Digital Art Festival by Portion's Founder, Jason Rosenstein, and Louis Parker. The first-time artists from all around the globe were able to sell their work on the CryptoArt platform with the Rare Pepe Wallet launch. Digital art was also the first to have inherent worth for the first time.

2017: CryptoPunks

John Watkinson and Matt Hall, the founders of Larva Labs, began creating unique characters produced on the Ethereum blockchain as trade-in Rare Pepes increased. The number of characters would be restricted to 10,000, and no two characters would be identical. As an ERC721/ERC20 hybrid, the project is named Cryptopunks after a Bitcoin experiment from the 1990s.

Although ERC20, the most widely used Ethereum Token Standard, provides rules that enable tokens to communicate with one other, it isn't the greatest for developing unique tokens. ERC721, a standard for NFTs on the Ethereum blockchain, was introduced. Using ERC721, a single smart contract can keep track of the ownership and movement of its tokens.

Using ERC721, CryptoKitties NFTs were off to a flying start. They are a virtual game built on the Ethereum blockchain that lets participants adopt, breed, and trade virtual cats. CNBC and Fox News were among the first to show them on their airwaves, and they quickly became an internet sensation. Axiom Zen, a Vancouver-based firm, produced CryptoKitties, which swiftly went viral and attracted financing from prominent investors due to the growth in their user base. Dapper Labs, a spinoff of Axiom Zen, was formed from CryptoKitties.

2018-2021: The NFT Explosion

Before widespread usage begins in early 2021, NFTs will gradually become known to the general population between 2018 and 2021. The crypto-supposedly community's subterranean activity gradually becomes more popular art. When artist Kevin Abosch joined GIFTO for a charity auction on Valentine's Day 2018, this transformation reached a tipping point. The Forever Rose, a stunning piece of CryptoArt, sold for $1 million due to the collaboration.

Artists other than Abosch have embraced this daring mode of expression. Slowly but surely, it's gaining hold among artists eager to test the limits of their imaginations. Using the Ethereum network and his blood in a project dubbed "IAMA Coin," Mr. Abosch proceeded to increase the stakes.

Compared to current asset transfer methods, the NFT market is more efficient and liquid. There is a slew of new online sites that cater to both makers and collectors. Traditional art brokers, such as auction houses, often charge up to 40% of a buyer's purchase price for their services. This is the primary area of disruption. The open sea is one of the essential online markets for art, music, domain names, and other memorabilia. To simplify the minting process for creators, the Mintable platform is designed with this goal in mind. With its $PRT governance token, Portion aims to become an NFT platform that connects the Defi ecosystem, NFTs, and the decentralized autonomous organization (DAO). Niftex, for example, enables users to acquire "shards" of NFTs, which are ERC20 tokens that represent a portion of the complete NFT and may be purchased on other platforms.

NFT Fundamentals

Cryptocurrencies are based on blockchain technology, such as non-fungible tokens (NFTs). Some digital item, such as a game artifact or a piece of digital artwork, is represented by an NFT. The majority of NFTs have been developed on Ethereum, with a few recent examples employing alternative blockchains, such as Flow, in addition to the Ethereum platform.

A non-fungible token's most distinguishing feature is that each one is individually unique. NFTs, unlike cryptocurrencies, cannot be easily exchanged since they represent unique and distinct items with varying values. For a non-fungible token, its value is based on the perceived value of its underlying item. As with a real-world artwork, the value is frequently subjective and relies on the taste and personal preferences of the owner or a possible buyer. Like real-world collectibles, it might be linked to a product's rarity.

The blockchain ensures the uniqueness of an NFT, making it an unchangeable asset. An NFT's ownership must be safeguarded with the help of these features. The authenticity and provenance of an NFT can be easily verified using blockchain technology, giving the owner complete peace of mind that they are holding an original and one-of-a-kind item.

An increasing number of digital goods, such as digital art, games, music, and even Defi, are now part of the NFT market. An Ethereum-based initiative called CryptoPunks published the first NFT in 2017 with a collection of 10,000 distinct digital characters. There have been more than 10,000 transactions of CryptoPunks in the past year, with an average price of $10,000 for a character. As a digital game by Dapper Labs, CryptoKitties is one of the first examples of NFTs becoming popularised in the digital world. Cats are famous on the Internet, and CryptoKitties, a game based on Ethereum, grew so popular that it clogged up the Ethereum network.

Nft Uses

In the early stages of the blockchain, non-fungible tokens were used as currency. The entertainment and creative sectors are fast adopting them as a new tool.

In gaming and digital collectibles, NFTs have their first use case. In 2020, the global gaming sector was expected to be worth $160 billion, according to estimates. NFTs are an excellent method for ensuring fair and transparent transactions in the gaming industry since many games entail collecting artifacts, virtual possessions, or even experiences. The entertainment and sports industries are also using NFTs. For example, the NBA's Top Shot Moments – legally sanctioned digital collectibles that have racked up about $230 million in sales – and Actor Trek star William Shatner recently debuted their NFT cards.

Digital art is another use for NFTs. In recent years, there has been a tremendous rise in the popularity of digital creative arts. One theory is that the tendency towards greater accessibility of art will lead to its democratization. Ownership may be found in digital and real-world art, but the two mediums are distinct. When it comes to protecting intellectual property rights and verifying the authenticity of digital artwork, NFTs are a dependable and straightforward solution. Several platforms, including OpenSea, Nifty Gateway, and Raible, provide a market for NFTs to enable the production and exchange of digital art.

Non-fungible tokens may be used in domains like digital identification, Defi, and yield farming because of their immutability and uniqueness. These nonlinear functional transforms (NFTs) may depict the distinct characteristics of various yield farming methods in this configuration. The term "yield farming" refers to those who receive incentives by storing their crypto assets in a DeFi service.

NFT Outlook

The existence of non-fungible tokens is unquestionably an unusual occurrence in the crypto sphere. Investors and consumers alike are fast adopting NFTs, despite their novelty and lack of established valuation measures. An estimated $355 million has been spent on these assets, with an average token price of $66.

NFTs may be accelerated by variables such as the rising gaming business, the rapid development of new technology in games, such as virtual reality, and the exploding popularity of digital art. Another indicator that NFTs are becoming more widespread is Christie's recent sale of an NFT artwork by digital artist Beeple.

NFTs also depends on how well the technology can withstand time, how thriving infrastructure can keep up with expanding popularity, and how effectively NFTs combine scarcity and convenience to adapt to user demand in the long run.

Chapter 2:
Non-fungible token

The term "Non-Fungible Token" refers to a data unit that may be used to record and verify digital material, such as films, music, and photographs, on cryptocurrency blockchains, most notably Ethereum. Every transaction on the blockchain has a record of the content's origin and pricing history that can be readily accessed. NFTs are primarily responsible for simplifying acquiring and reselling digital material.

- NFTs are one-of-a-kind cryptographic tokens that cannot be copied on a blockchain.
- Artwork and real estate may be represented with NFTs.
- As a result of this "tokenization," these real-world physical goods may be exchanged more quickly, with less risk of fraud.
- Individuals' identities and property rights may also be represented via NFTs.

Background of Non-Fungible Tokens

Anything labeled as 'fungible' may be swapped out for anything else. Any token that may be exchanged for another of a similar kind is said to be fungible. As a result, NFTs are one-of-a-kind and cannot be used in any situation.

An essential component of blockchain and cryptocurrencies is tokens. They come in various shapes and are used for a variety of purposes. Different token types exist, but non-fungible tokens offer unique characteristics and may be used in multiple situations. It is vital to concentrate on fungibility since most cryptocurrencies seek to be a common medium of exchange.

When exchanging currency, for example, a US dollar might be exchanged for another US dollar and the British Pound. There is no requirement to return the identical dollar with the same serial number if you give someone money. The opposite of non-fungibility is lending someone a unique piece of art and expecting them to return it with the same work.

All major cryptocurrencies, including Ethereum and Bitcoin, have fungibility built in. NFT, on the other hand, has developed into a new token type with several fascinating features and uses. Non-fungible tokens, on the other hand, are a relatively new idea that is difficult to grasp. As a result, there may be substantial skepticism about the concept of non-fungible tokens, as well as their characteristics, uses, and prospects.

Understanding What is NFT

NFT stands for what? Cryptographic hashing techniques are used to create a unique digital asset that can't be copied, and blockchain technology connects the token to that digital asset. Monero, Ether, and Bitcoin all have non-fungible tokens that vary from non-fungible tokens. NFTs can't be swapped for another NFT because of their unique properties.

The unique and exclusive data that distinguishes NFTs from other tokens may be stored in smart contracts within the NFTs. The indivisibility of NFTs is another well-known property. Non-fungible tokens cannot be exchanged in more small amounts like Bitcoins. As a result, you cannot transfer a portion of an NFT to another party. NFTs may play a revolutionary role as companies embrace blockchain technology and integrate it into their operations. Because of this, non-fungible tokens play a particular function in the blockchain ecosystem. Furthermore, NFTs have a higher relevance when it comes to blockchain's drastic move to the next phase of digital transformation.

Token Standards

Let's look at some non-fungible token usage cases now. It's fascinating to see how versatile NFTs can be. Tokens on the blockchain may be created from both digital and real-world entities. It's critical to grasp one element of NFT operations before moving on to a more in-depth discussion of actual usage cases. Developers must adhere to specified blockchain token criteria to build a successful token application. For example, Ethereum provides a wide range of ERC standards for developers to choose from. Let's take a look at the various blockchain token standards that are critical to the operation of NFTs.

ERC-20

Ethereum-based cryptocurrency tokens use the ERC-20 token standard. To ensure interoperability and compatibility with exchanges and wallets in the Ethereum ecosystem, the ERC-20 standard is a set of rules and laws that individual objects must adhere to. In October 2020, the Ethereum network had over 300,000 ERC-20 tokens, and that figure continued to rise rapidly.

ERC-721

It is a separate asset that cannot be interchanged, unlike the ERC-20 token standard. Including certificates and asset tokenization that cannot be divided serves to represent assets. Information is stored in the smart contracts of ERC-721-compliant coins.

It's possible to use smart contracts to store an asset's ownership and identification information. ERC-721 offers more excellent ownership transparency, security, and immutability despite the absence of a set mechanism for issuing tokens. Non-fungible ERC-721 tokens are, in a nutshell, tokens that can't be exchanged.

ERC-1155

In addition to establishing the groundwork for NFT use cases, ERC-1155 is another essential token standard. For installing new assets that may be transferred between wallets, ERC-721 is unquestionably the best option. ERC-721 tokens, on the other hand, are often inadequate and sluggish.

A collection of ERC-721 tokens may not be enough if a person exchanges various artifacts, like weapons and skins, for a single character in a game. The ERC-1155 standard comes in handy in these types of situations. As the 'next-generation multi-token standard,' ERC-1155 can have revolutionary effects on the development of NFTs. ERC-1155 is unique because it allows for both fungible and non-fungible token applications to be implemented.

Different uses Of NFTs

Non-fungible tokens have been the subject of much conjecture in the blockchain community over the years. While this may seem counterintuitive, the reality is that NFTs can demonstrate evidence of genuine ownership of certain assets on the blockchain. NFTs can control, prohibit access to, or limit the use of specified assets by persons. Consequently, NFTs have a long road ahead of them, and their applications are expected to rise over the following years.

NFTs, on the other hand, are now seen as advantageous in a broad range of business blockchain applications. It would be best not to underestimate their ability to verify originality and the scarcity of information on internet sites. After saying that, let's look at the many non-fungible token use cases in detail as follows:

Art

Recently, the blockchain community was rocked by the revelation that digital artist Beeple had sold an NFT of his work for an astounding $69 million at Christie's. After a series of progressively pricey auctions, the NFT went for a world record price. In October, a pair of NFTs sold for $66,666.66 apiece in Beeple's first batch of sales. A collection of his artwork was later auctioned for a total of almost $3.5 million. For Beeple's work and NFT as a technology, Christie's, an auction house with a history spanning 255 years, places a fair value on both.

Tokens that can be used to create programmable art are the most prevalent non-fungible token use cases. Currently, there are several limited-edition artworks available for purchase. Indeed, they provide a degree of programmability that may adapt to various situations. Blockchain-based digital assets' price movements may be reflected in artwork created using smart contracts and oracles.

Consequently, non-fungible tokens might be used in the realm of legacy arts by tokenizing real-world assets and various works of art. Scan a code on a tag affixed to artwork to register ownership on the blockchain using the combined strength of blockchain and IoT. As a result, people could explore the artwork's whole history, including prior prices and ownerships.

Fashion

Blockchain has been successfully integrated into the fashion industry to ensure that the whole supply chain benefits. To prevent counterfeiting, consumers may quickly check the ownership information of their goods and accessories online. Apparel and accessory price tags might be scanned using a QR code in the form of an NFT.

Carbon dioxide emissions have been significantly reduced due to the use of blockchain in the fashion industry. Because of this, customers could obtain a sense of the asset's origin and where it was generated. Additionally, customers may see information about the previous owners of an item before purchasing. Thus, they can safeguard their clients and their employees simultaneously. As a result, NFT has the potential to build a new sort of blockchain for the fashion supply chain.

Licenses and Certifications

Verifying licenses and certificates is another area where NFT may be pretty useful. Successful applicants may choose between digital or paper-based course completion certificates, as with any other degree or license. To get a job in a business or an educational institution, universities and companies want copies of the certificate of completion from the course as references.

With the use of NFTs, administrators may save a great deal of time. NFT certificates and licenses alleviate the strain of record-checking and verification by eliminating the need for paper documents. As a result, keeping proof of course completion or license will be more straightforward using this technique.

Collectibles

Non-fungible tokens may also be used for collectibles, one of the most notable examples. One of the first ways individuals learned about NFTs was via online collectibles like Cryptokitties. Since they caused the Ethereum network to become overburdened in 2017, the popularity of Cryptokitties has grown significantly.

These virtual kittens may be bred to produce a variety of different kittens. Each crypto cat has a unique hair pattern or eye color that makes it stand out from the others. Users may buy a Sire and a Dame cat for breeding by clicking on a button.

Genetic Algorithm, or GA, gives the new kitten its unique identity. The rarity of their genetic composition determines the value of crypto kitties. Cryptokitties' worth is also determined by the number of times a Sire has been used for breeding other kittens.

Sports

Some of the most pressing concerns facing the sports business are counterfeit tickets and goods. As an ideal substitute for addressing such challenges, blockchain technology is emerging as a leading contender. Fake artifacts and tokens can be avoided because of blockchain technology's immutability.

Blockchain-based tokenized sports tickets highlight how NFT use cases might improve the sports market. Every key is the same, and they all include data that can only be accessed by the ticket's registered owner on the blockchain. With several tokenizations of successful sportspeople on the blockchain, sport NFTs are increasingly popular. Based on their achievements, tokens representing successful athletes have a higher worth.

Unstoppable Domains and the Ethereum
Name Service
Both Unstoppable Domains and the Ethereum Name Service provide crypto addresses as non-fungible (NFT) tokens. Tokens like my name. Crypto and my name. Eth is a famous instance of non-fungible token use cases. Users' crypto addresses are comparable to their Twitter or Instagram handles in that they are all unique.
Popular names tend to be more valuable than those that are less popular. Hundreds of individuals may attempt to get the same handle name if the name is very prevalent. Even while Twitter and Instagram prohibit users from selling their username handles, Unstoppable domains and ENS may assist in purchasing and selling bitcoin addresses freely.

Memberships
As a membership, NFTs may also be utilized to acquire access to limited-edition items and services, as well as special events. An NFT membership is easy to buy, sell, and swap for any other asset on the blockchain since it is frictionless and transparent in its objective.
Having all of your membership cards in one wallet makes it simple to keep track of all of your memberships. If you're a member of many clubs and organizations, you may leverage your memberships to enhance your brand and reputation.
The Bored Ape Yacht Club is a well-known example of an NFT that allows members to view exclusive content (BAYC). The BAYC NFT collection is like a swamp club for apes, and it's free to join. You'll notice a lot of holders of BAYC NFTs using their assets as their profile picture on social media, which is a perfect illustration of how some NFTs may help you build your brand.

Gaming

Game makers have shown a lot of interest in NFTs. Players may profit from NFTs since they can give away to document ownership of game objects and drive in-game economies. You may purchase goods for use in your game in many regular games. When you're done with the game, you might retrieve your money if that item was an NFT. If the thing gets more popular, you may even earn money.

Games may earn a commission every time an item is sold in the open market by becoming issuers of the NFT. As a result, both players and developers benefit from the secondary NFT market, which is mutually beneficial.

This also implies that even if the creators stop supporting a game, the goods you've gathered are yours to keep. Your in-game purchases may outlast the games you play. All of your things will remain in your possession even if the game itself is no longer being updated. To put it another way, in-game items now have a monetary worth outside the confines of the game. It is possible to acquire virtual plots of land in Decentraland, a virtual reality game with NFTs.

Advantages And Benefits of NFTs

As far as new types of digital assets go, non-fungible tokens are the best bet. NFT auctions with starting bids of $1 million are familiar, yet one-third of all NFTs sell for less than $100, which creates an interesting dichotomy. Since NFTs are so valuable, it's logical to investigate what elements are responsible for their high worth. The advantages of NFTs demonstrate this. Non-fungible tokens provide several benefits, including the basis for their value.

Ownership

Non-fungible tokens have a significant benefit over fungible tokens in that they can be shown to be owned. With NFTs on the blockchain, ownership may be linked to an individual account. NFTs, on the other hand, cannot be divided up among several owners since they are unassignable. The ownership benefits of NFTs guarantee that customers are protected from the problems of counterfeit NFTs.

Those who are critical of NFTs have said that it is possible to sell or give away images of NFTs simply by taking photos of them. The NFT may be seen in a photograph. However, it is critical to determine whether you own the item first. A picture of the Mona Lisa downloaded from the internet does not make you the proprietor of that image.

It is essential to keep in mind that with NFTs, ownership overvalue is ensured. To put it another way, NFTs have the potential to change the way assets are verified and managed fundamentally. You can transfer ownership of NFTs since they can be found on a blockchain network. You may also reap the benefits of NFTs' quick asset ownership transitions in a wide range of real-world settings.

Authenticity

To demonstrate their worth, NFTs have a fantastic set of characteristics. The uniqueness of non-fungible tokens is a significant factor in their advantages. The creation of NFTs on the blockchain implies that they are linked to unique data. NFT developers, on the other hand, have the option of releasing just a limited amount of NFTs to create scarcity.

Some NFTs allow makers to make numerous copies, similar to how tickets are created. Furthermore, the blockchain on which NFTs are kept is immutable, ensuring the legitimacy of the NFTs stored there. The immutability of blockchain-based NFTs assures that they cannot be changed, removed, or replaced. As a result, NFTs can quickly demonstrate their authenticity as an essential attribute.

Transferability

NFTs' transferability is the second most frequent response to the question, "What is the advantage of NFT?" NFTs may be easily traded freely on certain exchanges with a wide variety of trading possibilities. For example, when it comes to gaming, NFTs may help. In-game objects are every day in video games, and gamers often spend real money to get the most out of them. Players may only use in-game things in the fun, and they cannot use them anyplace else. Furthermore, if the game goes out of style, gamers may lose their investment in the in-game treasures or things they have purchased. With NFTs, game creators may issue in-game goods that players can keep in their digital wallets. After then, gamers may use or even sell the in-game things for profit. Using smart contracts to transfer ownership of NFTs is simple since they are based on smart contracts. There are intelligent contract requirements that must be met before the transfer of ownership may be performed.

Creation Of Economic Possibilities

To date, most NFT experts have concentrated on their core characteristics. NFTs are now widely used in the digital content industry for various purposes. Because of the industry's fragmentation, NFTs are a viable option in the digital content sector. It is common for content producers to worry about rival platforms swiping away their revenues and revenue opportunities. For example, a digital artist who publishes their work on social networks might generate money via advertising to the artist's followers on the site. While the artist receives their fair share of attention, the platform does not assist the artist make any money.

New creator economies might emerge due to the advantages provided by non-fungible tokens. The goal of the creator economy is to enable content producers to avoid having to hand up ownership of their material to the platforms they use to promote their work.

NFTs enable content ownership to be embedded into the content itself. In this way, the money generated by the sale of material goes directly to the producers. NFT information contains the inventor's address, so profits from token sales may go to the original creator. Smart contracts may be used to pay the inventor of the NFT royalties if the NFT is sold to a new owner.

Boost Inclusive Growth

The fourth and most essential benefit of NFTs is that they foster equitable development. All players in the ecosystem may benefit from NFTs' ability to bring together content providers from various industries. In the first place, NFT creators can get the total value for their work and communicate directly with their customers. NFTs, on the other hand, allow purchasers to access liquidity in a variety of asset classes.

One notable example of guaranteeing liquidity is via NFTs for precious metals. Real-world assets, such as property, might be represented by NFTs that reflect the growth potential. Real estate agents might issue NFTs with partial ownership in the support they represent. If certain circumstances are met, a single property might be owned by numerous purchasers.

While NFTs benefit a wide range of stakeholders, they may also provide certain general benefits. For example, NFTs effectively promote broad-based economic growth, as shown by the many examples of their use. Most importantly, the creators stand to gain significantly from NFTs in increased royalties, which bodes well for future development.

Composability

In a sense, NFTs may be compared to interlocking Lego pieces, which is fun. Because of this, new NFTs may be launched that builds on the success of existing NFTs.

It is possible for a second NFT collection, say 10,000 programmatically produced avatars, to be created for that previously launched collection if the first author decides to make an NFT collection of accessories. 3D Fluff NFTs may be used as a Jetpack to soar across the metaverse!

Composability also makes it possible to create NFT-only material that the owner of another NFT can only access. An NFT project may be seen as a component of a linked ecosystem because of its inherent composability.

Security

NFTs are immutable digital signatures that provide collectors with unparalleled trust. They must be aware of the hazards associated with dealing in art. For a seamless transaction, they need to investigate the piece's history and take further security precautions before buying it. NFTs, on the other hand, may be exchanged in a fashion that is both safe and transparent.

This trust in the future of art extends as well. No censorship or physical degradation may affect digital works on the blockchain, although adequate storage is still required. The use of blockchain technology also makes it possible to safely and openly transfer massively valuable assets between continents and throughout the world.

NFTs ensure the legitimacy, uniqueness, and ownership of unique assets in the same way that blockchain technology developed a protocol of trust that enabled the establishment of digital money.

Accessibility

Digital collecting becomes more and more valuable as more of us begin to work remotely, reject consumerism, or decrease our baggage while traveling. With the DoinGud app, all you need is an email account to browse your art collection on your smartphone – and no wall space is required.

Isn't it time to go beyond the 2D digital realm? There are also 3D immersive art shows in VR settings for people eager to go farther into the metaverse. Fans, for example, may stop by the gallery of our partner MOCA at Somnium Space for a look.

Chapter 3:

Different Types and Uses of NFTs

One of the most talked-about subjects in 2021 is NFTs or non-fungible tokens. In recent years, blockchain-based digital assets have grown more popular. Consequently, there has recently been an increase in people wanting to learn about the various NFT kinds.

People are interested in NFTs' economic possibilities rather than a vision for a radical shift in asset management. Non-fungible token developers and investors stand to benefit significantly from the market's current trend of steady growth. A greater understanding of the various forms of non-fungible tokens will help you make smarter choices along the way.

Sudden Rise of NFTs
In the realm of technology, digital tokens are nothing new. In reality, it wasn't until the digital artist Beeple auctioned off his artwork at a Christie's auction in March 2021 that NFTs began to attract international recognition. Twitter CEO Jack Dorsey and Tesla CEO Elon Musk have also spoken out supporting NFTs. To put this in perspective, the first NFT was issued in 2014, and just six years later, in the first quarter of 2021, the NFT market valuation is already close to $2 billion! Nearly $250 million in sales are expected to be generated by the end of the year in question. On a blockchain, NFTs are just digital or cryptographic tokens with the capacity to retain their uniqueness. NFTs can be tokenized versions of physical goods or entirely digital assets.

Common Categories of NFTs
Several variables might confuse newcomers to NFT: the link with art, for example. Non-linear functional transforms (NFTs) aren't only for art. There are several kinds of NFTs, each with its features and applications.

- The essential NFT type categorization is based on broad categories. NFTs may be broadly classified into three broad categories:
- An original or a replica of a work that has been recorded on a blockchain network or distributed ledger technology (DLT).
- Non-financial transactions (NFTs) are digitally native, which means they hold ownership rights to the labor that constitutes the NFT's NFT metadata.

Non-fungible tokens may be broadly classified according to various characteristics, as shown by the most prevalent forms of non-fungible tokens. One of the essential factors in categorizing non-fungible tokens is NFT information. NFTs built from the ground up are stored on a blockchain network and cannot be shifted. Digitally native NFTs are assets in which numerous individuals with ownership rights to the asset are issued NFTs. Therefore, the NFT is not yours; you receive the right to use it.

NFT on Ethereum

The Ethereum blockchain's first non-fungible digital asset standard was ERC-721[104]. It is possible to generate new ERC-721-compliant smart contracts by simply copying a reference implementation of the standard. Using ERC-721, a unique identifier's owner may be tracked, and the asset can be transferred to others only with the owner's explicit authorization.

Additionally, the ERC-1155 standard provides "semi-fungibility" and ERC-721 functionality (meaning that an ERC-721 asset could be built using ERC-1155). A class of assets is represented by the unique ID of an ERC-1155 token, as opposed to a single asset by the unique ID of an ERC-721 token, and the quantity field indicates how much of each class a wallet has. The user may move any quantity of assets from one class to another, and the assets are interchangeable. The high transaction costs (known as gas prices) imposed by Ethereum have led to the development of layer two alternatives for Ethereum that also allow NFTs:

- Using ZK rollups to avoid gas expenses, Immutable X is Ethereum's layer two protocol exclusively for NFTs.
- A polygon is a three-dimensional shape. NFT markets like OpenSea use Polygon's proof of stake blockchain, formerly known as the Matic Network.

What is ERC-721 Token?

There is a standard for tokens on the Ethereum platform known as ERC-721, or simply ERC721. Ethereum Request for Comments 721 is the acronym for the name. "Non-fungible tokens" (also known as "NFTs") are a typical moniker for these types of assets. "Non-fungible" indicates that they are one-of-a-kind. A surge in interest in NFTs occurred throughout 2020 as individuals started to speculate on their worth. Thus, ERC721 tokens became more popular than ever before due to this development. It's unclear, though, what the ERC-721 token standard is and what it means.

The ERC-721 standard makes it possible for smart contracts to use the Ethereum API for NFTs. Because of the criteria, NFTs may be exchanged and monitored, allowing for accurate documentation of the token's ownership. Tokens based on the ERC-721 standard and non-fungible tokens (NFTs) indicate ownership of many assets, including real and digital ones. They may, for example, represent virtual collectibles like CryptoKitties, real estate like homes, or even assets with a negative value like debt. However, it's important to remember that NFT contracts do not include any data, such as photos, in the contract itself. Examples of this include digital art, such as an image. However, a unique ID is associated with the picture found in the token.

As a result, a link to another picture housed elsewhere is included in the token's ID and information. Consequently, NFT tokens point to external resources and maintain track of the ownership of an item on the blockchain. The deed does not include the home; it declares that someone owns the land. This is not a novel idea, and it functions similarly to a house deed.

How to make ERC721 Token?

A more excellent grasp of ERC-721 tokens now allows us to go further into the process of creating an ERC721 NFT. For this work, we'll look at the process of constructing a dApp that can mint NFTs regularly, which isn't too tricky. As a result, we won't go into too much depth on how to transfer ERC721 tokens since the objective of this post is to describe what they are and how to do so.

We'll be utilizing Moralis to create an ERC-721 token. Thus, there are five stages to follow:

1. An example of a smart contract that may be initialized.
2. It's time to create a website's index page.
3. Create a way for users to log in.
4. Add the ability to upload files.
5. Create a function for mints.

A dApp will create more than one ERC-721 token when these procedures are followed. There is also no requirement for previous development experience since we're working with Moralis throughout the process. However, prior experience with JavaScript and Solidity would be beneficial since this would speed up the development process.

ERC-721 vs ERC-1155

The introduction of the ERC-721 standard increased the dynamic nature of the Ethereum network and opened the door to the development of new and creative solutions. Developers might utilize the standard to improve the efficiency of the real estate market, for example, or to introduce bonds into the cryptocurrency market. While the ERC-721 standard increased the network's dynamic capabilities, it was still conceivable to make Ethereum development even more flexible due to the standard. Token contracts based on the ERC-721 standard are meant to create just one particular sort of NFT, which might restrict the usefulness of a token in certain situations. Tickets for concerts are an example of how the limits of the ERC-721 standard may become a source of contention. This would imply that NFTs be created for this purpose and that the contract would include seat IDs linked to the seats' purchasers. So far, so good; but, when we have more than one concert. If we have numerous shows, this will imply that we would need to implement a new ERC-721 token contract for each new event, which would be a significant time commitment.

Another token standard, on the other hand, has evolved to address this problem. This standard, known as "ERC-1155," is considerably more dynamic than the previous one. It is feasible to have numerous distinct NFTs inside a single, smart contract, thanks to the ERC-1155 token standard. Furthermore, it is also possible to add additional NFTs as you go through the process. This implies that you will not have to make a specific decision about which NFTs you wish to include when the contract is implemented. As a result, ERC-1155 tokens are far more dynamic and capable of dealing with a more significant number of characteristics than the ERC-721 standard.

The disadvantage of this dynamic, on the other hand, is that an ERC-1155 token is far more sophisticated. As a result, we propose that new developers begin producing ERC721 tokens as soon as possible since they are substantially more straightforward to work with than other types of tokens.

Move Over Ethereum

Since the sale of Beeple's Everyday NFT collage for a record-breaking 69.3 million dollars in February 2021, the popularity of NFTs has soared. NFTs have become popular and can be purchased on many markets and supported by several blockchain technologies.

Some of the most popular NFT-enabled blockchains are listed below.

Bitcoin Cash

Bitcoin Cash is a cryptocurrency created as a fork of the Bitcoin cryptocurrency. Bitcoin Cash is a cryptocurrency launched in 2017 as a spin-off or alternative to Bitcoin. Bitcoin Cash was further divided into two cryptocurrencies in November 2018, with the names Bitcoin Cash and Bitcoin SV. Bitcoin Cash is traded on digital currency exchanges under the Bitcoin Cash moniker and the BCH currency code, which stands for Bitcoin Cash currency code (bitcoin). The Bitcoin Cash trade pairings BCH/BTC, BCH/ETH, and BCH/USDT were all banned from the OKEx exchange on March 26, 2018, citing "insufficient liquidity." As of May 2018, the number of Bitcoin Cash transactions per day is around one-tenth of the number of transactions per day for bitcoin. Coinbase offered Bitcoin Cash on its platform on December 19, 2017, and the coinbase platform witnessed price anomalies that prompted an inquiry into insider trading practices. BitPay, Coinify, and GoCoin are all accepting Bitcoin Cash payments as of August 2018, and further payment service providers are on the way.

Zilliqa

The transaction times of early blockchains like Bitcoin and Ethereum are well-known to the crypto-community. A sharding-based blockchain, Zilliqa, was launched in 2017. Because of Zilliqa's enhanced scalability, as the network grows, so does transaction speed.

By proposing and voting on ideas, Zilliqa community members with gzip governance tokens may help define the blockchain's future. NFT music platform Token||Traxx is only one of Zilliqa's many NFT-related initiatives, including its support for NFTs. Zilliqa's $10 million Creator Fund encourages NFT and Metaverse space innovation, which is fascinating.

Flow

For NFTs and other consumer applications, Flow is a proof of stake blockchain. One of the earliest NFT-based games was CryptoKitties, developed by Dapper Labs in 2017. The Ethereum network became crowded due to CryptoKitties transactions in 2017. There is no better way to assure low-cost, fast transactions than Flow's multimode design. It is possible to trade, stake, and vote using the FLOW token. More and more high-profile firms are joining the Flow network to sell their digital assets because of the platform's built-for-purpose architecture for consumer applications. The likes of UFC, NBA, and CNN have all jumped on the bandwagon to market great moments from their networks.

Tezos

An open-source proof of stake blockchain called Tezos was launched in 2018. Since Tezos wants to foster long-term innovation and upgradability, it urges its users to become involved. Compared to Ethereum, Tezos boasts about how much less power it needs and how little XTZ it takes to produce an NFT, two million times less than Ethereum does. Even though Tezos is one of the less-known blockchains, it is nonetheless making a presence in the NFT market with recent collaborations like OneOf, Raible, and Ubisoft launching their first NFT project on Tezos.

Solana

Solana promises to be the world's quickest proof of stake blockchain. Solana's scalability is one of its most appealing characteristics since it ensures that no transaction on the network will ever surpass $ 0.01. The NFT community has taken a shine to Solana because of its stated goal of being the blockchain of choice for crypto applications. In addition to launching new NFT initiatives, Solana has formed collaborations with notable firms like Opera Browser.

Cardano

Cardano is a decentralized blockchain with an open-source proof of stake model. As the co-founder of Ethereum and the creator of Cardano, Cardano has a strong team behind it and focuses on the necessity of regulatory compliance and scaling. In addition, it touts itself as the most eco-friendly blockchain. Cardano's cheap transaction costs and scalability make it a popular option among NFT users. In addition to Verlux and CNFT, several well-known NFT markets have been developed on the Cardano blockchain.

Types of NFTs

Speculations about the potential of NFTs, their worth, and the hazards they entail have grown into significant conversation points. With the capabilities of the blockchain, non-fungible tokens can show the true origins of an item. NFTs might be used to limit, deny, or restrict an individual's access to his or her assets, thereby assuring exclusivity. It is possible to see NFTs being used in a wide range of industries because of the rising infrastructure and possibility for innovation. As a result, new kinds of NFTs may be expected. You may look at some of the more noteworthy NFT kinds currently popular for the time being.

A list of non-fungible tokens would contain the following, among others:

- Collectibles
- Tickets to the Artwork Exhibition are on sale now.
- media such as music
- Gaming
- Items that are only available in the virtual world
- Assets that can be found in the real world.
- Domain names and identity memes

Let's look at these many non-fungible token (NFT) versions as a starting point.

Collectibles

Cryptokitties, virtual collectibles are the most prominent example of NFTs. In actuality, Cryptokitties is the first known use of NFTs by the general public. In 2017, Cryptokitties got so popular that Ethereum's network became jammed. One of the most interesting additions to the non-fungible tokens list in the digital collectibles area is the Cryptokitties token. In essence, these are digital kittens with unique characteristics that make them more popular than others.

Artwork

NFTs are a good fit for various visual media, including artwork. As the name suggests, programmable art is one of the most prevalent sorts of non-fungible tokens in this area. Many limited-edition works of art are now available to be programmed under particular circumstances. Artists might benefit from using oracles and smart contracts while making artwork for blockchain networks. The legacy arts sector has also been encouraged to participate via digital art NFTs.

Tickets for an Event

A new form of NFT that seems potential is event tickets. These forms of NFTs make it easier for festival-goers and concert-goers to prove their identification and tickets. Event organizers may create a limited number of NFT tickets on a particular blockchain platform. Customers can buy tickets via an auction and keep them in their phones' wallets for simple access on the go.

Music and other media

The music and media industries are experimenting with NFTs, creating a new category of NFTs in the process. Raible and Mintbase are two of the most popular sites for musicians who want to mint their tracks as NFTs. Using NFTs, music and media files may be linked to an individual's ownership claim, making them accessible. Listeners enjoy a premium experience while artists have the opportunity to connect directly with their fans and attract new ones. It's one of the most common reasons for incorporating classic vinyl record characteristics into NFT music. An increase in the number of non-fungible tokens (NFTs) for music might provide solid solutions to music piracy issues and intermediaries.

Gaming

In the gaming industry, NFTs have attracted a lot of attention. Most importantly, NFTs in the gaming industry aims to provide gamers with a broad range of advantages. Gamers often employ non-fungible tokens in the form of in-game currency. In-game economies may benefit from their inclusion of ownership records, which they can provide.

In contrast to in-game collectibles, NFTs may significantly impact the value of a game's collectibles. You may easily make money by selling in-game products like NFTs to other players. On the other side, authors of games or NFTs might receive a commission on every item sold on the open market.

Assets in the real world

NFTs may be used as real-world tokens, even though there aren't many NFT varieties to choose from. The tokenization of real estate and luxury items, for example, is a current focus of several NFT initiatives. An NFT deed may be used to buy a vehicle or a house, allowing for more flexibility in the purchase process. Cryptographic proof of ownership may help NFTs that reflect real-world assets take advantage of the prospects.

Identity

Scarcity is an essential characteristic of non-fungible tokens. Each NFT is a one-of-a-kind token that cannot be exchanged for any other. Like how event tickets NFTs work, identity NFTs do the same thing. It is possible to use them as unique identifiers for identity management systems.

Certification and licensing are two areas where identity-based NFTs may find frequent use. The identity management industry may alter if certificates, licenses, and NFTs prove and authenticate an individual's data were minted. Individuals would also store proof of their identification using identity-based NFTs without fear of losing it.

Memes
One of the most critical developments in NFTs in the last few years is the marketing of memes as NFT. Memes have been linked to NFTs, despite their widespread popularity in popular culture and their status as an immediate hit on the internet. As a result of NFT sales, unique meme-makers have shown their ability to engage in an expanding future ecosystem.

Domain Names
Non-Financial Transactions (NFTs) include domain names, which have grown more popular recently. Unstoppable Domains and the Ethereum Name Service (ENS) are two of the most prominent decentralized domain name NFTs. To simplify onboarding for new users, ENS can assist in converting lengthy and complicated user addresses into an intuitive and comfortable experience.

Chapter 4:
Platforms to buy NFTs

Nfts are fast becoming the most profitable and innovative segment of the cryptocurrency industry, not just in profit but also in creativity. Every day, pictures of pixelated figures (Cryptopunks) and bored apes (Bored Ape Yacht Club) sell for more than the price of practically any automobile or most homes combined, according to Forbes. To this point, corporations like Nike, Budweiser, and Pepsi are embracing NFTs quicker than they have done with any other blockchain technology. Almost all of the top NFT collections are mainly traded on OpenSea, which is the most widely used NFT trading site. Although OpenSea now leads the market, it still has a slew of faults, and a new platform that performs better while offering the same functionality may easily displace it and its enormous user base.

NFT Marketplace
An NFT marketplace is essentially a website that allows for NFT trading transactions. Several websites come under this category, and the majority of them provide significant advantages over their rivals. A nonfungible token, also known as a nonfungible coin, is a token that exists only on a cryptocurrency blockchain and can be shown to be unique. Through play-to-earn games and visually appealing profile images, the technology provides functionality. They are also highly handy for digital collectors since they don't have to worry about counterfeit items or demonstrate that their collection is genuine, which is a huge convenience.

Almost all non-financial technology platforms are connected with a widely used blockchain. Most of them are based on Ethereum, which might be problematic for smaller investors due to the high fees incurred. Others support blockchains that are far less expensive, such as Solana or Polygon. Different markets charge different fees, support various wallets and NFT collects, and provide a diverse range of trading capabilities and statistical data. NFT traders should exercise caution while selecting the most suitable trading platform for their needs since the platform might be critical to their performance.

How to buy NFTs?
Cryptocurrencies are required to purchase NFTs, and a cryptocurrency wallet is necessary for their storage. Signing up for a cryptocurrency exchange such as Binance or OKEx will allow you to build a free cryptocurrency wallet for you. After this is completed, the coins you purchase will be saved in your wallet. Take note that you will not purchase NFTs with all cryptocurrencies since most of them are constructed on the Ethereum blockchain. You will only be able to pay with cryptocurrencies built on the Ethereum blockchain. In some instances, credit card purchases are permitted on marketplaces.

It's as simple as signing up on the appropriate NFT marketplace and connecting it to your wallet after you've completed the initial setup of your wallet. You may now browse around the marketplace, mint NFTs, and put them for sale on the website. In most NFT markets, there are two types of systems: a fixed pricing system, where you may purchase an NFT at the advertised price, and an auction system, where you can bid on an NFT and hope that your offer is the highest one.

Where to buy NFTs?

Creating new markets for artists' work and an automated method of recouping a portion of resales via royalty agreements are two of the most significant benefits of NFTs. Financially supporting artists, flexing digital art collections, and speculating in an industry undergoing phenomenal expansion are just some of the ways investors who are optimistic about the technology perceive NFTs. NFTs are a type of cryptocurrency that is backed by blockchain technology.

What is the rate of growth in the market today? Market Watch reported in August 2021 that the online marketplace OpenSea had a total transaction volume of $3.4 billion on the Ethereum blockchain. According to Mark Cuban, the chief executive officer of Salesforce Marc Benioff, and the venture capital business Andreessen Horowitz, the NFT economy is more than a fleeting fad. Despite this, there have been several reports of theft and fraud. Various fees and commissions must be paid in addition to the energy used to run the Ethereum network, which contributes significantly to global warming pollution. Before spending their time and money, the market players should approach it with wide eyes, appreciating the need to scrutinize marketplaces, including perhaps inconspicuous FAQs and service agreements.

If you're looking for a place to start, here are 17 online marketplaces and what they have to offer both buyers and sellers.

SuperRare

SuperRare is a p2p marketplace for single-edition digital artwork that allows users to purchase and sell artwork from other users. It is a well-trafficked site with sellers, such as a Time Magazine cover that sells for three hundred thousand dollars, and it has a carefully chosen collection of artists and companies to choose from. The site has the sense of an online magazine thanks to features such as rich social media, a schedule of upcoming exhibitions, and a high-touch editorial section containing bios and remarks, for example. Arts, list prices, sale prices, and time auctions are shown in a tiling of windows similar to an Instagram profile, identical to an Instagram profile. The Ethereum network's native coin, ether, is used for all transactions.

Foundation

In February 2021, the Foundation's NFT sales featured Nyan Cat, Pak's Finite LP, and artists such as Nadya Tolokonnikova of Pussy Riot, Aphex Twin, and Edward Snowden. Using an array of postcards, each artist's work may be seen, with the most popular bids first, followed by those who have been acknowledged. An additional 15 minutes of the 24-hour bidding period is awarded if bids are entered during the final 15 minutes of the listing time, in addition to the reserve price. Before creating an artist profile, minting an NFT, or purchasing artwork from the MetaMask market, users must first have ether in their MetaMask account loaded.

Mintable

For NFTs, Mintable is a two-way marketplace akin to eBay, supported by Marc Benioff's Time Ventures and billionaire investor Mark Cuban. Buyers may build cryptocurrency wallets using MetaMask, integrated inside the site based on the Ethereum and Zilliqa blockchains. Alternatives for many producers include free "gasless" NFTs, short-printed series, and standard transaction-based items of many kinds of kinds. Buyers may purchase things featured on the site or bid on auctions after creating profiles and loading their wallets with funds. Winners of auctions are informed through email.

OpenSea

OpenSea is the world's first and most significant marketplace for buying and selling non-financial tokens (NFTs). Because of this, it is interoperable with the blockchains Ethereum, Polygon, and Clayton. More than 34 million non-traditional assets (NFTs) are available on this platform, organized into various categories ranging from digital art to collectibles, video game objects, virtual worlds, and domain names. To join up for OpenSea, you'll need an Ethereum wallet such as MetaMask, Coinbase Wallet, or Fortmatic, as well as the ability to pay a one-time setup charge to get your account up and running. Many NFT systems collect gas costs in advance of use. A gas fee is the cost of verifying transactions on a blockchain network, and it is charged for each transaction. Because the NFT is not transmitted to the blockchain until the purchase is completed, OpenSea allows inventors to mint NFTs without paying any gas fees. That implies you may convert a digital file into an NFT for free and only have to pay the gas price when the item is sold, saving you money. After the NFT has been sold, OpenSea additionally receives a 2.5 percent commission. The buyer is responsible for the cut; the seller is responsible for the amount for auctioned items. All transactions on OpenSea are atomic, which implies that either the whole transaction is completed or none of it is completed at any point. In contrast to eBay, where the buyer must pay for the products in advance, there is no need here. Consequently, the Wyvern Protocol ensures no difficulty with trust, regardless of whether the side initially takes the initiative.

NBA Top Shot

This NBA-licensed game will enable fans to collect and trade digital "moments" from league players and coaches starting in early 2020 as a trial. Open trading in the broader marketplace and limited-edition bundles (costing $9 to $230) are the two ways. Moments are available for purchase. Highlights from games, player statistics, and box scores are all included. With the help of the company's blockchain technology, collectors may swap assets display and track their carefully chosen collections. According to CoinDesk, the NBA Top Shot app has one million users as of May 2021, with an average of between 150,000 and 250,000 people checking in each day.

Axie Infinity

Axie Infinity is a video game inspired by Pokemon developed by the Vietnamese company Sky Mavis. Players may gather cartoon creatures, combat other players, and establish agricultural kingdoms in this Pokemon-inspired game. In a statement on its website, Axie Infinity said that it had an average of more than twenty-three million monthly gamers between September and October 2021. NFTs are used to encrypt both characters and land parcels. On an online marketplace, collectors and gamers may purchase them, with some virtual land parcels fetching more than Twenty Thousand dollars and animals selling for hundreds of dollars.

Sorare

A cryptocurrency-based fantasy soccer league in which fans may acquire player cards in the form of NFTs and then utilize them in online tournaments, Sorare is gaining traction. There are 180 recognized groups on the platform, including some of the most popular teams in the world's top leagues, and all transactions are made in the Ethereum cryptocurrency. NFT collectibles, although being more affordable, provide a significant advantage over the competition owing to their unique scoring multipliers. A Kylian Mbappe card from Paris Saint-rookie Germain's striker's set was acquired for $65,000 in December as an example of the high prices that certain cards may get. TechCrunch reports that Sorare has raised $600 million in a new round of funding, led by SoftBank's Vision Fund 2, which values the company at $billion. SoftBank's Vision Fund 2 was the driving force behind the deal.

Venly

There is now a second version of the NFT platform, which enables gamers to buy and trade virtual goods without bitcoins. Venky has a user base of over Two Hundred Thousand gamers that utilize it. The Sandbox, Ethermon, and Vulcan Verse are among the blockchain games that allow players to buy and trade assets via digital wallets. Other blockchain games may be purchased and sold by linking accounts to digital wallets. Thanks to a contract signed with Polygon, strategic development for linking Ethereum-compatible blockchain applications and virtual currencies like Binance, PayPal purchases in US dollars are now accepted on the blockchain-agnostic market.

Nifty Gateway

An American dollar marketplace called Nifty Gateway works with artists and companies to create Nifties, an acronym for non-financial tokens (NFTs). Collections are made available for a limited time — usually three weeks — before being pulled from the market to facilitate sales. Drops and artworks may be sold back to users through the site's P2P marketplace once they've been completed. Beeple, Cam Hicks, and Playboy are among the artists and brands featured on the site, which operates at a high rate and includes:

A discovery page.

A detailed statistics dashboard shows sales and appreciation figures.

An activity journal contained a record of site-wide activity.

Zora

Zora Auctions is dedicated to helping a person recapture the value that labels, galleries, and large companies have conventionally received in exchange for their services and products as an auction house with a political mandate. The linked Ethereum wallets such as MetaMask, WalletConnect, Coinbase, and other networks of cryptocurrency exchanges allow buyers to find and purchase digital content like as music, video, photographs, GIFs, and text NFTs. Since the ERC-721 standard is the most extensively utilized for decentralized digital currency systems, Zora also serves as an open-source protocol. NFTs may be purchased and resold from any site that can communicate with the protocol, and creators can define royal percentages for sales in the documentation.

Decentraland

"The first-ever virtual world controlled by users," Decentraland claims to be. It offers a builder tool that allows users to construct land holdings and gain power and influence over others while incorporating the metaverse idea. Using a VR headset or internet browser, the game operates as a marketplace where participants may resell the property, castles, character clothes, and Ethereum-registered identity tokens. According to the Nonfungible sales database, 196 transactions were placed on the site between October 11 and October 18, 2021, for a total of more than $491 000.

Rarible

Rarible is a non-financial-transaction (NFT) platform where we can create, purchase, and trade memorabilia ranging from GIFs to animated movies honoring sporting accomplishments such as boxer Floyd Mayweather Jr.'s 50-0 record. Currently, Rarible is a centralized autonomous organization evolving to a decentralized independent organization, which the Ethereum blockchain's regulations will eventually manage. Top sellers, trending collections, and live auctions are all shown in a scrollable stack of columns similar to Spotify's design in layout.

The Sandbox

The project's stated goal is to "disrupt existing game makers such as Minecraft and Roblox by providing creators true ownership of their creations as nonfungible tokens." An ethereum-based cryptocurrency known as SAND serves both the game's use charge and its utility token. Users may upload, publish, and sell items developed in Vox Edit, a 3D modeling tool, via a web-based marketplace for non-traditional toys. It is possible to put creations that have been acquired or made using the editor on land parcels, therefore changing the game dynamics via programmed actions.

MakersPlace

MakersPlace is a digital art gallery organized around collections of artists and biographies of those artists. The webpage includes short videos, ecstatic motion graphics, photographs of lunar landscapes, reinvented statuary, and mythological gods, among other things. Each item is issued and signed by the artist, and it is forever documented and validated via the use of blockchain technology. The site's detailed artist biographies, clearly traceable possession data, and searchable tags make it both descriptive and straightforward to travel through. Work may be acquired via fixed-price purchases, with ether or a conventional credit card serving as the payment method of choice.

GROW.HOUSE

A recent briefing was provided with Built-In characterized GROW.HOUSE is the "first-ever digital metaverse for fans of cannabis, cryptocurrencies, and decentralized banking," according to the company. Assume Farm villa and Roblox, but marijuana as the primary virtual cash crop transacted in cryptocurrency. The game, which is being led by brand maven Branden Hampton, who is best known for creating a fictional David Chappelle account, is being developed on the Polygon and will allow players to grow virtual cannabis, earn dollars, and grows tokens, purchase NFTs, and learn about farming techniques. Following its starting dex offering (IDO) in June, the firm received money from Polygon, Juicy Fields, and other investors. After going online, the GROW.HOUSE marketplace will enable users to purchase cannabis NFTs as well as other things.

Zeptagram

Artists may sell a stake in their recordings to fans and other investors by tokenizing them as nonfungible tokens (NFTs) via Zeptagram, a Stockholm-based start-up created by Christina Lö Wenstrom and Johan Forsman Lö Wenstrom. Using smart contracts, musicians and fans may earn royalties on second-hand purchases. Payments for royalties and trades in music copyright rights are made using Zeptacoin, the company's cryptocurrency on the site. A public sale campaign is about to commence with artists including Wylie Ligomeka and Taurai Mudamburi, who are offering possession shares in the virtual market.

Valuables

With the help of Valuables, a place developed by Cent, anyone can auction off their tweets in exchange for Ethereum. Buyers may put bids by typing the URL of the tweet or the user's handle into a search window on the website. The bidder is routed to the seller's tweet after placing a bid, where they may notify the user that they have placed an offer. Unless the seller has specified a reserve price, the bare minimum offer is one dollar.

What's the Right Marketplace for you?

Finding the correct NFT marketplace for your needs may be difficult, particularly since there isn't a single perfect answer as to where you should join up for services. The first step is to define your use case - what are you interested in, and what precisely are you seeking in terms of technology? Are you a sports enthusiast who wants to capture the best moments from live games? If this is the case, NBA Top Shot is the most apparent marketplace to consider. You would benefit significantly from Foundation and SuperRare if you are a professional artist who wishes to be a part of an exclusive NFT marketplace. For gamers looking to join a gaming metaverse, Axie Infinity, Venly, and Sorare are three characters that might be suitable choices. Any well-known NFT marketplace with a low transaction cost that allows you to mint NFTs for free will be ideal if you do not have a particular use case in mind. For the ordinary NFT maker, OpenSea, Rarible, and Mintable are all excellent possibilities to consider.

Chapter 5:

Discovering and Analyzing

Projects

To begin with, NFTs have the advantage of being able to be used in a variety of different applications produced by various firms and being readily sold on secondary markets for other NFTs. These qualities allow for new business models and use cases to emerge.

Since Dapper Labs formalized NFTs in 2017, the topic has been widely investigated. Adoption, on the other hand, has been a letdown. About 20,000 people use NonFungible.com monthly, 40% of the anticipated Defi users. It's because NFT features aren't being used to their full potential. There are four main ways in which the value of an NFT is calculated. Each of these four components is weighted differently depending on the asset the NFT represents. Using this framework, investors and NFT developers alike can determine if an NFT is worth their time and money and develop creative methods to raise the worth of NFTs. Developers and asset owners alike will benefit greatly from the numerous new possibilities opened up by NFTs.

Value: The value of the NFT is based on how it may be utilized. Game assets and tickets are two of the most valuable categories. According to recent sales of Crypto Space Commander battleships, a single NFT ticket is equal to the cost of one event ticket. The use of the NFT in a different application is another aspect of its usefulness. Using the same ship in another game would increase its worth significantly.

Possession History:

As far as value is concerned, it all comes down to who owns NFT and who issued it in the first place. High-value NFT ownership pasts are often produced or published by well-known artists or corporations. The increasing value may be achieved in two ways. The first step is to work with firms or people with a famous brand to create NFT coins. As a result, the ecosystem sees an increase in traffic and users.

Future Utilities:

Valuation changes and cash flow forecasts are used to determine an NFT's future value. There are instances when speculation is the primary driver of price appreciation.

Liquidity Premium:

NFT's value rises in the presence of a significant level of liquidity. Tokens generated on the blockchain should be worth more than tokens created because of the liquidity premium.

Discovering NFTs

Using NFTs in the Metaverse has established a solid use case. In 2021, there will be a significant increase in the use of NFTs. Too far, the NFT market has generated USD 19 billion in sales, up 29% in the past month alone, according to CoinMarketCap.

Primary sales account for around 57% of total revenue in this sector. This suggests that early adopters of NFT Investments can benefit from their discovery and then re-sell it for a profit. All NFT Projects are in jeopardy. Neither do we. In this environment, only a select few will be able to flourish. Finding the appropriate Project at the right time is critical.

Twitter

Identifying NFT initiatives early on Twitter is the best way to do so. The NFT community is housed on this platform. As a result, you'll be able to identify who the most popular influencers and purchasers in your industry are. Accounts like bobbyquinn, which have been around since the NFT frenzy, utilize an analytical approach to pricing NFTs and accounts like BAYC, which trade well on conviction. Users may use lists to organize and branch out on common themes in this situation. Users may also observe who is interacting with whom and take action accordingly. Finally, Twitter spaces allow you to interact with the people you follow in real-time and see what they think. Whether you're a fan or hater of a project, here is the place to discuss it.

Discord

When it comes to finding NFTs, Discord is a better option than Twitter. There's a Discord server for it somewhere, no matter what you're working on—or who you're working with. Servers with close-knit communities that freely debate new initiatives may also be found, for example:

- Announcing impending free mints on servers like Free Mint Club. Individual NFT collections have dedicated servers.
- Become a member of the BAYC server to connect with other BAYC enthusiasts.
- Talk to the Cool Cats devs on the Cool Cats server.

When it comes to finding out what the community wants and needs, there's no better method than to join the Discord community.

Nansen.ai

To find NFT diamonds, it's essential to use data that can be analyzed. This is why Nansen makes this ability available to its consumers. Opensea's buyer data is aggregated by Nansen and presented in visually appealing graphs and statistics. To put it another way, users can see what the most prominent purchasers on the market are purchasing and holding. It's also possible to set up notifications when specific wallets mint new collections or when you acquire a unique collection of those wallets. You can also check which groups are the most popular for each week.

RyzeNFT
Before being used in NFTs, Ryze Solutions was a hidden tool. To locate discounted NFTs, RyzeNFT is a costly but effective tool. The NFT addon provides access to a wide range of handy tools.

- Allows you to check how rare an item is right on the open sea.
- Mint's sniper tools Allow you to mint from the contract as soon as a mint opens, avoiding any gas wars that may ensue.
- The OpenSea sharpshooter lets you set a maximum price for underpriced NFTs so you can sweep the floors with them.

If somebody publishes below the floor searching for immediate liquidity in Ryze's collection, Ryze alerts you so that you may acquire it swiftly.

OpenSea Activity
Another option is to use the OpenSea and other websites' capabilities. To keep track of the most popular collections in Open Sea, use social media platforms like Twitter and Discord. Using this method is both cost-free and straightforward. Look for the collection, and then choose the activity tab. Statistics such as the average price, current owners, and more may be seen minute by minute. All OpenSea activity may also be followed manually. To sort by a chain, go to stats, activity, then sort by the chain. In addition, users may keep an eye out for trends, sales spikes, and repeat purchases. If you spend enough time on OpenSea, you'll be able to identify practically every collection. For the first time, customers will monitor the trending collections of whales that are scooping up rares from a collection. Watch for recurrent collections in your feed, too, to see how everyone else is doing.

The Road Map
A Project's roadmap map is a vital document made available to the general audience. It's time to get ready for the Project's future events, drops, and important dates! One of the most revealing indicators of a successful NFT project is the roadmap. If you want to invest in a project for the long run, you should look for a roadmap that includes long-term solid events. Red flags include roadmaps that promise unrealistic short-term outcomes. These are often used to inflate the price before a downward price adjustment. These promises are made in the form of free airdrops, tokens, perks, and more.

Icy Tools

NFT market trends are given minute-by-minute by Icy Tool, a membership service. Allow Icy Tools to aggregate all of your data instead of utilizing OpenSea to keep tabs on trends. Icy Tools gives hourly and daily movements in the free plan. You may examine 15- and 30-day trends, follow wallets, and get notifications when they purchase, sell, mint, as well as hot mint alerts, all for the low monthly fee of $62. A single lead on a hot mint may pay for your whole year's membership, so it's not as expensive as it first seems. Analytical traders who want an easy-to-use interface can choose Icy.

Rarity Tools

Rarity Tools is a great resource to locate new mints and underpriced rarities. In this way, users may get a sense of what the community is looking forward to in the next weeks by looking at the Calendar's curated list of forthcoming mints. In addition to this, users can see who is following these projects and branch out from that. One or a few coins may be produced. Make use of this as a launching point for further exploration.

NFT Calendar

It's impossible to keep track of all the forthcoming NFT drops without consulting the NFT calendar. In addition to a list of planned NFT mints, projects may apply to be included on the site. As a result, this list is about to become absurdly overcrowded. NFT Calendar accepts submissions from the public for consideration as a featured artist. Remember that sellers have the option of paying to have their projects appear at the top of the list.

NFTs Project Analysis

The NFT industry is now experiencing unprecedented growth. Since May 2021, at least one NFT project has been launched on the chain every day, according to NFTGO data. Similar to Defi, the quality of NFT projects varies widely, and investors may be tempted to fall victim to the "liquidity trap." In your opinion, how nice is the project that a buddy spoke of? Let's talk about this NFT Game that has been making headlines lately. How clear is my vision of the NFT universe? Which NFT should you buy? If you're a newbie or an investor in the blockchain, you may use facts to avoid "hearsay" and make your own decision on which NFT to purchase.

First Step

Elements: The fundamentals of knowledge

- an overview of the categories
- Capitalization and total issuance of securities

Before putting money into a project, you need to know the project's fundamental profile and placement. Using the Ethereum (ETH) Network, CryptoPunks, a Collectible project, comprises 10,000 distinct NFTs pixel art graphics. CryptoPunks now has a market value of $424 million, with a total circulation of 9,999* and an average price of $40,000 for one NFT. With a four-year history of project management and the pioneering position of underlying NFT technology, CryptoPunks has a $400 million price tag.

Second Step

Trading Data from the NFT

In the second phase, the project's trading conditions are examined. The transactions of the project may be analyzed using the following factors.

- In terms of volume, 24 hours a day, seven days a week, how is the liquidity of NFTs? After purchasing, how will they resell?
- When it comes to the highest, average, and lowest trading prices, where do NFTs stop and start?
- Is the project on the rise in sales volume, trading frequency, and the project's price trend?

Quantity and interdependence of all participants in the market (including both consumers and sellers) Is the initiative getting additional investors?

Third Step

HODL: NFT holdings data.

This is the third phase, verifying the project's basic logic, establishing its development scale, establishing its liquidity, and determining its revenue range.

The following levels of analysis will be performed on the project's NFT holdings.

- There are a large number of persons in the market who trade NFTs.
- It's hard to tell whether they're speculators or long-term investors who trust in the project's potential.
- How many there are, what they possess, and how many NFTs do they invest in – what sort of individuals are they, and can we track them?

Fourth Step

Token: The Project Data

- Capacity, Ranking
- Trading volume, issued volume, and Circulating volume.
- Investing in the market's movement

With tokens, we can analyze the progress of initiatives by tracking their token price movements. A group of cautious investors invest in FT because of the higher liquidity offered by tokens than NFTs.

Fifth Step

Inter-project comparison data is used to rank the projects.
In the fifth phase, we may use several rankings to assess the market position of CryptoPunks. Cryptopunks has the highest market capitalization, with a share of 29.58 percent, and is well ahead of Art Blocks, which is in the second position. Punks have eight spots in the top 10 and 14 in the top 20 on the Top NFTs list. Eight of the top ten addresses on the NFT Whales list are CryptoPunks. The NFTGO website has rankings and particular guidelines. As of right now, CryptoPunks' volume share has surpassed the long-term average of 33.67 percent (thanks in large part to the two trading booms in early August).

Sixth Step

Project data from the media.
In the sixth phase, we may look at the primary media platforms of a project to see how many active users they have, and this can help us get a sense of the project's trader profile (investment preferences, project loyalty, etc.), which can help us predict the future trend of a project.

Punks, a division of Larva Labs, now has 48,300 Twitter followers and a count of 300, steadily rising. There are more than 25,000 members of its official Discord discussion forum, the number of online users is over 1,000, and the number of daily discussions is more than 100. Senior NFT investors and new high-net-worth investors outside the business make up the bulk of the traders' roster. Several active and well-funded traders (particularly the former) can help develop the project.

Three Major Sites for Project Analysis

nftcatcher.io (collecting airdrops)

As a reward for taking part in an event or making a purchase of a digital asset, cryptocurrencies, tokens, or NFTs are sent through airdrop to a web3 wallet address. In most cases, airdrops are used to enhance a product or service or to bring attention to a particular brand or event. The most typical application of an airdrop is to promote a new cryptocurrency or blockchain-based community, such as a DAO, by giving away free tokens.

Art, music, and any other digital object may be found in NFTs at this location. Investors and collectors often put in long hours in the office.

In addition to these features, the platform provides the following:

- With the finest market liquidity, this is a simple exchange.
- If you're a cryptocurrency enthusiast, you may utilize dollar-cost averaging (DCA) to invest in your favorite tokens regularly.
- To speed up the process of remittances for contractors and enterprises, you may set up automated payments.

Rarity Tools (rarity)

Rarity Tools is a great resource to locate new mints and underpriced rarities.

In this way, users may get a sense of what the community is looking forward to in the next weeks by looking at the calendar's curated list of forthcoming mints. In addition to this, users can see who is following these projects and branch out from that. One or a few coins may be produced. Make use of this as a launching point for further exploration. Ranking, grading, and retrieving information are all possible using rarity.tools. The webpage is updated often. It's possible to learn about a wide variety of new initiatives, including well-known ones like CryptoPunks and Bored Apes, as well as lesser-known ones. Additionally, customers can inquire about upcoming things offered on the site. Users have the option of sorting their NFT collections by rarity once they have selected a number of them.

Rarity.tools calculate the series' overall rarity by evaluating each of the series' traits, which it then adds together. NFT collector, number, qualities, overall rarity, and so on may all be requested, and a clear floor price is shown for each of these attributes. The rare reference will be enhanced with "hidden features" based on input from several NFT communities, such CryptoPunks, and BAYC's "feature totals," Waifusion, Chubbies' "tops," Download matching," and so on. These "hidden features" will be included to the rarity reference. Rarity.tools evaluate these NFT projects based on past seven-day transaction volume, the total volume of transactions, average price of transactions in the previous seven days, and the total number of users.

Freshdrops.io

A new sniping website, freshdrops.io, is a fantastic resource. Freshdrops.io is the most incredible browser addon for sniping top rarities. Auto-buys may be triggered at preset price and gas levels; you can see the ETH you'll spend on the purchase in OpenSea. For free, you should have a look at it. Because the transactions are safe and confidential, you don't have to put your faith in the other person. It is possible to keep track of your favorite collections, access the history of any wallet in real-time, and study any collection with this app. In addition, you may go through the collections of your favorite artists and obtain project analyses.

Chapter 6:
Make money with NFT

From $162.4 million to $12.6 billion, the market for non-fungible token (NFT) purchases grew significantly in 2021, becoming a prominent sector in cryptocurrency. Additionally, hefty gas prices make the creation and sale of NFTs on Ethereum a costly endeavor. A single NFT on Ethereum will cost you roughly $98.69 in gas fees, while a collection of NFTs would cost you around $900 on average to mint. Many investors and producers attempt to sell their NFTs on secondary markets like Open Sea to earn some money to offset these expenses. However, there are more ways to make money with NFTs than just selling them for more than you bought or developed them.

The world of cryptocurrency investment is maturing, and several emerging ideas show symptoms of being the next big thing. It is becoming more common in the blockchain industry for cryptocurrencies Non-Fungible Tokens (NFTs) to be used as a passive investment vehicle. Several well-known companies, celebrities, and investors have already launched or planned to launch NFTs. NFT has had a similarly transformative effect on the game industry. The best NFT games, such as Guild of Guardians, Axie Infinity, and Illuvium, can be found on this page. As a result, not all non-fungible tokens (NFTs) are created equal. NFT's popularity is increasing at an incredibly rapid rate, according to recent data. Total NFT sales value in 2020 was $250 million, while in the first quarter of 2021, the total sales value was $2 billion.

Ways to generate income from NFTs
Renting out NFTs
Renting out your NFTs, especially those in great demand, is one way to generate passive revenue. Players may borrow NFT cards in several card trading games to increase their chances of winning. Intelligent contracts manage the conditions of the agreement between the parties concerned. NFT customers may thus choose the length of the leasing agreement and the rental fee they choose. One of the most popular platforms for renting or lending out NFTs is reNFT, founded in 2012. Presently, daily rates range from 0.002 to 2 wrapped ethereum (WETH) on average for lenders to establish maximum borrowing lengths. Ether's native cryptocurrency, WETH, is the ERC-20 version of the Ethereum (ETH) token.

NFT royalties
Royalty fees may be imposed on the secondary market when NFTs are sold using the underlying technology of NFTs. In other words, even after selling their works to collectors, the artists may still reap the benefits of passive revenue.

They'll get an ongoing percentage of the NFTs' sales price if they're successful. In other words, every time a digital artwork is sold to a new buyer, the original author is paid a royalty of 10% of the selling price. Observe that the NFTs' designers typically establish these percentages during the minting process. Even more importantly, smart contracts, which are self-executing computer programs that execute contractual agreements, oversee the whole process of distributing royalties. As a creator, this eliminates the need to enforce your royalty conditions or monitor payment manually.

Stake NFTs
Staking NFTs is one of the advantages of combining NFTs with decentralized finance (Defi) protocols. Depositing digital assets into a Defi protocol smart contract and waiting for a return is staking. Depending on the platform, you may receive staking token rewards in the platform's native utility token without purchasing native NFTs; however, this is not always the case. The following are some examples of platforms that make it easy to stake NFTs:

• Kira Network
• NFTX
• Splinter lands

- Only1

Staking tokens may be used as part of stake remuneration in certain situations. As a result, these token holders have a say in the future evolution of their ecosystems via these protocols. Staking NFTs yields coins that may be reinvested in other yield-generating protocols rather often.

Earn NFTs by providing liquidity

Liquidity may now be handed out in exchange for NFTs, thanks to the integration of NFTs and Defi infrastructures occurring for some time now.

So, if you supply liquidity on Uniswap V3, AMM will give you an ERC-721 token, also known as LP-NFT, detailing your percentage of total funds locked in the pool. The NFT also contains the token pair you deposited, the token symbols, and the pool's address. Liquidity pools may be liquidated by selling this NFT.

Use NFT-powered farming to increase yields.

Using NFT-powered items, customers may now grow crops in their AMMs and get the benefits of increased yields. Yield farming is a strategy that uses various Defi protocols to maximize the return on your digital assets.

AS SEEN IN THE EXAMPLE ABOVE, the LP-NFT tokens we provided as liquidity provider tokens on Uniswap may also be used as collateral or staked on other protocols to generate extra yields. This opens the door to a multi-tiered revenue model that's great for farmers who want to maximize their yields. Think of it as a way to gain more money on top of an already profitable strategy.

NFTs and smart contracts are still in their infancy, so keep that in mind. As a result, many of the apps that provide the possibilities discussed in this article are still in the early stages of development. Due diligence and an understanding of the risks associated with any of the aforementioned techniques should be carried out before implementing any of them.

NFT Video Games

Changing video games from paying to winning to playing and earning is a significant advantage of blockchain technology, which is also being used to develop NFTs for video games. Creating NFT games is the best approach to reach a broader audience and improve income prospects with highly sought-after incentives. The games offer features that enable you to trade, sell, or trade your valuables in the game. Even though there haven't been any very successful games, the potential is excellent.

Video games with NFTs that allow players to buy and sell in-game objects have the potential to be major winners. It's worth noting that the producers of NFT video games are also ambitious NFT creators, which might help advance NFT technology further. In comparison to other NFTs, in-game NFTs are the most sophisticated. As a result, these games are sophisticated, dynamic, and constantly evolving as the player's character grows and develops.

Licensed Merchandise

Using NFTs to tokenize valuables is among the most potent and apparent niche applications of NFTs. Collectors of actual treasures, such as trinkets and memorabilia like trading cards and sports memorabilia, no longer need to differentiate their products. Because NFT may demonstrate rarity, collectibles with NFT have a far greater market value than those without.

Sports cards have proven to be the most popular collectibles so far. It was only possible to trade licensed footballer cards via the sports card project. NFT cards have also been introduced by the National Basketball Association (NBA). Sport NFTs will soon be available in a more extensive range of sports, and collectors will have more options.

No one is saying that there aren't more popular items out there. Tokenized assets, such as actual collectibles, may be created by converting them into digital tokens and then trading or selling them as such. Because NFTs only exist in digital form and are safely kept on the blockchain, they never lose their quality, unlike actual collectibles.

Profiting from Your Inventive Ideas on NFT

While it's possible to make a million dollars with one NFT, no one can guarantee that you will. However, there is a potential that you may encounter collectors who are willing to make significant investments in your original works of art. Consequently, the following are some of the top NFT business ideas.

- Aim for perfection. The first thing you should focus on is making art. An easy way to create your own NFT is to ensure that you possess the rights to your unique media property. What may these mediums be used for? Most of the time! Take, for instance, a photo you took over the weekend or a funny animation you made. However, if you are a creative artist and have a basic understanding of how blockchain works, this option is for you.

- NFT Airdrops are a great way to get NFT. Is it possible to profit from NFT without generating your token? Yes, NFT Airdrops are an excellent way to generate money. You should keep up with current events in the NFT business and become involved in NFT initiatives if you want to succeed. Do not miss the opportunity to get your chosen NFT for no cost or at a fair price, and then sell it to make money.

The well-known blockchain project Avalanche's Don Wonton, for example, routinely holds NFT lotteries. Participation is open to anyone who follows the company's Twitter account. You'll need to retweet the contest post to achieve this. After that, leave a comment with the URL of your electronic wallet. Up to 20 cards are picked for each promotion. Everyone is entitled to a share of the coinage.

- Playing video games may win you NFT goods. Several popular games use blockchain technology, and you may play these games and make money while doing so. You don't have to spend a lot to generate money from NFT Gamers. On e-marketplaces, NFTs may be exchanged for other assets. Axie Infinity is an apparent effort in this field.

- Invest in NFTs on reputable exchanges. Purchasing NFT tokens is no more complicated than buying other types of assets. It is a strategy used by investors to buy low and sell high at the right moment. The problem is figuring out how much money you'll make. Inferior liquidity means that you may hold onto virtual assets for a lengthy period.

There is a marketplace where you may purchase and sell NFT products for profit. So, how can you profit from NFT? Purchase an NFT at a lower price on one platform, then resell it for a higher price on another. Keep in mind that you may not be able to resale NFTs fast or readily. As a result, the best course of action is to choose digital art that you like and would be proud to possess. Seek for works of art that are now in style and can appreciate in the future.

Making Money with NFT: Strategies for Success
You must first choose a digital asset, such as a painting, a photograph, or a music recording. The following steps are registering the product in the marketplace and adding a description and price. Assets may be created when you press "Create" on the website.

It's a great way to get in on the NFT token craze by creating your currency and trying to figure out how to start making money with NFT? The OpenSea platform, for example, allows for this kind of functionality. To get started, you'll need to link an Ethereum wallet. After that, you may begin making a coin. The system will automatically fill in all fields when you click "Create." You'll also need to design a logo and record a cover and double-check everything.

Do you want to know how to earn money on NFT even if you have difficulty creating your tokens? Creating and designing your assets isn't required to trade them. Giveaways are an excellent method to get free coins. Companies and initiatives in the cryptocurrency space use social media to promote themselves like retailers do with product samples. Additional aggregator sites provide extra points for the purchase of digital items.

The business is increasing. To summarise, there are several ways to profit from NFT. If you need ideas for your creation, peruse the list of popular NFT collections on Top NFT Collections and the table of the most recent additions.

NFT Market Place Buy and Sell
In the cryptocurrency arena, NFTs represent development and an improvement over current monetary systems and other businesses. A dollar may be used interchangeably with any other denomination of the same denomination of money, which means that money is fungible. There is a tendency to switch stocks from the same firm and similar grade items. A piece of art or an in-game item can't be replaced by any other investment since NFTs are non-fungible and represent unique physical and digital assets. It is impossible to trade one non-fungible token for another since each has a unique identification stored on the blockchain.

NFTs may eliminate intermediaries and link content producers directly with their viewers by allowing digital representations of particular products paired with the advantages of smart contracts. A significant shift in the crypto and art world may be expected thanks to NFTs.

When it comes to art and collecting, what makes non-fungible tokens appealing? What are the best places to purchase NFTs, and how to do so? When selling an NFT, what are the best ways to do so? Let's have a look at the answers to the questions posed above.

Buying non-fungible tokens (NFTs)

The purchase of PNG or GIF files for hundreds of millions of dollars may appear unreasonable to some people. Despite this, many are still eager to pay a hefty price for something they can watch, screenshot, and download for free from the internet. Why?

Due to its status as "investment-as-status," NFTs are one of the most effective ways to maximize social capital in the crypto world by creating more ties and relationships. NFTs immediately link social and financial capital to create a network of ties among individuals and prove community participation. Authentication is integrated into the blockchain's immutable records. With the ability to "digitally sign" their NFTs, content producers may now interact with their fans, share their favorite works of art, and become a part of an online community.

Even if a picture or piece of music has been shared hundreds of times online, when a collector purchases an NFT, they buy something unique and uncommon - the ultimate requirement for any serious collector.

Collectors don't purchase original material since they don't own its rights, but they buy licensed copies of it. Instead, by buying NFTs, collectors are acquiring the most valuable asset: a link between their identity and the work of the content producer on the blockchain. As a result, collectors may possess original artifacts recorded on the blockchain as evidence of ownership when they purchase NFT tokens. In the future, if the item is sold again, the content creator may claim royalties from the NFT platform because of the technology's ability to protect their copyright.

Where to buy NFTs

Not all of them work in the same way, provide the same features, or use the same kinds of NFTs. Non-fungible tokens may be purchased and sold on several different online markets in the crypto realm. As a result, most platforms are built on the Ethereum network. Other non-Ethereum NFT services, such as Cosmos, Polkadot, or Binance Smart Chain, belong to blockchains other than Ethereum, such as these.

In addition to supporting NFT standards and file formats, NFT platform accessibility, a fee to generate (or mint) an NFT, and other aspects that may be more essential to content providers than purchasers, there are variances amongst NFT markets. No matter how they operate, most NFT marketplaces provide a large selection of NFTs to choose from. Non-fungible tokens are also a consideration for seasoned purchasers when selecting a marketplace.

Choosing a crypto wallet and cryptocurrency to fund a wallet

To purchase NFTs from an NFT marketplace, collectors must first register for an account on the market. However, consumers must first link their cryptocurrency wallets to the selected NFT platform to buy or sell anything.

An essential component of any blockchain system is a crypto wallet for storing digital assets. To utilize blockchain services, access multiple platforms, sign transactions, and maintain one's balances by the foundations of the blockchain, members of the crypto community need wallets. Their operations become more accurate and safer by eliminating the need to retain users' account information on all crypto platforms and NFT markets.

Make sure your wallet is compatible with the cryptocurrency you plan on using before you begin the process of setting one up. Since most NFT services are built on Ethereum, the native cryptocurrency of Ethereum, Ether (ETH), is accepted as payment. Many kinds of bitcoin wallets exist, including hosted wallets, private wallets, and hardware wallets.

Hosted Wallets: It's widely regarded as the most user-friendly and straightforward to set up a hosted wallet, also known as a custodial wallet. In the same way that banks maintain money in savings and checking accounts, it is dubbed "hosted" because it automatically stores the crypto belonging to its customers. A custodial wallet's major drawback is a lack of control and the loss of privacy. Since a third party handles the security of a user's cryptocurrency, users may rest easy knowing that even if they misplace or forget their password or private key, they will never be without their cryptocurrency. This sort of wallet often suggests that users conduct Know Your Customer (KYC) verification, a form of identity verification. Customers should also verify the reliability and competence of the web hosting business before entrusting their data to them.

Non-Custodial Wallet: There is no third party involved in the non-custodial wallet's security. As a result, they have complete command over the safety of their cryptocurrency money. Users don't have to submit a request each time; they may pick the transaction charge, either the default or a higher price depending on how quickly they want the transaction to occur. Users are solely responsible for remembering and safeguarding their passwords when using a bitcoin wallet. Passphrases, also known as mnemonic and seed phrases, are the only way users can access their wallets if they lose or forget them.

A set of 12 to 24 words created at random is a "seed phrase" (arranged in a specific order). Wallet software generates this token, which users use to recover access and control over their crypto assets on the blockchain. You should retain a duplicate of the seed phrase offline to protect it. It's a good idea to keep a copy of the information in a safe place. You should avoid keeping the seed phrase stored on a computer or any other device linked to the internet. A bad actor will have complete access to a wallet's crypto assets if he obtains the user's seed phrase. With non-custodial wallets, complex cryptocurrency activities like staking, lending, borrowing, and more may be performed by users without the need for an intermediary.

Hardware Wallets: As the name implies, hardware wallets are physical storage devices similar to USB flash drives. Users' private keys are safely stored on a hardware wallet, eliminating the security issues associated with internet wallets. Even if the user's PC is compromised, crypto money may be kept safe in a hardware wallet. Using this kind of wallet is a bit of a challenge, and it's also a little pricey.

There are several factors to consider when selecting a wallet for collectors, including their tastes and the level of security they are prepared to put up with. Collectors have the option of using a hosted wallet, a non-custodial wallet, or a hardware wallet to safeguard their crypto assets. The decision is totally up to the collectors.

If you have enough crypto assets in your wallet, you may link it to an appropriate NFT marketplace, make an account, and begin purchasing New Fiat Tokens (NFTs).

Buying NFTs: Options

Many of the possibilities for purchasing non-fungible tokens resemble an eBay auction. As a result, the process of buying NFTs is easy enough for the average collector to understand.

An auction is the most prevalent method of selling goods. As an auction house, most NFT markets operate. Auctions are available in two varieties. The first is a traditional English auction, in which the bidder with the highest final offer gets the item. During a timed auction, each lot may be bid on for a certain amount of time, and the highest bidder at the end of that period wins and purchases an NFT. A different sort of auction is known as the "Dutch Auction." The price of an NFT begins at a given level (the ceiling price). It then steadily decreases by a predetermined amount over a specified period (e.g., 0.1 BTC every 10 minutes). The NFT Dutch auction finishes when a user bids the current price.

NFT drops may also be used to buy non-fungible tokens. To avoid missing out on the opportunity to acquire NFTs when they are dropped, collectors must join up for the specific NFT site and fill their crypto wallets in advance. Collectors will have to wait until one of the drops is disclosed before attempting to get their hands on one of the few remaining NFTs.

Additional features include a "purchase now" option on specific NFT platforms. It refers to the direct selling of non-fungible tokens at a predefined price specified by NFT designers. For collectors, fixed-priced purchasing may be the most convenient option since they do not rely on auctions or wait for a predetermined drop time. Aside from the currency and format, collectors need to pay attention to what's stated in decimal cryptocurrency (for example, ETH) and what's listed in fiat (for example, USD). The volatility of the cryptocurrency market means that buyers should be aware that this dollar value is subject to frequent fluctuation.

The cost of processing and validating transactions on the blockchain, known as "gas costs," must be paid. Because of this, users have to pay for the energy required to run it. On top of that, collectors must have enough cryptocurrency in their wallets to cover the transaction charge or gas fee they incur when purchasing an NFT.

Selling non-fungible tokens (NFTs)

Two ways of selling NFTs

- For content producers, selling minted NFTs is the preferred method of selling NFTs.
- For collectors, selling NFTs, they've previously purchased and are now willing to trade is also an option.

First Way to Sell NFTs

Non-fungible tokens (also known as "minting" or "creation") may be created in a variety of ways. The term "minting" refers to a quick and painless process in which material like artwork, collectibles, lyrics, memes, and other forms of original content is converted into a non-fungible token (NFT) and "tokenized." Digital things may now be exchanged and sold as NFTs, and they can be monitored digitally when they are resold.

To begin minting, only a Mac or PC, a cryptocurrency wallet that accepts NFTs, and an account on a blockchain-focused NFT marketplace are required.

Before pressing the "Create" button, double-check everything is a good idea. To finish the process of minting, the NFT creators must sign and pay the gas costs. Finally, content providers may view their freshly minted NFTs on their profiles on the selected NFT platform when the transaction has been verified.

It is also possible to specify a royalty proportion for selling NFTs on NFT markets. Every time an NFT is sold to a new collector, they might earn a specific commission thanks to royalties. Because of the fundamentals of non-fungible token technology, royalties have the potential to provide content creators with recurring streams of passive income for the rest of their lives.

While minting a token, most NFT markets allow users to choose a selling mechanism or set a token price. Consequently, it's common to think of newly created NFTs as being placed on the market for sale straight away.

Second Way to Sell NFTs

Alternatively, content providers must go into their NFT marketplace accounts and find the digital things they want to sell. They will need to click on the NFT objects after they locate them. Performing this action will bring up a "sell" or "list for sale" button for you. An auction or a set "buy it now" price may be selected by clicking on this option once it's available.

With the support of NFT platform representatives, they may have a chance to build a drop for their non-fungible tokens, which will likely add some exposure and help them sell their inventions.

Mint And Airdrop

Airdrop
An airdrop is a free distribution of a cryptocurrency, token, or NFT given to a web3 wallet address in exchange for an experience or a digital asset purchase. In most cases, airdrops enhance a product or service or bring attention to a particular brand or event.
Promoting an NFT project or other blockchain-based community like a DAO or a freshly formed coin is the most general purpose of airdrops.

NFT Airdrop

Several factors may lead to the start of an NFT airdrop. To get an NFT airdrop, you may hold a particular NFT in your wallet or participate in some promotion, or you can even receive a present that is more of a marketing technique than an actual gift.

Even so, NFT airdrops have the potential to be tremendously profitable. The Bored Ape Mutant Serum is an excellent example of a useful NFT airdrop. The Mutant Serum NFT was airdropped to holders of Bored Ape Yacht Club NFTs.

As soon as these Mutant Serums were airdropped for free, they started selling on secondary NFT markets for over 3 ETH (thousands of dollars). Mega Mutant Serum sold on January 2, 2022 for $1,542.069 ETH ($5,907,542.97).

Nonetheless, not all NFT airdrops are worth the time and effort required to participate. In some instances, they might be a waste of time and money. It's essential to exercise great caution when receiving a random NFT in your wallet from an unknown source and to avoid selling or trading the asset altogether.

NFT Minting

To put it another way, Minting NFT is the process of converting a digital file to an Ethereum blockchain-based crypto collectible or digital asset. An object or file saved in a distributed database can never be modified or deleted since it is permanently kept there. Making fiat currency by minting real coins is known as "minting," whereas putting an item on the blockchain is known as "uploading." Alternatively, we may say that "NFT Minting" is the process by which your digital artwork or digital material is added to the Ethereum blockchain and becomes publicly available. Non-fungible tokens are "minted" in the same manner as metal coins are: when they are generated, they are "minted." Simple files are transformed into crypto assets, which can then be sold or purchased directly on the internet without the need for a middleman.

NFT's author may plan royalties from future sales during the minting process, which will be a fee he can get if his work is sold to another individual or exchanged on the secondary market. NFT

How To Mint an NFT

NFT art or NFT assets may be created from almost any digital information or file. This means that anyone who creates digital art or works in the creative industries can quickly turn their work into a collectible crypto asset with real-world value.

NFT markets and blockchain applications use Metamask as their default wallet; therefore, if you're using Google Chrome, you may quickly install the browser extension "Metamask." However, it would be best to have Ether (ETH), the Ethereum blockchain's native coin, in your wallet. In the majority of big markets and NFT systems, this is the default setting: To begin creating your own NFT, follow these steps.

Connect your wallet to the NFT marketplace.

After connecting your Metamask wallet, you'll be able to establish a username or display name, upload a profile picture or cover photo of your collection, and link to any of the Ethereum-based NFT marketplaces you've chosen (OpenSea NFT, Rarible, Nifty Gateway, Foundation, or super rare).

Upload your file

A file may be uploaded in several formats: a picture in PNG, JPG, or GIF format, a sound file in MP3 or WAV format, an MP4 video file, or a 3D model in a GLB file. Finding the "Create an NFT" page on your preferred marketplace is all it takes to get started.

As a reminder, keep in mind that an NFT is just a representation of the digital file or information.

It would be best to ensure that the NFT tokens representing your files are being kept adequately on the Ethereum blockchain, which will be there for a long time. Decentralized databases like IPFS are better to store the digital file (InterPlanetary File System).

Your files might be in danger if you use cloud-based databases like those offered by cloud hosting providers. Cloud storage systems like Google Drive may not be the best long-term option for digital objects that have been converted into nonfeasible tokens (NFTs).

Upload your file

Here, you may add or provide a title and a description to your digital artwork after you've uploaded it, before clicking the "Mint NFT" or "Is for sale" button, as appropriate.

Approve Gas Fee or Transaction Fee

The Ether (ETH) coin is used to cover the costs of all Ethereum network transactions. Therefore, to finish the minting of the NFT, you will need to authorize a gas cost or transaction fee in your digital wallet.

To be clear, gas costs are not fees imposed by the NFT platform or marketplace you are utilizing but instead are paid to use the Ethereum network.

Wait until your NFT is minted.

Minting begins automatically when the file has been uploaded and paid for gas. The Ethereum smart contract will run a piece of code embedded in your artwork on the Ethereum blockchain throughout this process.

Chapter 7:

Famous NFT

To comprehend NFTs, you must first grasp the distinction between fungible and non-fungible assets. For example, gold, a Bitcoin, a barrel of oil, or a dollar are all goods that may be exchanged for one another without any further processing.

A non-fungible asset is a property that cannot be traded for another piece of property. Plots of land, artwork, and trade cards are examples of non-fungible assets. Users may verify the validity of non-fungible assets on the blockchain by tokenizing them and storing them in a blockchain-based database. Although digital collectibles, art, and in-game objects are currently the assets exchanged via NFTs, the potential uses for NFTs are almost endless in the future. It's vital to remember that a non-fungible token has no intrinsic value on its own. The media associated with NFTs is responsible for the value acquired by them. Among other things, a CryptoPunk NFT is as valuable as a CryptoPunk, and a plot of land on Decentraland gains value based on the location and size of the ground inside the virtual world.

The cryptocurrency boom of 2021 not only brought new tokens to the forefront, but it also ushered in new marketplaces, such as the one for digital collectibles and non-fungible tokens, which have since taken off (NFTs). This last year has been a watershed moment in the business, with these one-of-a-kind digital objects fetching millions of dollars for every piece sold at auction. According to NonFungible.com, sales of non-fungible materials will reach $14.4 billion by 2021. Stand-alone pieces of art included the disaster girl meme, which went for half a million dollars, and the beetle NFT, which sold for $69 million at the Christie's auction house in New York. The greatest winners, though, were collections of thousands of NFTs and initiatives hidden behind the scenes, such as the avatar-generating CryptoPunks, the metaverse Decentraland, and play-to-earn blockchain game Axie Infinity, to name a few examples. The total trading volume on OpenSea, the world's largest marketplace for NFTs, has already reached $13.25 billion, a significant increase over the $24 million recorded in the whole year 2020. A total of 1.25 million traders operates on the platform, with the all-time average price of NFTs traded on the platform standing at $933, which is almost 70,000 rupees – more than the average monthly pay.

What makes NFTs so popular?
NFTs are digital tokens that are one-of-a-kind or non-fungible and operate on smart contracts on Ethereum and other blockchains. They may be used to distribute assets and verify the legitimacy of those assets via the usage of the blockchain.
The idea of NFTs was initially proposed in 2015, and the first experiments were launched in the following year. A non-fungible token project is being utilized to sell unique products online, such as collectibles, which are not available elsewhere. Given that each token is one-of-a-kind and cannot be duplicated, the use of NFTs promotes scarcity, increasing their value to collectors, artists, and other merchants. ETH BTC and fiat cash are accepted as payment methods at auctions to buy and sell (BTC). Using NFTs as collateral for loans or as financial contracts for insurance, stock options, or bonds in the future may be possible in the nascent area of decentralized finance (Defi). Artwork, rare antiques, and even estate might be utilized as collateral.

Trends in the NFT industry
The bitcoin explosion has spawned a new generation of billionaires seeking other digital assets with the potential to grow in value in which to invest their fortunes. The best NFT ventures in 2021 will generally be those that deal with the sale of rare and limited-edition items like visual painting, music, collectibles, and other collectibles. On March 11, Christie's sold a piece by Beeple for $69 million after a succession of NFT auctions of digital artworks and music by high-profile artists, including Grimes. The piece was designed by Beeple and sold at Christie's for $69 million.
It is being argued that new NFT initiatives represent the future of product sales and a method for artists to retain ownership of their work in the age of streaming and file sharing, as well as a way for game creators to benefit from the creation of in-game economies.

Notable NFTs

A new NFT project is launched every day, and the number is growing. Everyone, from world-renowned artists to movie stars and public figures, is investing in digital assets and parading them on social media, which is resulting in an exponential surge in NFT sales, according to the NFT Association. Here are the best NFTs projects:

- VeeFriends
- CryptoPunks
- Bored Ape Yacht Club
- Crypto Baristas
- Moon Boyz
- Meka Verse
- Nouns
- Creature World
- Adam Bomb Squad
- Claylings
- Autograph.io
- Decentraland

CryptoPunks

Background

A total of 10,000 distinct CryptoPunks (6,039 males and 3,840 females) have been created via blockchain technology, and all of them have been rendered digitally rare. Each one was created algorithmically by computer code; thus, no two characters are precisely the same, and specific characteristics are more common than others. They were first made available for free, and anybody having an Ethereum wallet may claim them at that time. The only expenses associated with claiming a CryptoPunk during its original release were Ethereum (ETH) "gas fees," which were insignificant due to the limited usage of both the Ethereum network and general understanding of the project at the time of the release.

What Exactly is CryptoPunk?

Last year, John Watkinson and Matt Hall published a total of 10,000 punks that were made using an algorithm. The evidence of their ownership is stored on the Ethereum blockchain, distributed ledger technology.

CryptoPunks are 24x24 pixel art pictures primarily of punky-looking men and women, with a few more unusual characters thrown in for suitable measures, such as apes, zombies, and aliens. Watkinson and Hall produced these pixelated figures known as CryptoPunks, who come in various haircuts, headgear, and spectacles. Since then, they have started another project known as Autoglyphs, a generative artwork. In addition, they have established the Larva Labs firm to support their different initiatives. Before today, CryptoPunks had a small but dedicated network of supporters. Everyone from Silicon Valley to YouTubers to poker players and celebrities joined crypto in their love of punks this year, and the mainstream fans followed suit. Logan Paul, a YouTuber, recently showed off his CryptoPunk, which he purchased for $170,000 in a video posted in March. According to the non-financial transaction monitoring website CryptoSlam, the CryptoPunks platform has witnessed approximately $2 billion in transaction activity since its introduction, increasing from $200 million in April of this year and only $11,500 in June last year. CryptoPunks were given out for free at the time of its inception, even though they are presently being sold for 6-7 figures. That's correct if just one person has shown interest or conviction in them before their arrival. Because there is only a limited amount of CryptoPunks available, possessing one has become a "digital flex" as the value of the cryptocurrency has risen. Several proprietors have even turned to parade them on social networking sites like Twitter by posting pictures of their punks as avatars.

Valuation of a CryptoPunk

Beauty, like physical art, is in the eye of the beholder, and every piece of art has a varied value to various people who appreciate it. When evaluating any art, including NFTs, there is also the consideration of hedonic value, which refers to how much pleasure one derives from one's work. NFTs are no exception to this rule. When it comes to CryptoPunks, there are a variety of additional considerations that are taken into account when determining the value of the NFT.

Scarcity

First and foremost, there is a lack of quality. Just like there will only ever be 21 million Bitcoins and no more, there will only ever be 10,000 CryptoPunks in the whole history of the world. It is entirely up to the NFT creator whether they want their NFT to be a rare collectible or release several copies of their NFT. Nonetheless, the legitimacy of the NFT can be verified in both circumstances thanks to their distinct IDs and information. There are no two punks who are alike in CryptoPunks. Some are wearing a headband, some are wearing hats, others are wearing tiny sunglasses, and several are wearing gold chains. The characteristics of each punk varied, and some were more common than others. Simply said, the more the rarity of an object, the greater it is worth.

Popularity

In addition to popularity, another critical component in an NFT is the amount of money that the NFT is worth. After maintaining monthly sales between $5k and $50k until September 2020, CryptoPunk finally reached six figures for the first time with $2.96 million in sales. August 2021 was a record-breaking month for CryptoPunk, with around $680 million in transaction volume recorded throughout the month. In terms of monthly statistics, Cryptopunks had over 1200 unique customers, surpassing the 213 individual buyers in January 2021 and the 15 unique buyers in March 2018, respectively. This is because CryptoPunks only became well known in the latter half of 2020 and into 2021. Earlier this year, the payments giant Visa stated that it had purchased CryptoPunk #7610 for the sum of $150,000 (USD).

How Costly is CryptoPunks?

Larva Labs maintains a comprehensive listing of all CryptoPunks presently available for purchase. A selection of CryptoPunks, together with their accessories and current market situation, is shown below.

2022 for Cryptopunks

Even though NFTs have seen a fall in both value and volume since their peak in early 2021, they are still here to stay. Undeterred by the avalanche of projects such as Art Blocks, Bored Ape Yacht Club, Meebits, Cool Cats, and hundreds of others, CryptoPunks is one of the collections that have a promising future. It has maintained its position as the most popular and influential brand on the market.

CryptoPunks have simply become a part of the social status game since they are only available to a small number of individuals who can afford to get them. Finally, as time passes, the value of this collection is expected to rise in value in the long run. As a result, I expect to see the expansion of fractionalized ownership of CryptoPunks shortly, as it becomes the primary mechanism for most individuals to acquire this kind of NFT.

Bored Ape Yacht Club

It's hard to think of another club like the Bored Ape Yacht Club. In this virtual lounge, there will never be more than 10,000 members. As with CryptoPunks, the Bored Ape Yacht Club uses NFTs as online avatars. The project offers cartoon apes with various qualities and rarity. The cheapest Apes cost roughly 75 ETH ($250,000). You could buy an Ape only a few months ago for just a few ETH, making this NFT collectible one of the most rapidly rising. Since its inception, there are now floor values of 6 ETH and 15 ETH for holders of the Bored Ape Kennel Club (BAKC) and Mutant Ape Yacht Club (MAYC) NFTs.

The Strokes and Lil Baby played a private performance at New York's Bored Ape Yacht Club for token holders. Each NFT has its distinct characteristics, including its dress, headgear, expression, and more. ERC-721 tokens are used to hold these NFTs, like other Ethereum NFTs. At this point, they are the most popular NFT project for profile pictures (PFP) and have been utilized by several celebrities, but we'll get into that later.

Why to buy BAYC?
You may enter the so-called "bathroom," a virtual hangout area that's only available to wallets having at least one Bored Ape NFT in them, by purchasing the NFT. Owners may use this area to express themselves in whatever way they deem proper. Paint one pixel every fifteen minutes, and the ape-holders may do it as many times as they choose. An ape NFT is essentially membership in an exclusive club with a membership cap that one may purchase.
An NFT that is well-known and valued in the community may be compared to purchasing a priceless artwork. Ultimately, its value is based on what it represents to the owner. Also, keep in mind that no two Bored Ape NFTs are the same; there will never be another. These NFTs are also seen as an investment by some people who purchase them. Because there's a limited quantity on the market, they may become a profitable investment because they may continue to increase. This has so far been confirmed to be the case as of January 2022, when this article was written.

Unique and Revolutionary NFT

Beyond the uniqueness of each NFT's proven and verifiable characteristics, the Bored Ape Yacht Club is an intriguing undertaking for additional reasons. The project began with a precise plan in place from the beginning. The Bored Apes' sympathetic characteristics made them ideal for online avatars, and the project quickly evolved to be the largest PFP ever. The number of NFTs is also sufficient to create a healthy NFT community. Owners will also be granted the ability to economically exploit the Bored Apes, which is essential to the project's continued growth.

With each passing day, the BAYC community becomes stronger and stronger. Not only has a large number of well-known individuals joined the bandwagon, but this gets us to our following issue.

Today's Cost of BAYC

Among the non-traditional tycoons, Bored Apes is likely to be one of those that gave early investors the most excessive returns. They were released in April 2021 at the cost of 0.08 ETH apiece. Open Sea's floor price now stands at 77.99 ETH, representing a return of about 100,000 percent as of this writing. Many apes went for six and even seven figures, but it seems that Bored Ape #3749 is the costliest of them all. 740 ETH was purchased for $2.9 million at the transaction time. It appears as follows:

Other significant references were Bored Ape #2087, which sold for $2.3 million, Bored Ape $8585, which sold for $2.67 million, and so on.

Future

The practice of "play to earn" became very popular by 2021, and it quickly took over the market. However, even if most of the project's goals have been achieved, a big part of the project's enduring appeal is the team's relentless pursuit of new possibilities. The Bored Ape Yacht Club has partnered with Animoca Brands, a prominent P2E developer, to create a blockchain-based game. Yuga Labs had this to say about their involvement in the partnership:

"WE'RE PLEASED TO COLLABORATE WITH ANIMOCA BRANDS TO INCREASE THE BAYC UNIVERSE AND IMPROVE THE USEFULNESS AND ADVANTAGES GIVEN TO ALL BORED APE NFT HOLDERS."

All in all, the initiative seems to be moving along at a steady pace since ape owners have the commercial rights to their NFTs, and it is in their best interest to keep moving forward.

Chapter 8:
Interesting Projects

The world has moved inexorably toward modernity throughout history. Humans' inventive nature is seen in adapting to new ways of life. People worldwide are in awe of these innovations since they aim to make life better for everyone. Similarly, NFT Projects were created by a human being's intellectual reasoning. We've been keeping tabs on the global buzz around this word. It has provided relevance and vigor to the people of our planet's population. With this site, you can use your digital cash to purchase or sell everything from art to music to images to films. This means that you can buy anything you want, but you can't trade it for something else. Any time you exchange one card for another, you will get a new one. The notion is unique in fungible tokens. One Bitcoin may be exchanged for another in the same way. As of 2014, NFTs have become a global sensation. An everyday use is for the purchase and sale of digital artwork.

Research conducted by nonfungibletoken.com in 2021 shows that NFTs cost $75.736.378 between May 10th and June 10th of that year alone. There are no limits to what an NFT can be. It doesn't matter whether it's a piece of digital art that catches the eye of everyone. Yes, you are on the correct road with your views. NFTs also include the sale of high-quality tweets. For a mere $3 million, Twitter's creator sold one of his own. You may believe that digital art collectors have a strong desire to amass a collection. As a comparison, think about the guy who paid $390,000 for a brief Grimes video and the one who spent $6.6 million for Beeple's film. The owner of an NFT can make a duplicate, but the original work of art will always be linked to the original owner.

NFT-Utility:

An NFT gives a purpose to a digital asset that goes beyond simple ownership of a work of art. You can get a tangible piece of art that matches the NFT you bought, or you can get exclusive in-person memberships, or you can utilize it in the digital world in the future if you acquire a utility NFT.

Assume you can locate a project with a purpose you can identify with and is also useful somehow. In this situation, you are obtaining more than just digital ownership of an asset via the purchase of NFT (art, photo, video, audio, etc.).

So, how do you know what to look for in a good project? Listed below are some of the great projects by now:

- Cryptopunks
- Cryptoadz
- Sneaky vampire syndicate
- Bored Ape Yacht Club
- Cool Cats NFT
- Lazy Lions
- Doodles
- The cryptoDads
- Mutant Ape Yacht Club
- Capsule House
- Veefriends
- Avarik Saga Universe
- Doge Pound Puppies

Doodles

Burnt Toast created hundreds of unique aesthetic features for use in Doodles, a collection of 10,000 non-fungible tokens. Skelly, cats, aliens, apes, and mascots are among the Doodles drawn by hand. Also included in the Doodles collection are a slew of unusual heads, costumes, and hues of the artist's palette. New adventures like Space Doodles are unlocked exclusively by avid collectors every year. We're expanding our brand all the time, so collectors can look forward to getting first dibs on the hottest new items, gear, and events. You may vote on community-driven features, goods, and events if you own a Doodle. The Doodle bank allows the project's leaders and Doodle holders to develop the project's plan.

Team
The designer of this series is the well-known but not very renowned artist Scott Martin (aka burned toast). On Foundation, he has previously shared NFT artwork in the same manner as the doodles. There's also Evan Keast on the team, a former Kabam Games employee who previously worked at Dapper Labs (the firm behind NBA Topshot and Cryptokitties).

The Doodles Roadmap
Doodles have quickly established itself as a "community-driven collectible NFT project," as its creators claim. An online forum has been set up for the Doodles community to propose ideas for the roadmap and get comments on them. So yet, the formal vote is just on one proposal: a temporary contract for a Doodles animator. However, the community wallet will be seeded with 420 ETH from the first sale and a percentage of any secondary sales. As a result of this funding, the Doodles brand will be further developed via community-driven activities, including the payment of moderators and artists and marketing.

Beyond employing an animator, nothing is known about the future of this collection and the Doodles brand as a whole, but that's probably for the best. As a result of donors asking for a timeline, several profile images projects have gone beyond their ambitions. Doodles are all about creating likable art that evokes a sense of wonder in the viewer. Also, it's giving us a new approach to establishing a community via NFT initiatives. A staff understands how to do things well due to their expertise in the NFT sector. There may one day be airdrops, friends, or further enhancements to the rainbow-filled environment when an animator joins the team. For now, all that matters is that you're a Doodle and that you're spreading the word about this unique brand to other collectors.

Why invest?

Let's go back to some solid arguments for purchasing many items from this project:

- Before its official introduction, the Doodles were introduced with a large community already on Discord.
- This is a well-thought-out, practical plan.
- A solid strategy for future bids (here's an example of a request for proposals for hiring an animator).
- Equitable allocation of resources. As part of the public mint, the remaining 10,000 pieces were given out randomly. There are 4600 owners as of this writing, which is excellent. There are 5700 shareholders in the BAYC project.
- The mood is light and upbeat. In general, I like NFT artwork that is cheerful and lighthearted, and this piece is the epitome of that aesthetic.
- Nice blend of characteristics. A wide range of facial features, hair, physical qualities, and backdrop characteristics are available in special effects such as rainbows or animals.

Things to watch out

It's a somewhat limited license compared to, say, BAYC. Use for commercial purposes is very difficult. If you acquire an NFT, you have the right to show it on social media services like Twitter and Discord as your profile picture. Doodles LLC, the firm that created the Doodles, owns the copyright. Since we've already seen derivative projects and PFP holders making modifications to their PFPs, the Doodles team decided not to pursue these kinds of usage. The words themselves seem to be at odds with enforced and perceived. The reason for my request is that I believe an open license would be much better for Doodles' long-term prospects; therefore, I've been lobbying the team to rethink.

Capsule house

The Gachapon NFTs in Capsule House are digital versions of the famous Japanese collector toys. Each Capsule NFT includes a verifiably uncommon and unique gachapon artwork, with over 120 performances and limitless combinations of features. Those who have the Capsule are granted access to all CAPSULEVerse expansions and future drops from their team.

In January, artists Seerlight and Kaejunni will convert the capsules into a profile picture-style work of art. Those with the original capsules may only claim the capsule. Each pill will contain one pfp. The deployment will be done species by species. There are four types of capsules. According to the latest information, the Yokais will be the first to hatch. Over the next several months, the remaining species will hatch.

Team
- **Artist**: Seerlight
- **Artist**: Kaejunni
- **Developer**: Oksami

Avarik Saga Universe

Over 300 different hand-drawn qualities were used to create the 8,888 NFT personalities of knights, archers, and wizards that make up the Avarik Saga.

This medieval nation is filled with stories of a hero who would lead his faction to victory and put an end to the ceaseless conflicts between the fiery Ignis, the kind Terra, the sluggish Glacia, and the ethereal Tenebris. These legends are said to be true.

Team

It is a Japanese RPG NFT P2E & PvP metaverse game.
CEO: Kevin Cahya

Super Interesting Games Project

Cryptocurrency has risen to become one of the most important marketplaces, with NFTs representing the leading edge of technological innovation in this field. NFTs are also a field with a great deal of overlap with the gaming industry. Although NFTs are specifically designed for gaming, the technology has many applications, including usage inside video games. These games go above and beyond what can be done in the greatest crypto mobile games available on the market. The most popular NFT games incorporate technology into their gameplay mechanics, resulting in a new gaming experience. NFTs provide new gameplay dynamics and provide a means for gamers and developers to monetize in-game objects.

The finest NFT games utilize the underlying technology NFTs to provide a more enjoyable gaming experience than you'd get from a standard game. These are games that make use of NFTs to improve your overall experience. We're doing more than simply selling NFTs with gaming themes on them here. Gameplay using NFTs is seen in a wide variety of different genres. Non-fungible tokens, often known as non-fungible coins, represent an intriguing new frontier in cryptocurrencies. They have a great deal of promise, particularly in the gaming industry. Here is a list of the most popular NFT games available right now.

Types of NFT Games
Play to Earn NFT Games
The best NFT games raise the bar on what it means to play a video game. There is already a lot of attention paid to the play-to-earn paradigm in the finest NFT games. Play-to-earn is one of the sorts of NFT games where players concentrate on gaining money rather than winning. The things that players gain have a proven scarcity and are solely theirs. Through the multiverse concept, players may utilize their stuff in other games. The built-in rewards are what sets it unique from other conventional games. Because of these incentives, gamers with higher ability levels gain control over the game's publishers.

Games for Players (Reward: In-game Coins & Transaction)
NFT games that need players to gather in-game assets are the second category. Some of the game's in-game objects have some kind of real-world worth. The finest NFT games in this category tokenize in-game assets, letting players acquire them as non-fungible tokens (NFTs) (non-fungible tokens). Games for players let users gather and sell in-game items that may be used in several ways, including weapons, characters, vehicles, and more. NFTs are the only means of trading. Players are given two options based on the game they are playing regulations. Alternatively, they may hold onto their NFTs until they return the crypto incentives they received, or they can sell them for profit.

Free To Play Games (User Experience & Players-Teenagers-Coders)

Gamified learning is commonplace in the greatest NFT games. A wide range of instructional information can be accessed via a game-like user interface that aids learning. No money is required to begin playing a free-to-play NFT game. Most free-to-play games, like Gods Unchained and Splinterlands, let you earn money without having to make a financial commitment to the game. Some of the most popular free NFT games rely heavily on RNG mechanisms. Alternatively, some games may include pay-to-win systems where the greatest in-game assets are locked away behind paywalls.

Illuvium

The Illuvium DAO is a decentralized autonomous organization (DAO) developing a fantasy role-playing game on the Ethereum network. A "decentralized, NFT collecting and auto battler game based on the Ethereum network" was defined when the project was initially launched in January 2017. Open-world exploration and capturing mythical creatures known as Illuvials are central to Illuvium's gameplay. NFTs on Ethereum's blockchain reflect the Illuvials that players gather and have a real-world value. Players use illuvial to compete against each other to win (ETH).

IlluviDex

The IlluviDex, an online marketplace run by the Illuvium DAO, is part of the Illuvium ecosystem. Players of Illuvium may use this marketplace to purchase and sell NFTs, such as Illuvials, weapons, armor, and skins. NFTs from Illuivum, like those from any blockchain, may be listed and sold on other markets.

What are ILV and sILV?

Two ERC-20 coins, ILV (Illuvium) and sILV, support the Illuvium game and help keep it running smoothly. The ILV token lets holders participate in the Illuvium DAO's governance, yield farming, and staking. If you want to stake your tokens, you may choose to be paid in ILV or sILV. One year is the lockup time for ILV incentives if holders wish to receive them. Because of this lockup period, trading pairings between ILV and other cryptocurrencies will remain active. There is no lockup time for sILV; however, it can only be used to buy in-game items. In-game purchases and other sources of money are utilized to support the prizes offered to ILV stakeholders.

How to stake Illuvium?

The ILV token allows its owners to stake their tokens for network incentives. ILV token holders who are staking their money to the network get in-game earnings. Because of the 12-month lockup on ILV, only sILV may be used immediately in the game. An Ethereum wallet is required to stake ILV. Defi wallet MetaMask browser plugin is one of the most regularly used ethereum wallets in the Defi market because of its ease of usage. If you want to stake your ILV, all you need to do is transfer your tokens to a MetaMask or MetaMask comparable wallet, and then go over to Illuvium and link the wallet with your ILV tokens. After that, players should choose "core pools" from the drop-down menu and follow the on-screen instructions. It's crucial to know that staking incentives are now on hold until the introduction of staking V2. It is expected that incentives will be computed for individuals who continue to stake throughout the next weeks and that these benefits will be carried over to V2.

Development team

Its development team comprises more than 75 people with a wide range of expertise. Co-founders Kieran and Aaron Warwick, brothers of Kian Warwick, who created the Defi protocol Synthetix, are key team members. Nate Wells' former job was producing Illuvium's popular games like Bioshock, The Last of Us, and Rise of the Tomb Raider.

When does Illuvium come out?

Although Illuvium is yet to be released, enthusiastic players may not have to wait too long to get their hands on the game. In late 2021 or early 2022, the first private beta was expected to be launched. Private beta two is expected for mid-Q1 2022, followed by an open beta in late Q1 2022 that anybody may participate in. The game will also be released on mobile devices at some point in late 2022.

Although it's now in a semi-private beta, Illuvium: Zero will be released with the main game in Q1 2022. These release dates may change at any moment, so anybody interested in staying on top of the latest release information should keep an eye on Illuvium's Discord channel for announcements and sign up for the game's website to begin with.

Chapter 9:

Nft and Crypto

Non-fungible tokens (NFTs) were the first blockchain technology application to gain public awareness in early 2021. The ownership of digital assets (such as photos, music, video, and virtual creations) is documented in smart contracts on a blockchain. It may be traded as an NFT (non-fungible token). We investigate if NFT pricing is linked to cryptocurrency price since the NFT market was born out of cryptocurrencies. According to a spillover index, only a little volatility is transmitted between cryptocurrencies and NFTs. Nonetheless, wavelet coherence analysis suggests a correlation between the two sets of markets regarding their movement. This shows that studying the price behavior of cryptocurrencies might help us better understand the pricing patterns of NFTs. In addition, the low volatility transmissions further imply that NFTs might be regarded as a low-correlation asset class separate from cryptocurrencies.

This research aims to analyze the interrelationships between cryptocurrencies and non-fungible token (NFT) markets based on this concept of trader crossover. Compared to other cryptocurrencies, Bitcoin has the most significant capacity to transmit volatility shocks, as shown by Moratis (2021). We look at whether bitcoin volatility spills over to NFT markets, given the cross-trading between cryptocurrencies and NFTs and the possible leading effect of NFT pricing on cryptocurrencies. The co-movement between cryptocurrency and NFT returns has been proved to be a prominent element in cryptocurrency markets; thus, this inquiry will be strengthened by looking into whether there is co-movement there as well (Qiao et al., 2020). Because of this, scholars and practitioners alike will benefit from uncovering ties between the two sets of markets, allowing them to evaluate cryptocurrency price patterns as guidance on NFT market developments.

3 Best Crypto to Invest in 2022

Sandbox

It's not clear what the source of this remark is. It has released iOS and Android smartphones and Windows PCs by Pixowl as a sandbox game. A PC version was released on June 29th, 2015. Animoca Brands obtained the brand in 2018 and renamed a blockchain-based 3D open-world game after it.

Blockchain Version
As part of Pixowl's Sandbox platform, users may develop and construct virtual objects in the manner of a video game. The Sandbox blends the capabilities of decentralized autonomous organizations (DAO) with non-fungible tokens to create a decentralized platform for a healthy gaming community (NFTs). As stated in the official Whitepaper, Sandbox seeks to integrate blockchain technology into mainstream gaming successfully. The platform encourages using "play-to-earn" models, which brings together players and creators. The Sandbox has created the SAND utility token, which uses blockchain technology to streamline network transactions.
Uniqueness
Sandbox is the first platform to use blockchain technology in the gaming industry. Since then, it has established a name for itself in the world of online gaming. As early as 2011, Pixowl saw that the gaming industry had a lot of potential for blockchain adoption. With the Sandbox, gamers will produce and collect blockchain-based commodities, transforming the industry.

The Sandbox creates a metaverse of participants who actively contribute to the platform's evolution by emphasizing user-generated content. With the introduction of the SAND token, which allows users to share their views and opinions on the project's development, Sandbox also fosters decentralized governance. Due to technological improvements, decentralized governance is becoming more necessary for blockchain-based enterprises. Several big-name gaming companies sponsored and invested in the firm while getting started. Atari, Helix, and Crypto Kitties are a few examples that spring to mind.

Sand coins in Regulation

It is possible to manufacture 3,000,000,000 SAND tokens. In March 2021, there were 680,266,194 SAND tokens in circulation, which is 23 percent of the total supply. A corporative reserve was established with a quarter of the total token supply. An additional 17.18 percent of the token's seed sale was put aside. One-third of the total token supply went to the founders and members of the team. The Binance Launchpad Sale took up little over 12 percent of the total supply, while the remaining 10 percent went to advisor rewards.

How is the Sandbox Network Secured?

Because it is built on the Ethereum blockchain, the Sandbox virtual world is secured via the proof-of-stake consensus mechanism. Because SAND tokens are based on the ERC-20 standard, they may be staked and rewarded as a result. A significant amount of computing or electrical power is not required to verify transactions using PoS, unlike Bitcoin's Proof of Work (PoW) consensus method. A significant number of SAND token holders is critical. To ensure the safety of staked assets, the PoS consensus approach may be used for many different purposes.

Where can you buy the Sand coins?

Investors and consumers have shown an increasing interest in SAND token trading on various platforms. SAND may be purchased using Uniswap (V2), Gate.io, and LATOKEN. As of March 2021, the total trading volume of SAND/BUSD on Binance was $7,015,941.

Transaction:
Artists and gamers may use $SAND to buy and sell assets on the Sandbox Platform. $SAND is the only currency accepted in all Sandbox Marketplace purchases. Artists are charged $SAND for uploading materials to the Marketplace.

Governance:
The Sandbox will be run by a DAO, which will use the $SAND governance token to do so. For token owners, the platform's future is at stake. Concerns like how Foundation grant money is credited to content and game producers and platform Roadmap additions are prioritized are all part of this. SAND account holders may delegate voting power to whomever they want.

Price History:
To say that early investors in the $SAND cryptocurrency have garnered significant gains would be an oversimplification. The $SAND token IEO was conducted in August 2020, and each token was sold for $0.0083. SAND is now trading for $5.91, a 72,050 percent return on investment from the coin's inception. There will be an all-time low of $0.028 for this coin in November 2020. IEO investors were the primary culprits for the token's price decline since the token had already earned a 10x return at launch.

Until early 2021, the token's price fluctuated between $0.03 and $0.1 per token. This year's bull cycle saw the SAND token hit an all-time high of $0.84 in March, but that's nothing compared to the $8.44 it reached in November during the second half of the 2021 bull cycle. Due to a significant inflow of institutional money into metaverse firms, the majority of this price movement has occurred. As soon as Facebook announced that it would be renamed "Meta," the crypto markets went into overdrive with enthusiasm over blockchain games and the metaverse. However, even though the token is experiencing a significant downturn, we may expect a more considerable upside in 2022 or 2023 with the game's full launch and the public market.

$SAND has a circulating supply of 919,498,319 (i.e., 30.64 percent of total supply) of its 3 billion total units (i.e., 30.64 percent of total supply). Sandbox's token unlock schedule indicates that all of its supply will be unlocked by 2024. According to the developers, the goal of the Sandbox is to become a community-run DAO that is self-governing; this might mean that the firm eventually sells all its tokens to the community. Sandbox's token unlocks timeframe, and this sale pressure may indicate that, despite $SANDs expected to rise, it may not be as stratospheric as its previous pumping.

Sand Market Cap

SAND might be a beneficial investment choice if you seek virtual currencies with a high rate of return. On the 22nd of May 2021, the Sandbox price was equivalent to 0.298 US dollars. A five-year investment is predicted to provide a return of roughly +1778.19 percent.

Decentraland

A non-profit organization called the Decentraland Foundation would run the virtual world from February 2020 onwards. Decentraland is an open-source virtual world platform. Users may buy virtual pieces of land on the site using the MANA cryptocurrency.

History

Decentraland was started in 2015 by Ari Melech and Esteban Ordino and has been under development ever since. In 2017, parcels of virtual land were sold for $20, while mana tokens were sold for $0.02. A total of 90,601 pieces of land are available in Genesis City, the game's first location. An initial coin offering (ICO) in 2017 garnered $26 million for the firm. Following a spike in interest in NFTs in April 2021, pieces of NFT land sold for anything from $6000 to $100,000. In June 2021, Sotheby's auction house created a digital reproduction of its New Bond Street headquarters for an exhibition of digital art at Decentraland. Two hundred fifty-nine plots of Decentraland were purchased by Republic Realm for $913,228 each parcel, based on the Tokyo shopping district Harajuku. It may soar to $5.79 when events like Facebook's overhaul to Meta and good press help the currency.

Purchasing Mana

Consider using the company's virtual currency, MANA, if you want to buy virtual property, do commerce with other users, or participate in the program's growth.

Decentraland's blockchain, which maintains and controls the ownership of digital land, is one of the ways it empowers its citizens.

Difference Between Buying and Trading Mana

MANA trading and MANA buying are often used interchangeably, although there is a big difference between the two terms. To complete both jobs, MANA tokens must be purchased, but the execution of each is separate. The following vital distinctions are critical:

Buying

- For the sole purpose of resale
- This procedure may be performed on almost any platform that has MANA capability.
- There is less significance when markets open and shut or when prices change.

Purchase MANA quickly and easily. If you use eToro or a similar site, you may search for MANA and select how much to invest in it. You're not likely to examine charts or keep track of price changes before purchasing. So, you'll decide on how much money you can spend and how long you want to retain MANA in your possession. That is all there is to say.

Trading

- In a short period, many transactions may occur.
- There are just a few systems that can do this.
- Fees, volatility, and market activity are becoming more significant.

Trading is a full-time career for many people, not just a pastime. Cryptocurrencies like MANA, which are still in their infancy, can bring in a lot of money for good traders. To trade MANA, you must continually watch the market and be ready to act at a moment's notice. This is a time-consuming endeavor. Knowing what you've been up to can help you stay out of the sights of shady merchants who make a rash of trades quickly.

What to consider when buying MANA?

In 2021, Decentraland Mana had one of its most successful years. In November 2021, the value of the Metaverse currency reached an all-time high of $5.41, but Mana has since dropped by almost 40% and is presently trading at slightly over $3. After Axie Infinity, Decentraland Mana is the second most popular game cryptocurrency. During the first week of January 2021, Mana was trading at roughly $0.08, and by the end of the year, it had surpassed $5. However, the token's value has solidified at a little over $3 as of January 2022.

If we look at the past six months of Mana's performance against Bitcoin, it's apparent that Mana has outperformed the latter. Mana has grown by over 323% in the previous six months, whereas Bitcoin has increased by roughly 22%.

Sandbox and Mana were the two most popular tokens in the Metaverse in the previous six months. The Sandbox grew more than 1120 percent in the last six months, but Mana only gained around 323 percent. However, Axie Infinity has risen by 245 percent in the previous six months.

Financials

Decentraland Mana's all-time financials show that more investors have profited from their investments than those who have lost money. According to statistics from IntoTheBlock, 59 percent of investors have made a profit, while 30 percent have lost money after investing in the Mana cryptocurrency. Approximately 12 percent of investors are either in profit or at a loss. Since November 2021, when Mana hit its all-time high, more than 60 percent of investors have profited from their investment in Mana, while just around 26 percent have lost money. There is 13 percent of investors that are in the red.

Dominance of Whales

Whales dominate the Mana network. The whales own around 51% of the total supply of Mana tokens in circulation (14). As a result, there will always be apprehension about Mana hitting rock bottom if the whales abandon ship.

There are around 28% of total Mana tokens in Investor volume and approximately 20% of total Mana tokens in the retail market.

Gala

Founded in 2019 by Eric Schiermeyer, Gala aims to revolutionize the gaming industry. "There is no doubt that we are constructing the world's biggest decentralized gaming platform. Decentralization implies giving players authority, responsibility, and rewards. "According to the company's statement. Building an extensive and autonomous blockchain node network is the platform's goal.

GALA tokens are the Gala Games Ecosystem's digital utility tokens, ERC-20-compliant, and run on the Ethereum network. Cryptographically protected and utilized as an exchange medium between members in the ecosystem, the utility token is non-refundable. Since it's portable between users, they have complete control over its use.

For many users, the idea that they may vote on which names appear on the Gala Games platform after purchasing a node in GALA or ether (ETH) is exciting. An important aspect of Gala Games is the capacity of its users to engage in governance votes, which may influence the game's growth and playability.

GALA price analysis

According to CoinMarketCap, the GALA coin value surged 488 percent from its low of $0.021 on September 12 to its all-time high of $0.1236 on September 18. During the week of September 13, the price of the GALA crypto was soaring since the coin was listed on two cryptocurrency exchanges. On September 13, Binance, the biggest crypto exchange globally, listed it first. A digital asset trading platform called Bibox also included the Gala Games coin to its inventory of digital assets on September 16. CoinMarketCap is now valued at $1.2 billion and trades at $0.17 per coin as of today's date (January 24). There are just five optimistic signs on GALA compared to 24 negative indicators, according to CoinCodex's short-term sentiment study.

GALA token price prediction

Automated service for making weather predictions According to Wallet Investor's projections, the price will begin at $1.06 in 2023 and rise to $4 in five years. In 2022, Digital Coin Price estimates that the token will increase to $0.24. According to the company's predictions, GALA will reach $0.36 by the end of 2025 and $0.62 by 2028. Before investing, you should always do your research. Consider the possibility that algorithmic pricing projections may be incorrect. Use your research instead of looking at the forecasts. Never invest or trade money that you can't afford to lose.

Chapter 10:
Future of NFT

Before the outbreak, many individuals had never heard of non-fungible tokens (NFTs). Blockchain-based digital assets, like cryptocurrencies, began to attract gamers, artists, and influencers who realized how to use the technology to their advantage.

NFTs have become a crucial asset for content providers in the digital world because of their assurance of ownership and authenticity and their digital character. Creators now have greater control over their digital work since they can put something out that they genuinely own and gain recurring cash every time it is sold. A digital provenance is created for each NFT sale, which means it can't be tampered with.

Use Cases for NFTs
DappRadar, a company that tracks app transactions, estimates that consumers traded more than 85,000 NFTs worth $5.8 million in a single day in May. However, I believe that widespread acceptance is nearly impossible.
NFTs will ultimately replace industries that take pride in appropriating the hard labor of others, perhaps sooner rather than later. Consider the example of a record label. Like a checkmark on Instagram, NFTs will have become a status symbol for decentralized social media by that time.
However, NFTs are more than just a way to make a quick buck off of bored apes. Digital assets, in my opinion, have a more comprehensive range of applications, including those that may be used in the workplace. As a result of decentralized blockchain technology and the online exchange of digital certificates, corporate transactions may be more efficient and secure.

Additional features and incentives may be included in NFTs as well. Whether an experience or a tangible item is offered in conjunction with an NFT depends on the vendor. Creator coin NFTs, for example, might award top coin holders with special privileges if the number of people who care about a specific athlete or artist is large enough.

As it is, CryptoPunks are indeed selling for millions of dollars, Fidenza is turning into a collector's item, and Axie Infinity is employing people in underdeveloped nations via play mechanics that reward players more than game publishers.

NFTs, on the other hand, have a far more expansive and promising future than just gaming and the arts. Proof of ownership, license, social standing, exclusive access, and certification of authenticity are just a few of the ways NFTs may be used.

NFTs: The future of art digital

Tokens known as NFTS (non-fungible tokens) are unique digital assets that can be confirmed and differentiated by their information and ID codes on a blockchain (mainly on Ethereum). NFTs are distinct from bitcoin because of their "non-fungible" nature: if you exchanged bitcoins, you'd receive the same item, but if you traded one NFT, you'd get an entirely new commodity. The reason for this is that NFTs might differ in quality and kind.

This means that almost any valuable digital product may be an NFT, including art, in-game stuff, GIFs, design and clothing, websites, and even tweets. At the moment, it's a $40 billion market that draws developers and producers from all over the world by functioning as an auction house on a selected blockchain.

Too far, about a quarter of all NFT sales have come from large art buys, according to the market tracker NonFungible.com. An American artist is known as Beeple, Mike Winkelmann, sold his digital artwork at Christie's for $69.3 million, which placed him in the "top three most expensive living painters." He will be paid a royalty of 10% each time the NFT's owner changes from that point on.

Winkelmann's achievement in the digital world is certainly not unique. Earlier, CryptoPunk #7804, a 24x24 pixel art piece, went for $7.5 million, while Trevor Jones' Bitcoin Angel fetched $3.2 million in the same auctions.

Unlike the traditional art market, where galleries and agents take a significant portion of an artist's revenues, NFTs enable artists to produce more great money since they take a tiny (or even nil) part.

NFTs will soon replace traditional art.

Despite the technical difficulties of owning an NFT and the environmental concerns they bring (a single transaction produces 14 times more carbon emissions than sending an artwork). In addition to being an excellent investment, they may provide their owner's entry to elite neighborhoods.

It isn't easy to anticipate how NFTs will do against their physical counterparts in the future. NFTs may already be at their height, or they may be just beginning to take off at this point. On the other hand, some experts feel that traditional forms of art, such as sculpture and painting, will endure for some time to come.

Auction houses are joining the NFT arena because of the criteria for client verification and anti-money-laundering policies, forcing them to comply with the problems of curation and technology administration problems. Many consumers want to pay in cryptocurrency, which raises new legal issues.

However, the NFT market is expected to grow in several years. Before investing, prospective investors should be aware of the unique dangers of this particular field. When it comes to art, it's crucial to look at the item first and then at its attributes since there's no value in possessing something you don't like.

NFTs' prospective applications are nearly limitless.

Despite NFTs' recent emergence, the idea of storing digital artwork on the blockchain utilizing them has been around for five years.

In the Western world, items like evidence of ownership, proving authenticity, licensing, and property rights are taken for granted. As a result, we have access to conventional, solid legal and governmental structures that safeguard our rights.

Because of this, it is necessary to trust a central person to provide this level of safety. Using NFTs to unlock a person's rights to intellectual or physical property has the same effect on the value of those assets as does Bitcoin. Like Bitcoin, it lets you be your banker in managing your investments.

Over two billion individuals throughout the globe do not have access to a formal banking system, making this a critical value offer for those who do not have the security of a solid legal framework to safeguard their property rights.

As a result, the future of NFTs extends well beyond social status, jokes, or multimillion-dollar pieces of art that have been converted into profile images in recent years. Just the beginning of a worldwide revolution that began with banking and will now affect everything else.

The Mission to Decentralize

Creators may use the decentralized social media component of NFTs to communicate with an audience about their NFTs. After all, the idea of decentralization fits right in with the mission of NFTs, which is to make art ownership — a luxury hitherto reserved for the affluent — accessible to everyone. Even the once-exclusive domain of a select few art lovers is now open to the general public. Even if some are skeptical about NFTs, the wild nature of the technology inspires hope in the minds of those like myself. The future of NFTs is still up in the air, but my organization isn't going to lose out on the chance to get in now. Content creators, you're not dead. The digital entertainment industry's future is bright and blazing.

NFTs And Future

On blockchain networks, NFTs serve to exchange real-world goods for virtual ones. In the future, they might play a significant role in everything from virtual treasures to real estate to online dating to fundraising to tickets.

NFTs are very flexible and may be tailored to suit any need. More control over how their data is displayed on the blockchain will be possible with NFTs. Blockchain apps will also be simpler to use for those who are less computer savvy.

From both a customer and seller standpoint, non-fungible tradable tokens will be critical in the future of e-commerce. Using NFTs to exchange or transfer digital assets will become more common in the future. As a result of their use of the Ethereum blockchain, they've recently seen a surge in popularity.

On Crypto Kitties, a decentralized gaming platform, more than $200 million worth of non-fungible tokens (NFTs) have been traded. NFTs may seem complicated, but they may be precious to game creators and game users.

They represent the next stage in virtual asset development. However, many individuals have no idea what NFTs are or what they may be used for. Since its ICO, NFTs have been shrouded in obscurity. A wide range of sectors are now using them, and they're beginning to live up to their full potential. The general public will eventually catch on.

Conclusion

With NFTs, there is no limit to what may be achieved. Non-fungible tokens have the potential to represent virtual-world property objects and potentially become game-changers in the sports and fashion sectors, as well as gaming collectibles. In addition, with NFTs' increasing acceptance and appeal, platforms other than Ethereum will certainly prioritize NFT support in the future.

Even though NFT is still a relatively new technology, it already has a great deal of promise and offers artists advantages they have never had before. As a result, more musicians are expected to join the NFT industry shortly.

NFTs are unquestionably garnering a lot of attention as a profitable 'investment' possibility or for their capacity to provide new income streams for content producers or owners, which is why they have already been deployed in a broad range of industries. NFT is a potentially lucrative market, but it should be approached cautiously due to the myriad legal and practical issues involved, particularly concerning enforcement, ownership, and intellectual property rights.

NFTs are here to stay, and we need to pay attention to them. As a result, unique assets may now be monetized in previously unfeasible ways on any platform or metaverse, both in terms of traceability of returns and in terms of marketing and selling.

Eliminating the need for intermediaries unleashes an explosion of the invention. This will lead to a new economic-financial paradigm, just as Defi has done, in a short period. The possibilities are endless since we can tokenize anything: paintings, songs, short films, and podcasts.

Finally, if you can network with celebrities, business prospects, or new friends, NFTs may be affordable. If you're interested in NFTs, be aware that many people and businesses are jumping on the bandwagon. A comprehensive investigation of this NFT community/club is critically essential. Consider the advantages, the date of the listing, and the number of followers whenever you create an account on any social media platform. Check out the follower-like ratio on social media since it is frequently the case that there are phony and purchased followers. On the OpenSea.io platform, Ethereum is the most common currency used to acquire NFTs.

Hopefully, after reading this, you have a better idea of NFTs and how they function. Non-fungible tokens have been shown to have a variety of real-world uses, but are they a technology for the future?

It's difficult to predict whether or not NFTs will be extensively employed in the future. We can see that interest in them is at an all-time high and several possible advantages. Although the technology is relatively new, several obstacles need to be overcome.

As intriguing as NFTs are, whether or not they're the future of technology, they're an essential component of popular culture. NFTs, blockchain, and cyber security are just topics we cover in-depth in our training programs. Understanding the fundamentals of these new sectors might help you get a job in one of them.

In most situations, however, such royalties aren't hardcoded into the smart contract and are distributed to the intelligent contract owner via the NFT marketplace, which is noteworthy.

A novel usage of blockchain technology, NFTs, will continue to be adopted and used in commercial applications. However, there will be a need for legal assurance that the NFT fulfills the commitments it has made to shareholders.

Non-fungible Tokens don't seem to be a fleeting blockchain and crypto fad. Based on its wide range of applications, only a fraction of this technology's potential has been exploited. If basic visuals are now in demand, that means we don't know the full potential of this technology. The increasing popularity of NFTs may lead to the development of increasingly complicated tokens, leading to an explosion in the NFT industry. There is also a growing number of NFT developments in other fields. NFTs may be used in various sectors, including real estate, media, and entertainment.

Any blockchain experiment's future is uncertain. If affluent investors continue to invest in NFTs, experts believe that they will continue to develop beyond the realms of art and gaming.

Additionally, the rise of NFT may be linked to its characteristics that can represent evidence of ownership, give social status, allow exclusive access, manage to license, and guarantee authenticity. In the same way that Bitcoin lets you be your banker, it controls your goods.

The future of this blockchain project is primarily undetermined, as is the case with many others. Publications with a wide readership suggest that NFTs aren't going anywhere soon. It's conceivable that they'll grow more and more mainstream as affluent investors pour money into them.

Consumers may soon be able to purchase music rights without parting up to their hard-earned cash. Anything creative you possess has the potential to be valued as a stepping stone into the market. All kinds of things, from game sprites to music to photos to notable social media accounts, are examples of non-fungible assets (NFTs).

More than simply another fad in the crypto world, Non-Fungible Tokens are here to stay. NFTs have a wide range of possible applications, yet their full potential is untapped.

As more and more people and companies join the Non-Fungible Token ecosystem, it seems that the NFT gold rush is just beginning. As the most popular NFTs are still photos, the market is still undervalued, and the genuine explosion in NFT popularity may not occur until complicated NFTs exploring the full potential of the new technology becomes widespread.

As the last point, NFTs as investments have the same dangers as cryptocurrencies and other similar assets, such as volatility. Despite the high cost of NFTs, the breakthrough blockchain technologies that underpin them ensure ownership and provide a new avenue for networking and establishing relationships within the NFT community. NFT owners' pride and nepotism may lead to beautiful chances for community members, as was previously indicated.

METAVERSE INVESTING

From Beginners to Advanced, All You Have to Know about Metaverse, Nft and the best Crypto project for the Future

Easy Blockchain Academy

Introduction

Humans always been astonished by technology. The present advances in artificial intelligence, quantum computing, nuclear power, virtual reality, and augmented reality would have been unimaginable to someone who lived in the Stone Age. Despite this, technical advances are routinely predicted decades in advance, simply that it is difficult to forecast how everything will come together. This has been the case in virtual reality (VR), augmented reality (AR), and the Metaverse. Virtual reality (VR) was first proposed in 1838, but it wasn't feasible until the world's visuals and processing capabilities (as of today) caught up. In the late 1970s, the concept of a "metaverse" existed, although it was only an imagined successor or development of the Internet at the time.

People started talking about the "Metaverse" once Facebook was renamed Meta, but no one understood what it meant. There's been a lot of assumptions about how the Internet and other technologies would change for a long time. When discussing the development of the Internet, we often refer to Web1, Web2, Web3, etc. Now we're talking about the Metaverse. Nevertheless, let's consider a different scenario. Imagine being able to design your ideal alter-ego in a virtual environment where you have complete control over every element of your character's appearance. Your options are almost infinite, so don't be afraid to go for what you want. In various science fiction films and television shows, a situation was described. As a result of a lot of buzz in the business sector, it's possible that "The Metaverse" may soon become a reality. However, there is a lot of debate over the definitions of Web3 and the distinction between the Metaverse. Others suggest that following Web2, we'll witness a leap into a "Metaverse"-style immersive Internet known as "Web 3.0," which some believe is the next stage of the Internet. However, the debate over whether Web3 is crypto and blockchain or immersive Internet with virtual worlds will continue for some time to come.

Although the term "metaverse" has just recently become a buzzword, Tim Berners-Lee is well-known for inventing the World Wide Web in 1989. The term 'metaverse' was created by sci-fi writer Neal Stephenson in 1992 to describe a 3D virtual realm. Augmented Reality (AR), Mixed Reality, Cryptocurrency, and the Internet will construct the Metaverse in 2022. It's been 30 years since Philip Rosedale's "Second Life" online virtual world was launched, and Mark Zuckerberg's "Meta" (previously Facebook) metaverse concept was unveiled in 2020. The year was 1962, and television viewers were treated to a peek of what the future may hold. In a future megacity with flying vehicles, intelligent houses, an automated workforce, virtual reality, and an array of innovative living solutions, the American Broadcasting Corporation (ABC) broadcast a sitcom about a family. The Jetsons seem to be living a regular life 60 years later. Aside from our everyday routines, technology has become an integral element of every choice we make. A brighter future or perhaps a potential successor for the Internet–the Metaverse–had previously been envisaged by several engineers in the early 1980s.

It was thought that the Metaverse would change both the digital and physical worlds, including all of its connected services. Inventors in fields like gaming and communication are hoping Metaverse will revolutionize how digital and physical services function. This means it might have huge effects on society in all of these dimensions. Because companies like Epic Games and Facebook have shown interest, we may hold out some semblance of optimism while we wait for more concrete evidence of the Metaverse's existence. A tremendous step towards a reality that seems to be decades away has already taken place with the implementation of metaverse elements in games like Roblox, Fortnite, and Animal Crossing.

Meaning

Two words, "meta-" and "verse," make up the term "metaverse," a combination of the two. The prefix "meta" means "beyond" in Greek, while "verse" is derived from the Latin word "universe." Snow Crash by Neal Stephenson was the first time used in literature. Presented as a form of virtual reality where every online contact may directly influence the actual world, the Metaverse is described as the subsequent development of the Internet in this book. The Metaverse is well summed up in this book. This activity will give you an idea of how ambiguous and confusing the word "the metaverse" may be. Replace "the metaverse" with "cyberspace" in a sentence. In the vast majority of cases, the intended meaning remains primarily unchanged. We utilize technology in many ways now; thus, the word "interaction design" doesn't relate to any particular form of a technological solution. Even as the technology it previously defined becomes more widespread, the name "smartphone" may also become obsolete.

The Metaverse is a highly scalable, permanent network of virtual worlds where individuals may work, socialize, trade, play, and even create. AR, VR, haptic sensors, and other cutting-edge virtualization technologies are used to completely immerse the user in the virtual environment. As a result, the user may engage in real-time communication with a constantly available world. People who are proponents of "The Metaverse" think that in an ideal future, there would be a single platform from which you could visit various worlds, each with its persona, identity, and platform services. Many sub-worlds to choose from that allow you to join, quit or even construct your own for a fully functional economy in a virtual environment, there must still be a definition for a digital identity, digital currency, and the universal transferability of digital assets, such as a virtual currency. In this sense, the Metaverse might replace many parts of how tourism works, what it means to attend a concert, fine art exhibits, and mainly how people learn, study, interact and even make friends in real life. Virtual reality, which creates permanent virtual worlds that remain even when you're not playing, and augmented reality, which merges the digital and physical worlds, are two significant components of the Metaverse. That doesn't mean that VR or AR must be the only way to access these virtual worlds. A metaverse virtual world maybe something like Fortnite's battle royale mode, which can be accessed on PCs, consoles, and even mobile devices.

A digital economy is one in which people may make, purchase, and sell things digitally. You may even transport virtual objects like clothing or vehicles from one platform to another in more idealized conceptions of the Metaverse. A shirt purchased in the mall may be worn to the movie theatre. Currently, most platforms only enable you to establish a virtual identity, avatar, and inventory that can be used on a single platform. However, a metaverse may allow you to construct a persona that can be used on several platforms simply as a profile image.

Definition

The term "metaverse" refers to a digital realm that exists above and beyond our existing reality. As a portmanteau, "metaverse" is derived from the two terms "verse" and "meta," which mean "beyond." To put it more simply, the phrase "metaverse" alludes to a cosmos that extends beyond our own. Metaverse is a word used in technology to represent a computer-mediated cosmos that is not constrained by the physical world's metaphysical and spiritual dimensions. The term "metaverse" refers to a future Internet technology that goes beyond the limitations of existing technology and raises the bar for user involvement in the next generation. In the Metaverse, avatars may be used to engage with each other and with software programs. The Metaverse mixes social networking, AR, VR, online gaming, and cryptocurrency to create a virtual world where people may engage.

In its simplest definition, Metaverse is a "shared virtual world" that users may access through the Internet. Using holograms/avatars, individuals may immerse themselves in a virtual world and feel like they are in the same physical location. VR technology augmented reality, and 3d virtual environments will all be used to generate this sensation of presence in a metaverse. We want to leverage the Internet's potential to provide our users the feeling of engaging face-to-face. This will be a significant leap forward with the usage of virtual worlds to connect people around the globe in real-time for various objectives.

Users are linked in every area of their life through the Metaverse, an online, 3D, virtual realm. Users would view various websites on several platforms using a single web browser. The idea in his science fiction book Snow Crash. Metaverses were initially considered science fiction, but it now seems they may become a reality shortly. Users will be in command to take control of an avatar or character in the Metaverse using augmented reality (AR). For example, you might use an Oculus VR headset to have a mixed reality conference in your virtual workplace, then relax and play a blockchain-based game to unwind after work.

Some of the Metaverse's features may already be found in virtual video game environments. Online worlds like Second Life and Fortnite and programs like Gather. The town that lets us socialize at work together with many aspects of our daily lives. The Metaverse isn't precisely like these programs, but it's a close approximation anyway. The Metaverse does not exist at this time.

Additionally, the Metaverse will include digital identification, decentralized government, and a variety of other functions. User-created and owned valuables assist in building a single, unified metaverse today. Blockchain can fuel this future technology because of all of these qualities and capabilities. There will be a lot of avatars/holograms in the Metaverse. In virtual or computer-mediated worlds, an avatar is an appearance, embodiment, or manifestation of a person. A variety of styles are possible, including "character-like representations" that enhance a user's sense of self both in the physical and digital realms. It is possible to build and utilize various avatars for various reasons, for example, a gamer avatar, a professional/business avatar, a social/family avatar, and so on. Users will establish and manage social network accounts in the Metaverse using avatars. Using an interconnected network of interconnected areas and sites, the avatars may plan and execute planned and purposeful activities. Individuals and avatars develop expectations and experiences over time by immersing themselves in new environments, which they may then utilize to help create unique environments and procedures in the future.

How the Metaverse Work

Facebook CEO Mark Zuckerberg and others have framed the Metaverse as "an opportunity" to bring our virtual and real lives closer together. As Zuckerberg put it in October, "We'll be able to express ourselves in totally delightful, truly immersive ways, no matter how far away we are," he stated during a presentation on the Metaverse. AR and VR will be used to build a more immersive internet, where we'll spend more time participating in virtual locations and experiences rather than the real world. It was initially used in Neal Stephenson's 1992 science fiction book Snow Crash, but now Zuckerberg and other industry leaders want to make it a reality

MATTHEW BALL INTRODUCED THE METAVERSE LIKE THIS:

"At the moment, the internet is essentially a "push" medium." After being "pushed" with information (e.g., by email or notice), you open your device and check it out. It's an "embodied engine" that you're already "inside, rather than seeking out," Ball said of the Metaverse.

This implies that we will be disconnected from our actual surroundings, such as the workplace the living room, in a real-world sense. As an alternative, we'll don our VR headsets or some other kind of virtual reality headgear. Virtually altering your environment or even your physical appearance may positively impact how you feel about yourself. It may also be seen as a dystopian idea, as though the Metaverse is reserved for those who want to escape the harsh realities of the actual world (which is how it was envisioned in the novel Snow Crash). However, any discussion of the Metaverse is purely speculatory for the time being. If you ask Facebook, they'll tell you that it's still a baby. Even if it "doesn't completely exist" yet, Facebook's Oculus Quest 2 headgear, which costs $299, has drastically dropped the entry price point for VR devices, as stated by its founder and CEO. HP Reverb G2 Virtual Reality Headset presents $450, while the HTC Vive Cosmos is more than $600.

Many individuals may interact with one another and digital things while using virtual versions of themselves, known as avatars, in this network of always-on virtual settings. Incorporate virtual reality, massively multiplayer online role-playing games, and the Internet into one seamless experience. In the computer sector, the Metaverse is a sci-fi notion that many people envisage as a replacement for the current Internet. Facebook and other internet firms see it as the hub for a wide range of online activities, from work and recreation to education and retail. For this reason, Facebook is changing its Meta to emphasize its desire to rule the Metaverse in the new name. It is a homogenous mixture of meta and verse. In his 1992 book "Snow Crash," sci-fi author Neal Stephenson invented the phrase to describe the virtual environment in which the protagonist, Hiro Protagonist, engages in social interactions, shops, and defeats real-world foes through his avatar. Before "Snow Crash," William Gibson's revolutionary book "Neuromancer" popularized the term "cyberspace."

3-Key Aspects of Metaverse

The existence, interoperability, and standardization of the Metaverse are the three most important features of the Metaverse. Being present in a virtual realm and interacting with other virtual beings is what we mean when we talk about the concept of presence. This sensation of physical presence enhances the quality of online interactions, as has been repeatedly shown over decades of study. Virtual reality technology, such as head-mounted displays, is used to create a feeling of presence. If you have interoperability, you can move across virtual places with the same virtual assets, including avatars and digital objects. Apps like Animaze and Ready Player Me enable consumers to build avatars that can be used in virtual environments, including Zoom meetings. Virtual products can be transferred across virtual boundaries thanks to blockchain technology like cryptocurrency and nonfungible tokens. Standards facilitate interoperability across metaverse systems and services. Consistent technical standards are vital for their broad acceptance when it comes to mass-media technologies. The Open Metaverse Interoperability Group, for example, is a global group that establishes these guidelines.

Functioning

In the Metaverse, the real environment is combined with virtual worlds to create a collectively shared virtual space. The Internet, augmented reality, and virtual worlds were all part of it. Although "cyberspace" was first used in 1984 in William Gibson's Neuromancer, the metaverse idea may be traced back far earlier. The Metaverse is already present in online role-playing games like World of Warcraft, Minecraft, and Roblox. However unsettling it may seem to contemplate the idea of a metaverse, our physical and digital lives are increasingly becoming intertwined. Many of us currently spend most of our time in front of screens, whether for work or play. We're all aware that tech titans are working on this, even if it's 5 to 10 years away from becoming possible.

There have been considerable investments in AR and VR made by Meta, formerly known as Facebook Inc. The purchase of Oculus in 2014 is only one example. From 2022 forward, it will be known as Meta Quest for its Oculus Quest VR headsets. It's known as Horizon and Horizon Workrooms by Meta and is now in the open beta metaverse. Regardless of location, users can collaborate in the same virtual space using Meta's flagship collaboration experience. Virtual reality (VR) headsets enable teams to communicate with one other using virtual avatars in a virtual workplace. Team members may use avatars, digital whiteboards, and directional audio to communicate more effectively than they can with traditional video conferencing and a headset.

Microsoft is also preparing its metaverse vision by using HoloLens mixed reality headset technology and Microsoft's 2017 purchase of Altspace VR. Facebook changed its name to Meta, and Microsoft stated it was introducing its virtual reality technology, Mesh, to Microsoft Teams by the end of 2022. 3D animated avatars may be used with or without a virtual reality headset. Using the Teams platform, businesses will create their virtual worlds or metaverses. Windows Azure IoT and Digital Twins are also part of the metaverse technology stack provided by Microsoft.

Printing in the Enterprise Metaverse

Digital twins, IoT sensors, and mixed reality will all be needed to make the business metaverse a reality. It will enable the creation of workplaces that can be used for both physical and digital interactions. Companies can already unleash part of the Metaverse's potential by evaluating results and using AI to optimize and automate processes by analyzing data from linked settings. Using AR in predictive maintenance is already shown its full potential. In this case, ML may be used to monitor data from previous devices and forecast the future, which can lead to the replacement of things before they fail or to the prolonged usage of objects since failure is less probable. Companies may use Metaverse-based predictive maintenance to predict when a component will break and save downtime.

AR is beginning to be used in the printing business, although mainly in the service sector. Powered by Microsoft HoloLens 2, HP unveiled HP services on November 9th for its industrial printers. A virtual/real-world combination of HP services allows clients to contact HP engineers in a split second via mixed reality, advising them on any problem at any step in their print output, all through mixed reality.

Remote visual AR help may be instantaneously provided to customers, employees, and field personnel with Xerox careers. To be sure, in an already dwindling sector, printing faces competition from mixed reality cooperation. A virtual whiteboard in Horizon Workrooms, for example, allows you to use your controller as a pen to write on the whiteboard, whether sitting at a desk or standing in a group. It is also possible that "print" might be an electronic process, while "paper" could refer to data projection into a virtual reality world. If they want to be a part of Metaverse, print producers will have to use these digital print technologies.

The Immersive Workplace

The workforce expects suppliers to be agile and adaptable in terms of technology. A substantial shift in the way organizations deal with their suppliers is inevitable as technology advances. Even while the Metaverse has yet to reveal how it will reshape the world of work, the lines between the real and virtual domains are already becoming more blurred.

Because of the difficulty in simulating actual in-person interactions, virtual reality and augmented reality are going beyond the boundaries of online gaming. The Metaverse may be able to help companies create virtual office settings. Certain firms already use occupancy tracking, hot-desk scheduling, and intelligent heating systems to create low-touch office environments monitored by digital technologies. Remote and office-based employees might benefit from a more immersive work environment, which would provide an equal playing field for both groups. Data and privacy will undoubtedly be a problem, but it may be possible to create productive cooperation if people return to work through a hybrid office/home setting.

Using a headset for more than an hour is complex. Until lightweight, efficient AR glasses are available at a reasonable price, AR is likely to stay an environment for the tech enthusiasts and people with very specialized demands, such as surgeons who need the technology. A poorly maintained avatar or hologram isn't going to make us feel like we're engaging with a real person, so why would anybody want to do that? Taking on digital identity in this manner implies that our every move would be followed and scrutinized? The Metaverse may or may not portend a gloomy future, but it is still in its infancy. Many of the areas that engineers anticipated would be of great interest may be left behind as the technology matures and people discover what works best for them. However, we may expect other tech titans and a broad network of lesser point players to invest in metaverse goals in the future.

Chapter 1:
Augmented Reality

What is Augmented Reality

The use of AR-capable smartphones and other devices is on the rise, and this trend will only continue as more people have access to AR-ready devices. A digital overlay was placed on top of the real-world environment that we could see, such as trees swinging in the park dogs chasing balls, as well as children playing soccer. An extinct reptile could be seen swooping down to settle in the woods, dogs might be interacting with cartoon characters, and youngsters could be seen running past an extraterrestrial ship while on their way to scoring a goal. These examples aren't all that different from what's presently accessible on your smartphone, thanks to developments in AR technology. Many other applications for augmented reality are now widely accessible, from Snapchat lenses to apps that help you locate your automobile in a cluttered parking lot to many shopping apps that allow you to try on clothing without ever leaving your house. With its 2016 introduction and subsequent ubiquity, the smartphone game Pokemon Go is perhaps the most famous example of AR technology. Pikachu and pals appear in the real world, including on the street, in a watering hole, and your bathroom. Aside from gaming, we can find as many applications for augmented reality in our daily lives as Pikachus are roaming free in Pokemon GO. The following are only a few:

- Augmented reality is used to overlay a path on top of a real-time image of the road.

- To show and evaluate plays, football broadcasters employ augmented reality (AR) during games.

- Using IKEA Place, an augmented reality software, you can preview how a piece of furniture will appear and fit in your home before you buy it.

- They don't need to spend time peering down to view them since they have an AR projection on their helmet visor showing their altitude and speed.

- Neurosurgeons use an augmented reality (AR) visualization of the 3-D brain during surgery.
- AR can bring the past to life at historical locations like Pompeii in Italy by overlaying images of ancient civilizations on top of today's ruins.
- Using AR glasses, airport ground staff in Singapore may quickly examine information about cargo containers.

Understanding Augmented Reality

Virtual and audio/visual components are combined with the real-world environment to provide an improved experience known as augmented reality (AR). Particularly in mobile computing and corporate apps, this practice is becoming more popular. An essential purpose of using augmented reality is to emphasize and comprehend certain aspects of the physical environment to be used in real-world applications during growth in data collecting and analysis. Big data can be utilized by firms that make intelligent choices and learn more about what their customers spend their money on, among other things.

Augmented reality in a wide variety of applications is on the rise. Augmented reality has struggled to fight the notion that it is nothing more than a tool for marketing since its beginnings. Consumers are, however, starting to see the value in this feature and expect it to be part of the shopping process. For example, early adopters in the retail industry have created technology to improve the customer shopping experience. Catalog applications that use augmented reality allow customers to see how various goods appear in multiple settings. In the case of furniture, the product shows in the forefront if the consumer takes a picture in the correct room. In the healthcare industry, augmented reality's advantages might be far more significant. Hovering a mobile device over a target picture displays 3D images of various bodily systems, which may provide a wealth of information to consumers. Medical students and residents, for example, might benefit significantly from the use of augmented reality as a teaching aid. Wearable technology, according to some, might be a game-changer in the field of augmented reality. Unlike smartphones and tablets, smart eyewear can create full connectivity between the real and virtual world for users if it becomes widely used.

Working of Augmented Reality

A camera-equipped device, such as a smartphone, tablet, or smart glasses, loaded with AR software is the starting point for augmented reality. Computer vision technology analyses the video stream to detect an item when the user directs the gadget. Cloud-based information is subsequently similarly downloaded to the device to how web browsers load webpages. Rather than a 2-D page on a screen, the AR information is shown as a 3-D "experience" overlaid on the item. The user's experience, then, is a mix of the actual and the virtual.

With augmented reality (AR), users may see and interact with data streaming from their devices in real-time, whether via a touchscreen, speech, or gesture. To convey a command to a product, a user may, for example, press the stop button on the digital graphic overlay in an AR encounter or simply say "stop." With AR headsets, it's possible to view information about a robot's status and capabilities projected on top of the robot itself.

The size and position of the AR display dynamically adapt to the changing context as the user travels about the room." Other information is obscured by the arrival of new visual or textual data. A machine operator and a maintenance technician may both gaze at the same thing and have various AR experiences customized to their specific duties in an industrial context. The item's "digital twin"—a 3-D digital representation that lives in the cloud—serves as the link between the bright object and the AR. Computer-aided design (CAD) or technology that digitizes physical items may be used to generate this model. The twin gathers data from the development, business systems, and external sources to represent the product's current reality. In this way, the AR software can precisely position and scale the most up-to-date data on the item.

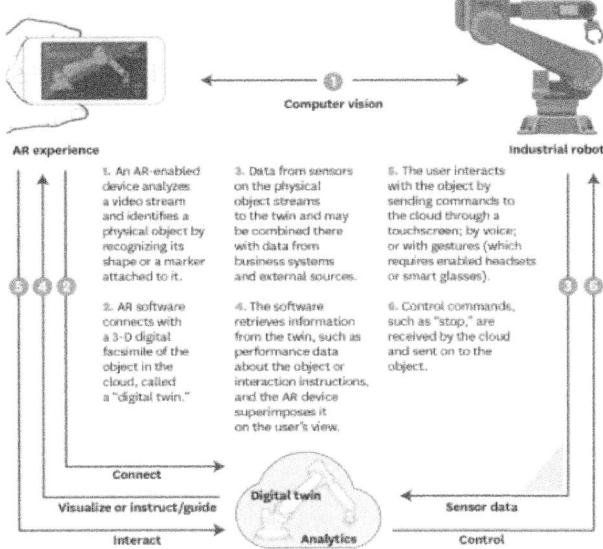

Merging Real and Digital Worlds

Computer vision

AR experience — Industrial robot

1. An AR-enabled device analyzes a video stream and identifies a physical object by recognizing its shape or a marker attached to it.

3. Data from sensors on the physical object streams to the twin and may be combined there with data from business systems and external sources.

5. The user interacts with the object by sending commands to the cloud through a touchscreen; by voice; or with gestures (which requires enabled headsets or smart glasses).

2. AR software connects with a 3-D digital facsimile of the object in the cloud, called a "digital twin."

4. The software retrieves information from the twin, such as performance data about the object or interaction instructions, and the AR device superimposes it on the user's view.

6. Control commands, such as "stop," are received by the cloud and sent on to the object.

Connect
Visualize or instruct/guide — Digital twin
Interact — Analytics
Sensor data
Control

AR Devices

The most widely used oxymoron could be Virtual Reality. It allows the user to get fully immersed in a computer-generated 3D representation. Head-mounted displays (HMDs) or fully immersive projection-based systems are the most common means of achieving virtual reality (VR). Using cardboard, plastic lenses, and a few other inexpensive components to create a smartphone-based VR experience, Google changed the game. Virtual reality experiences available exclusively to business and academic technocrats cost as little as $15 and could be enjoyed by anybody with a smartphone. A sensible and high-impact approach allowed the technology to be widely adopted and understood.

However, it's virtually probable that Augmented reality will be the more generally accepted technology despite the unrest. Like the smartphone, it allows people to incorporate technology into their everyday lives without obscuring the world around them.

Major Category Devices

Augmented reality dates back to the early 1900s, despite the term's comparatively recent emergence. Irish telescope builder Howard Grub invented the collimating reflector. Its primary goal was to improve shooting precision by focusing the crosshairs on the user's intended target. It aimed to address a fundamental problem in the human eye: it can only focus on one task at a time. Grubb's innovation influenced a variety of military gun sights.

Four major categories of augmented reality devices exist.

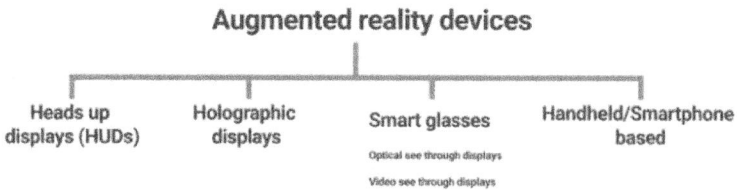

Augmented reality devices

Heads up displays (HUDs)	Holographic displays	Smart glasses	Handheld/Smartphone based
		Optical see through displays	
		Video see through displays	

Heads up displays (HUDs)

The number of sensors, avionics, and flight controls aboard planes grew as controllers got more sophisticated, increasing the information processing demands for pilots. Pilots need to keep their attention on the outside world rather than on the plethora of information in the cockpit. For mission-critical applications like flight controllers and weapons system dashboards, heads-up displays were primarily developed—transparent panels situated in front of the pilot display critical information. Instead of staring downward at their instruments, pilots may gaze out the window and see what's happening around them. Using a collimating projector, much as Grub's collimating reflector, HUDs attempted to address the issue of focusing shifts. This means that the pilot's eyes do not have to change focus to see beyond the cockpit since the information presented is collimated (parallel light beams focused on infinity).

Heads-up displays (HUDs) are becoming more prevalent in automotive designs. A typical HUD consists of a projector, a display (combiner), and a computer (symbol generator). Pilots benefit from HUDs because they reduce their time spent looking away from the road.

Helmet Mounted Displays

Moving from the windshield to the helmet was the next natural step for heads-up displays. Aviation and other sectors are increasingly using helmet-mounted screens that operate on the same principles as heads-up displays.

Holographic Displays

With light diffraction, these displays have become more popular thanks to films like Star Wars, Minority Report, and the Iron Man series. One of the most appealing aspects of holographic displays is that they don't need the wearer of any special equipment to observe them. Products like Looking Glass and Holovect have lately brought these displays out of science fiction and mainstream.

Smart Glasses

Smart glasses have been among the most popular augmented reality gadgets as the technology has moved from vital uses in the military and aviation to widely accessible items. These are amplification glasses, as the name implies. One of the two smart glasses is called "smart eyewear."

Optical See Through

If you have a pair of optical see-through glasses, you can see the actual world via holographic waveguides and other devices that allow you to overlay graphics on top of the real environment. Recent examples of optical see-through smart spectacles include Microsoft's Hololens, Magic Leap One, and Google Glass.

Video See Through

The built-in camera in the HTC Vive VR headset is often utilized to create augmented reality experiences on the device. Thanks to the display's one or two cameras, this sort of smart glasses lets the wearer see the world as it is. For the user, these images are mixed with computer-generated graphics.

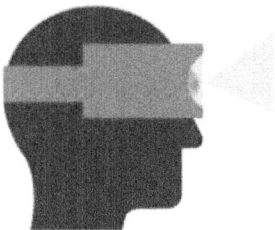

Optical see through displays   Video see through displays

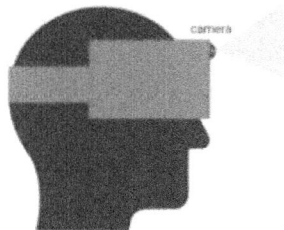

Handheld Through AR

Handheld AR's popularity has reached a tipping point, paving the way for widespread adoption. With the advent of augmented reality libraries like ARKit, ARCore, and Markit, anybody may now use cutting-edge computer vision techniques. You just need a smartphone to access a wide range of AR experiences on the go, whether you're using it for handheld or mobile AR. As a sort of video see-through, portable AR demands particular attention.

Current Leaders

Soon, mobile phones AR glasses, and headsets will cohabit in the same environment. Virtual reality (VR) can be used on smartphones, tablets, and desktops since it doesn't need any special hardware. We'll see more AR gadgets like this in the future:

Microsoft Hololens 2

Microsoft's Hololens 2 is the closest to a flawless augmented reality gadget. As the only AR device with dual 2K 120Hz displays, it can display 3D objects with more clarity than any other currently available AR gadget. In addition to tracking eye and hand movements, Hololens 2 lets you interact with the virtual environment naturally. The Hololens 2 can be the brave leader of Augmented Reality with more calibration and a size reduction.

Magic Leap One

When it comes to the most buzzed-about startups of 2018, Magic Leap came out on top. They released Magic Leap One, a groundbreaking augmented reality gadget, towards the end of last year. The Magic leap one costs about $2299, but it lets you experience AR graphics in the actual world. A gadget that doesn't completely isolate you from the real world seems like a sensible choice in today's technologically driven environment.

Epson Moverio

Epson Moverio AR gadgets, in contrast to Hololens and Magic Leap One, enable you to view a virtual display floating in front of the actual real-world environment. The display is based on your eyes and head rather than the environment in front of you. As a result, the screen will always be facing in the direction of the user's eyes.

Google Glass Enterprise Edition

When Google Glass originally came out, it was a flop. The device's advantages, such as the ability to capture video or take photos without alerting others, made it unappealing to consumers. Despite this, Google discovered a method to recover. Thanks to its AI capabilities and other benefits, doctors, mechanics, entrepreneurs, and anybody else may now use Google Glass. It enables individuals to work with both hands while still being linked to the virtual world, making things more efficient and productive.

Vuzix Blade AR

After discontinued Google Glass a few years ago, Vuzix Blade AR stepped in to fill the void. Unlike Google Glass, the Vuzix Blade AR camera features a red indication that lets everyone know whether or not the camera is active. Nevertheless, it features an integrated display in the center of the glass, rather than an inconvenient display in the corner. For the most part, it's controlled by Alexa, but it's also compatible with cellphones through Bluetooth.

Current Examples of AR

In the world of augmented reality, the possibilities are almost limitless. This technology will be commonplace in our daily lives in a few short years. Some organizations and businesses are already making enormous progress with this technology, but we're not yet there. We've rounded together seven of the most impressive uses of augmented reality technology so far.

IKEA Mobile App

One of the first firms to employ augmented reality effectively, IKEA is also renowned for its furniture with funny names that you have to build yourself an affordable Swedish meatball.

Nintendo Pokémon Go App

Shoppers could use an app to examine how tables and shelves would appear in different locations around their homes back in 2012. As part of its IKEA Place app, IKEA now lets you choose any item from the store's catalog and see how it would scale to any room in your home. Whether you're unsure whether or not a particular piece of furniture will fit in a specific area or if the color of your potential purchase will match the room's theme, this is an excellent resource for you.

Google Pixel's Star Wars Stickers

It's impossible to conduct a talk about augmented reality without bringing up Nintendo's Pokémon Go app. To make its debut in 2016, Pokémon Go allows players to capture their favorite Pokémon by scanning the virtual environment using augmented reality glasses. Up to 65 million people played the game at its height, making it a smashing success. It's possible that you spotted a large number of teenagers and young people walking around your area with their phones in their hands.

Disney Coloring Book

Star Wars is a movie; if you saw it in the cinemas or watched TV at all, you've undoubtedly seen this commercial: Google's Pixel phones include a camera function that allows users to add AR stickers to photos and videos, much like Pokémon Go. There is a possibility you have gotten at least one picture of a random Stormtrooper if you have a Google phone. For kids, Disney produced an augmented reality experience a few years ago to view their favorite characters from the movies in 3D. Using augmented reality (AR), a team of researchers created 3D reconstructions of colored pictures from a coloring book using a mobile phone or tablet. A whole new approach for youngsters to develop their imaginations might be ushered in by this technology that is still in its development and has not yet been made available to the public.

L'Oréal Makeup App

L'Oréal offers a mobile app similar to IKEA's that allows users to experiment with different cosmetics. It's a lot like a Snapchat filter, in that sense. The software scans your face and then shows you how a given shade or hue of a particular product might appear on you in a virtual environment

Weather Channel Studio Effects

For years, television news has used special effects to improve its programming quality. For example, weathermen have long used green screens, which project maps onto the screen, to communicate their predictions to the public. The Weather Channel is now using even more cutting-edge technology to better portray the consequences of severe weather. A virtual automobile was recently driven across the studio to demonstrate how cars lose control while driving on snowy or icy roads. This is only the latest in a long line of uses for augmented reality in the broadcast industry. Augmented reality in news, weather, and sports broadcasting are expected to grow in the coming years.

Technology

Although many people have seen it, the technology may be new. A smartphone, tablet, computer, television, or even eyeglasses or contact lenses may be able to show real-time information over live camera footage soon, thanks to this innovative technology. Watching a football game on TV is a great way to pass the time. The yellow first down line shown on the field for our convenience is a sham. You can only view it on television since it's an augmented reality display. Heads-up displays on aircraft helms, for example, are another type of augmented reality.

Geolocation and visual imaging are vital components of AR, which can be a significant tool for users. It is a fast-developing technology for entertainment, business, marketing, art, social networking, and activism. Also, this technology has a lot of potential for usage in treating mental health issues. Even though few studies have been done on AR, its impacts on users are apparent: Virtual reality is captivating, intriguing, persuading, and all-encompassing.

Even though augmented reality (AR) is now employed chiefly for entertainment purposes, it is a fast-expanding technology advancing quickly. AR development and programming is expected to see an increase in investment of more than $600 million by 2016. Several major tech firms are stepping up to create AR-capable products, including Apple, HP, Google, and Qualcomm. The US Department of Defense has made a significant monetary commitment to AR, and DARPA is researching to support the technology's future.

VR and AR technological advances should be of interest to psychologists because of their potential therapeutic and research uses. For example, imagine a patient with arachnophobia being exposed to augmented reality spiders while being able to alter the creature's appearance (size and form), color, and movement. Imagine having the patient engage with these virtual spiders, manipulating their activity and even picking them up, all in the virtual world!

Even though virtual reality has been used for therapeutic purposes for some time, the technology has significant limitations. The computer-generated world required a significant degree of disbelief for patients, and the development expenses were expensive. Virtual reality (VR) addressed these difficulties by being available to anybody with a smartphone, tablet, or computer. Application development software may be simple to use and even affordable in certain circumstances. Due to the ease with which accurate digital information may be projected into the patient's actual surroundings.

Application of AR

The usefulness of AR lies in its ability to comprehend, alter, and augment the real-time perspective of the world. Here are a few examples of how augmented reality is already being put to use:

Retail
AR's most significant usage for most users will be in retail applications, mainly "try before you buy." AR will enable buyers to preview how a thing will appear in their own homes before buying it, as more people shop from home and less emphasis is placed on public retail venues. Purchases may be made with more confidence thanks to this. Wayfair, Houzz, and Ikea are just a few of the many applications that let you arrange furniture and other items in your real-world settings.

Mapping and Navigation
With the business directory app, you can easily find your way around town. With its now-discontinued Monocle function, Yelp was an early adopter of AR. On your phone's screen, you may see information about nearby companies that Monocle has provided as an overlay. The locations of local eateries and basic details such as their distance were indicated through callouts. Rather than using the traditional HUD, Mercedes-Benz has developed an automobile that displays navigational information directly on the windshield, allowing drivers to keep their eyes fixed on the road.

Education
Traditional teaching approaches are being supplemented by augmented reality (AR). A smartphone may be used to scan a book's barcode and show supplementary information or 3D visualizations, for example.

Maintenance and Industry

Using AR to overlay essential information in a worker's field of vision while conducting maintenance or other chores offers enormous promise for decreasing dependence on paper technical manuals and increasing productivity at the same time. Using highlights and overlays, AR systems that are sufficiently sophisticated can not only comprehend context to display the correct information, but they can also aid in identifying components and processes. BMW, for example, is experimenting with using AR on the manufacturing line as part of a test program.

Entertainment and social media

It's not only for gaming that AR has a lot of promise. While Magic Leap has spent more than $2.6 billion building AR eyewear and an AR technology platform, the business continues to garner new financing even though it does not have a commercially viable product. TikTok has just offered branded AR effects that can be added to videos on smartphones. In the coming years, we may expect to see a scramble to produce even more appealing AR experiences that blur the lines between the real and virtual.

Common AR Use Cases

Training and Education

People can learn new skills more quickly and simply use AR-based lessons than standard training techniques (like instruction manuals). The potential for augmented reality training is enormous, especially as wearable technologies like AR-powered intelligent glasses, AR contacts, and AR headsets become more commonly accessible.

Entertainment

AR has been boosting entertainment for a long time, and it will continue to do so. Homage to Tupac Shakur debuted alongside Snoop Dogg on Coachella's main stage in 2012. An Instagram influencer who is also a totally CGI avatar was signed by CAA this year. As a result of the COVID-19 pandemic, Rcal Estate sponsored a "Quarantour," an AR-powered tour to replace the live events that had to be canceled due to international quarantine measures.

209

Gaming

Dozens of games now include AR features. Gaming was one of the most apparent early uses that many people saw for AR and VR capabilities, so it's no wonder that AR games are so popular.

Selling

Augmented reality applications allow customers to digitally try on or test out a range of products before making a purchase: You can virtually "try on" makeup from Sephora's app and see how it looks on your face in augmented reality. You can virtually "see" furniture from IKEA in your home. You can virtually "see" paint colors on your walls. You can virtually "try on" glasses from Warby Parker without visiting a store or order samples. They offered a means to improve customer experiences in-store or make their lives a bit simpler before the outbreak. Many firms may now sell to customers confined to their own houses because of the technology they've created. Augmented reality (AR) in eCommerce is on the rise.

Most of these augmented reality experiences are now made feasible by cell phones. There is a slew of potential uses for more sophisticated augmented reality (AR) gadgets on the horizon, including Apple's AR glasses and Microsoft's Hololens. New industries, such as healthcare, manufacturing, utilities, telecommunications, and education, are reaping the advantages of augmented reality. It's possible to imagine, for example, seeing IKEA furniture in the comfort of your own home through AR, purchasing online, getting it in the mail, and then using your AR-enabled glasses to see the assembly instructions projected directly onto the components in the box. With so many options, there's no limit to the fun.

Types of AR Applications

Solutions for monitoring the whole body, QR-codes, sophisticated graphs, and GPS data may all be used to identify a location, but some systems concentrate on one or the other. AR/VR systems with full-body motion tracking for sectors that need authentic, real-world interactions in their virtual world settings are an emerging technology.

Full Body Tracking Solution

Manus VR provides the most advanced AR/VR full-body tracking systems. To allow full-body tactile interactions in virtual reality, Manus has released the Polygon full-body tracking system, and the Prime II sophisticated glove system Motion capture expert Manus has entered a new phase of hyper-realistic immersive VR team collaboration with natural body motions and real touch sensations. Manus now offers customers a complete, durable, and efficient VR system created exclusively for teams in the business sector of automotive, manufacturing, engineering, and life sciences, including media and entertainment developers of virtual experiences.

Marker Based App

This is one of the most often used concepts in terms of AR software. Markers may range from primary geometric forms (frequently wrapped in QR-codes) to real sophisticated things (such as human faces) for digital perception. Many of these ideas need a significant amount of time and effort to implement.

Apps that Focus on GPS data

Apps that depend on GPS data take time to analyze multiple occurrences. In addition to a GPS connection, a high-speed web connection is required for this sort of solution. AR browsers and gyroscope-based applications are two examples of this kind of software.

Gyroscope-Based Apps

Another frequent technique to develop AR software is to leverage the gyroscope data from the user's smartphone. SLAM programs may use this built-in functionality to bring virtual 3D things to life on top of real-world items.

SLAM apps

Simultaneous Localization and Mapping (SLAM) combines data from several sensors into a single map (for instance, from GPS, gyroscope, accelerometer, etc.). Instead of employing markers, like in the preceding gyroscope-based app scenario, these applications create three-dimensional objects against a backdrop of real things.

Evolution of AR

- 'Ivan Sutherland' and his pupil, Bob Sprowle, created the first head-mounted display, or 'The Sword of Damocles,' in 1968, and this was the beginning of Augmented Reality technology.

- Myron Krueger made the next significant advancement in AR in 1974. This concept is called 'Video Place' and combines video cameras with projection technology to create shadows on the screen. This setup seems to be in a user-interactive space.

- Boeing researcher Tom Cadell coined the phrase "Augmented Reality" in 1990.

- 'Virtual Fixtures,' a system developed by Louis Rosenberg in 1992 at the USAF Armstrong Research Lab, was the first operational AR system. The data is kept out of the reach of the employees by a robotic system. An early prototype of current AR systems may be found in this system.

- In 1994, the first theatrical play was made to employ AR. Julie Martin's "Dancing in Cyberspace" included acrobats performing in and around computer-generated sets and props.

- In 1999, NASA's X-38 spacecraft employed the Hybrid Synthetic Vision System, an AR-enabled version of their Hybrid Synthetic Vision System. During flight testing, AR was used to aid in the development of navigation.

- When Hirokazu Kato of the NIST, Japan (Nara Institute of Science and Technology) was founded and published software with the name 'ARToolKit' in 2000, a significant advance in AR was achieved in the field. To capture real-world activities and merge them with virtual objects, this program is needed.

- Virtual down markers were inserted into NFL games using the Skycom in 2003, an excellent tool for overhead views of industries.

- Esquire Magazine and Robert Downey Jr. began using AR in print media in 2009. Readers may see AR material by scanning the magazine's barcode with their computer software. Fortunately, ARToolKit made AR available to all web browsers in the same year.

- Volkswagen began using AR in its automobile manuals in 2013. With the MARTA iPad app, consumers can see the vehicle's internal functioning and assist service technicians in figuring out what's wrong.

- A Google Glass with augmented reality (AR) was released to the public in 2014 by the world's biggest firm, Google. However, it didn't do as well as planned in the worldwide market. As a result, Google Glasses were discontinued in December of last year.

- When Augmented Reality (AR) first made its way into people's daily lives via video games in 2016, it was a worldwide craze. Pokemon Go, a famous augmented reality game, was downloaded by more than 100 million users through app stores. The primary goal of this mobile game application is to catch and employ monsters to compete against each other in Augmented Reality gyms. In the game, players may see their favorite Pokemon bouncing about their city.

- Using augmented reality, IKEA released IKEA Place, revolutionary new software that will have a profound impact on how we shop soon. Before making a purchase, users may use this app to get an idea of how they want their home to look with IKEA furniture.

- The "Harry Potter: The Hogwarts Mystery" mobile game has once again grown more popular throughout the globe in 2018. A Hogwarts-like atmosphere is created around the user, and they can cast and learn from Hogwarts professors with the use of this app. More than 10 million individuals have already downloaded this app from the Google Play Store.

- In celebration of Manchester City's 125th anniversary, the club's stadium featured an Augmented Reality installation in 2019. There will be an opportunity for audience members to sit close to the Manchester City manager, 'Pep Guardiola,' during the news conference. A 3D holographic screen and a 360-degree movie screen are also part of the tour, intended to deliver an immersive experience for the band's fans.

Present

As a cutting-edge technology, Augmented Reality is presently considered one of the most promising. In this day and age, most people automatically turn to their smartphones when the term "AR" is spoken. As an example, let's look at some of the things happening all the time. Just point your mobile device towards the exhibitor at your favorite music performance, and you'll get real-time information about announcements, future concerts, and ticket discounts and offers. Reading tiny characters on the label of your prescription medication container has probably caused some discomfort in most of you at some point. Never fear! This shift was made possible thanks to Augmented Reality. Patients may now quickly acquire dose, expiration date, adverse effects, components used in the drug, etc., using 3D glasses that are built utilizing AR to get the information quickly. Does watching sports with your pals interest you? Just aim your smartphone towards the coach or player, and you'll receive all the sports stats and information you'd get if you were browsing the Internet. All of this occurs as a result of AR. Using augmented reality (AR), you can now digitally try on garments and check whether the color and size work for you. With AR, it's easier than ever to shop for items from the comfort of your own home while still making a fashion statement. Assuming everything is in order, you may proceed with placing an order.

The societal benefits of Augmented Reality technology are many, but I'm not going to go into all of them here. An example of this is the Pokemon Go mania. Thousands of individuals could get out of bed and go for a jog because of it. In addition, AR aids law enforcement in catching criminals and in helping individuals deal with problems like despair and disease.

Future

AR and VR for brand awareness and consumer interaction is widely accepted as a novel, unique, and creative approach. A techie's life is a wonderful one. There is no question that the power and possibilities of Augmented Reality are limitless.

According to experts, tablets and smartphones will not be the primary platforms for augmented reality in the future. The development of contact lenses and other wearable devices with augmented reality (AR) capabilities continues apace. There is a general belief that smartphones will be replaced by AR-enabled devices, although it is unclear precisely what that replacement will look like. Even spectacles are gaining a new design as "smart glasses" for the blind are being created.

AR In Various Sectors

AR In E-Commerce
Almost all e-commerce firms will be incorporating augmented reality into their mobile applications and websites soon. Using a smartphone camera, users may quickly "dress" apps in clothing (such as coats, sunglasses, jewelry, and shoes)

AR In Digital Marketing
The way consumers interact with corporate brands is further enhanced through augmented reality. Marketing AR may be seen in various places, including video games, public signs, apps, and even packaging certain other goods and services.

Educational Resources
Educators are looking for methods to incorporate augmented reality into training scenarios in a manner that helps pupils retain information. Both the healthcare and military sectors are developing AR training simulators.

AR In Geolocation
Over time, mobiles/tablets that tell us about our surroundings have become more efficient. Everything from restaurant recommendations to on-the-fly travel advice is made more accessible with AR.

AR In the World of Extended Reality

The science-fiction origins of augmented reality may be traced back to 1901. Nevertheless, Thomas Caudell first used the word "technology" to describe it in 1990 while creating a tool to assist Boeing personnel in better perceiving complex aviation systems. Significant progress was made in the US Air Force's Virtual Fixtures AR system by Louis Rosenberg in 1992. Several consumer-oriented AR products followed, including ARQuake (2000) and the design tool ARToolkit (2001). (2009). There was a technology surge in the 2010s, including Microsoft's HoloLens in 2015, that went beyond what we traditionally think of as Augmented Reality (AR).

Mixed reality (MR) is a subset of XR, encompassing VR and AR (MR). The differences between AR and MR cause some misunderstandings. Each term's definition is contested, especially amid the 2020s' technological boom. Designing for user experience (UX) involves the following considerations:

In AR, you design for digital pieces to display on top of real-world views, sometimes with limited interaction between them, and most often through a smartphone. Developer kits for Apple's ARKit and Android's ARCore, as well as the game Pokémon Go, are just a few examples.

Design immersive experiences that separate people from the actual world, generally via a virtual reality headset. Gaming examples include PlayStation VR (PSVR), Oculus Rift (Oculus Rift), and Google Cardboard (Google Cardboard). Design features tied to a real environment are necessary for MR because digital items may interact with the actual world via AR and VR elements. For example, it is possible to learn how to mend things more directly using Magic Leap and HoloLens.

AR and MR are often used interchangeably by companies because of their similar interaction. "Augmented reality" is still popular, even though the basic meaning of AR design is overlaying digital features over real-world views, such as GPS filters/overlays on smartphone displays so users can locate directions from street views. There is no direct connection between the digital and real-world elements: Unlike with MR, the computer-generated material cannot interact with the real-world components that viewers observe. A good example of MR technology is the HoloLens, which integrates digital items with the user's physical world.

AR In Business

Unlike gaming, AR technology has a wide range of applications in other industries, including transportation, manufacturing, retail, and more. AR can improve almost every business process or activity that may benefit from a visual overlay.

Businesses are embracing AR. For example, Boeing tested AR instructions on an aircraft wing assembly with manufacturing trainees. According to the findings, time was reduced by 30 percent, and accuracy improved by 90 percent. Additionally, DHL is experimenting with AR-enabled smart glasses at one of its warehouses and is currently considering a wider deployment.

Retail is another industry benefiting from the use of AR technology to enhance the consumer experience. Customers can now see Ikea items in their kitchens and living spaces before making a purchase, thanks to virtual furniture from Ikea. As part of Lego's "Digital Box" initiative, the company is creating a device that will allow youngsters to manipulate a virtual replica of their favorite toy and see it from all sides.

Progress will be noticeable in the next several years, even if there is room for development in technology. Customers will eventually be able to check on items in virtual dressing rooms, receive personalized marketing and discounts at their favorite retailers, read extra virtual information at historic places, or study in 3D to improve accuracy and efficiency. A predicted 200 million people would be using augmented reality by the end of 2018, making it a more common part of our everyday life.

Brands

AR's promise of boosting sales is attractive. Still, it also presents a crucial question: what technology does a brand need to enforce augmented reality elements on its current website?

The simple answer is that new software on the market now makes integrating augmented reality into a website lot more straightforward, quicker, and more accessible than it was even a few years ago. It's worth remembering a few key points if you're interested in how AR may help your bottom line.

For augmented reality capabilities, customers don't want to download an app. To reap the benefits of AR features, remove any barriers to their use. Not in a separate AR app, but on your website, should be your AR capability.

There are several benefits to using AR-generating software. Until recently, every company interested in augmented reality (AR) had to construct the technology from the ground up. SaaS-based AR content creation is now feasible because of tools like Threekit. There is greater ease of access to AR as a result of this.

Create augmented reality applications for mobile devices. To reiterate, if you want to reap the rewards of AR, you must increase the likelihood that your clients will make use of it. AR experiences must be compatible with most consumers' technology, such as smartphones (such as iPhones and Android).

Commercial Opportunities

Even in the boundaries of the client's home, augmented reality can enhance many areas of the customer experience. In real-time, it merges the physical and digital worlds, enabling shoppers to see what they're getting in a store while also purchasing from the comfort of their own homes.

Because of the growing dependence on eCommerce, augmented reality (AR) is a valuable visualization tool that companies in a multitude of sectors can use to better connect with their consumers and, as a result, raise their profits. Even if we say so, don't simply believe us. AR's influence on business is only expanding, as seen by the data listed below:

- AR-enabled stores are preferred by 61 percent of shoppers.

- A whopping 71% of consumers said they'd make more purchases if AR were available.

- Using augmented reality in e-commerce may boost conversions by 40%.

Chapter 2:
Virtual Reality

What is Virtual Reality

The use of computer simulators to create a simulated 3-D visual or another sensory environment that allows individuals to interact with its users of **virtual reality (VR)**headsets, goggles, gloves, or bodysuits are submerged in a computer-generated world that mimics the appearance of reality. Wearing a stereoscopic headset, the user sees dynamic visuals of a virtual world on the screen. It is feasible to give the effect of "being there" (telepresence) by using motion sensors to track a user's motions and make immediate adjustments to the screen's display. It is possible to move about the virtual rooms, altering the vistas and perspectives in a way that is tied to the movements of the user's head and feet. In virtual environments, the user may even pick up and control items by wearing force-feedback gloves fitted with sensors that simulate the feeling of touch.

In 1987, Jaron Lanier created the phrase "virtual reality," and his research and engineering contributed to the early VR business with a variety of devices. The federal government, notably the Department of Defense, the National Science Foundation, and the National Aeronautics and Space Administration, was a common thread in early VR research and technology development in the United States (NASA). In domains like computer graphics, simulation, and networked environments, projects financed by these organizations and carried out in university-based research facilities produced a large pool of bright employees and developed linkages between academic, military, and commercial activity. This article explores the social and technical contexts in which this evolution took place.

5 Important elements of Virtual Reality

Content creation for virtual reality (VR) is a massive investment for many global organizations since it is the latest technological marketing trend. We're on the verge of a tremendous VR wave as VR headsets drop in price and become more readily accessible.

A virtual reality system must have a number of critical components.

1: Viewing Network

- If you really want the greatest virtual reality experience, you need a high-quality display.
- The viewing system is the final link in a chain, regardless of the number of users.

2: Tracking System

- For the ideal 3D world experience, virtual worlds need a sensor camera.
- This service is currently conventional on most high-end headsets.

3: Interactional Element

- There are many benefits to using virtual reality, but one of the most significant is that you can interact with your surroundings.
- An authentic experience was formerly unattainable due to a lack of technology available, but times have changed.
- An interaction's elements rely on its range, speed, and mapping.
- With the capacity to walk about in a virtual world and alter the environment, virtual reality provides the finest interactivity possible.

4: Artistic Proclivity

- Virtual environments should immerse consumers in a world they can't just leave.
- As a virtual reality artist, you should focus on creating an immersive experience by focusing on atmosphere, interaction, and entertainment.

5: Sensory Administration System

- Users should perceive slight changes in the virtual world, such as vibration, movement, or direction.
- Just about all high-end virtual reality headsets come equipped with this function nowadays.

Early Work

Artistic and entertaining skills have always been a source of fascination for artists, performers, and entertainers alike. Before the advent of virtual reality, there were several cases of audiences being willing to suspend their disbelief to experience a fictional world. Illusionary spaces have been built for homes and public areas throughout antiquity, culminating with the massive panoramas of the late 18th and early 19th centuries.

Panoramas created the feeling of immersion in the events they depicted by blurring the visual boundaries between the two-dimensional pictures showing the primary scenes and the three-dimensional areas from which they were seen. For similar effects, this visual tradition inspired the development of various media throughout the twentieth century—from futuristic theatre designs to stereopticons and 3-D movies to IMAX movie theatres.

As an example, Fred Waller's research of vision and depth perception led him to establish Cinerama, a widescreen cinema format developed for the New York World's Fair in 1939. When it came to creating an immersive virtual world, Waller's attention shifted to the importance of peripheral vision. His ultimate objective was to create a projection system that could replicate the whole range of peripheral vision that humans had. Multiple cameras and projectors and an arc-shaped screen were utilized in the Vitarama method to give the viewers the sense of being completely immersed in the place they were seeing.

For training during World War II, the Army Air Corps used Vitarama (then known as Cinerama) under the name Waller Flexible Gunnery Trainer, even though it wasn't a commercial success until the mid-1950s. It was a pioneering example of the connection between entertainment technology and military simulation that would advance virtual reality. Before computers, creating virtual worlds via sensory stimulation was a potential option. Morton Heilig got enamored with 3-D movies and Cinerama after the premiere of a promotional short called This Is Cinerama (1952).

After studying human sensory signals and illusions like Waller, he hoped that "cinema of the future" might be achieved. Designed to "stimulate the senses of an individual to simulate a real experience realistically," Heilig's Sensorama Simulator was patented in 1962 after he built it in the late 1960s. It had a variety of inputs, including stereoscopic images, a motion chair, audio, temperature changes, scents, and blown air.

Sensorama also built the Telesphere Mask, a "stereoscopic 3-D TV display" for the head that he patented in 1960. In the mid-1960s, Heilig produced a Multiview theatre concept patented as the Experience Theater and a similar system dubbed Thrillerama for the Walt Disney Company, despite his attempts to commercialize Sensorama failing. Three-dimensional interactive computer graphics and vehicle/flight simulation sowed the virtual reality seeds in the 1950s and 1960s.

When Project Whirlwind and its successor, the SAGE (Semi-Automated Ground Environment) early-warning radar system, both financed by the U.S. Air Force, began in the late 1940s, cathode-ray tube (CRT) screens and input devices like light pens (initially dubbed "light guns") were the first to be used. Until the SAGE system was used in 1957, air force operators had been utilizing these devices to show and modify aircraft whereabouts and associated information. Computers were presented in popular culture throughout the 1950s as calculating robots, electronic brains able to process data at previously inconceivable rates.

A shift in perspective occurred when second-and third-generation transistor and integrated circuit computers became more affordable, releasing the machines from a narrow focus on number-crunching tasks and instead focusing on ways in which computing could enhance human potential rather than replace it.

To better understand how people interact with computers, Joseph Licklider, an MIT professor of psychoacoustics, proposed the concept of a "man-computer symbiosis" in 1960. According to him, a collaboration between computers and the human brain would be more powerful than each of them functioning on their own. His work at DARPA's Information Processing Techniques Office (IPTO) allowed him to finance and support projects that fit his vision of human-computer interaction while also fulfilling military objectives, including visualization techniques and command-and-control systems.

Ivan Sutherland, an electrical engineer and computer scientist at MIT's Lincoln Laboratory, was another pioneer in computer graphics (where Whirlwind and SAGE had been developed). Sutherland produced Sketchpad in 1963, a device that used a light pen and a control board to allow consumers to sketch directly on a CRT monitor. Sutherland's technique was effective for interactive editing of pictures since he paid attention to the structure of data representation.

Computer images might be used to create realistic and fully detailed virtual worlds, according to Sutherland in 1965, who defined the qualities of what he dubbed the "ultimate display." Although he started with visual representation and sensory input, he went on to advocate for various sensory input methods. From 1968 until 1976, he supervised the computer graphics courses at the University of Utah, one of DARPA's most prestigious research centers, where he was in charge of IPTO.

At that time, DARPA funded projects including Timothy Johnson's Sketchpad III, which provided muti views of things, Larry Roberts's Lincoln Wand, which allowed users to draw in three dimensions, and Douglas Engelbart's creation of the computer mouse, which was an input device. In a short period, Sutherland developed the head-mounted 3-D computer display, which has come to be associated with virtual reality.

A servo-controlled infrared camera installed underneath the helicopter was tested in 1967 by Bell Helicopter (now part of Textron Inc.). The pilot wore a head-mounted display (HMD) to see the footage. His night vision and immersion were enhanced by the camera's ability to move with the pilot's head, which matched his field of vision with the pictures it captured. The term "augmented reality" was coined for this kind of device because it increased a person's ability to see the actual world. He started working on a tethered display for computer pictures in 1966 when he left DARPA for Harvard University. This was a head-mounted device with computer-generated graphics output seen via goggles. A suspension mechanism was used to keep the display in place since it was too heavy to be carried comfortably. The stereo 3-D visual experience was created by placing two small CRT screens near the wearer's ears and using mirrors to reflect the pictures to his eyes. As the user moved the HMD around, the right visuals were created to fit the wearer's field of view. A user could wander about in virtual space while still using the other senses because of the HMD's partial sensory deprivation.

Evolution of Virtual Reality

Stanley Weinbaum published the science fiction novel Pygmalion's Spectacles in 1935. Using only a set of goggles, the protagonist is transported to a holographic world that stimulates his senses and displays holograms. Virtual reality (VR) may have its beginnings in this narrative, which accurately predicted the goals and achievements of the future.

Though, it was not until the 1830s that the first VR breakthroughs were made; thus, this is where we commence our timeline:

1838

Sir Charles Wheatstone described stereopsis in 1838. His research on binocular vision, which contributed to the development of the stereoscope, was given the Royal Medal of the Royal Society. The studies found that the brain mixes two or more images of the same item taken from different angles to create a sensation of depth and immersion in the images (3-dimensional).

Wheatstone was able to create the first stereoscope because of this technique. Using two mirrors set at an acute 45-degree angle to the user's eyes, an image situated off to the side was mirrored in each mirror.

1965

Computer scientist Ivan Sutherland developed the Ultimate Display. The idea was to create a virtual world that was so similar to the real world that the user would not tell the difference. The user was allowed to interact with things as part of this. The virtual environment was created using computer hardware, and it was kept running in real-time.

In the eyes of many, his article constitutes the foundation of virtual reality. When the computer can create and destroy matter, it would be ideal for a display. In a setting like this, you might sit in a chair on a show. Handcuffs would be restrictive, and a gunshot would be lethal in such a setting.

The Wonderland that Alice wandered into may become a reality with the proper programming.

1975

The Milwaukee Art Center presented Krueger's VIDEO PLACE, the first interactive VR platform.

An immersive "virtual reality" experience was produced using big television displays in dark rooms. You didn't need goggles or gloves to utilize it because of its usage of computer graphics. The users' motions were recorded on camera and translated to the shadow, allowing them to witness their computer-generated silhouettes mimicking their moves.

People in other rooms could engage with the virtual shadows of others. Because of this, even if individuals weren't physically nearby, they could converse with each other in a virtual world.

1991

NASA scientist Antonio Medina developed a virtual reality (VR) technology to control the Mars rovers from Earth despite signal delays. "Computer Simulated Teleoperation" is the name of this system. Virtuality was developed by the Virtuality Group and released. A consumer-level VR entertainment system was accessible in mass production for the first time. These virtual reality arcade devices allowed players to immerse themselves in a 3D virtual environment. In a Virtuality pod, visitors may don VR headsets and see 3D pictures in real-time.

Multi-player games might be making use of the devices that are connected over a network. Some of the most popular arcade games, like Pac-Man, were eventually ported to VR.

2010

For Street View, Google has added a 3D stereoscopic option. 18-year-old entrepreneur Palmer Luckey initially prototyped the Oculus Rift headgear. To deliver visuals, it used a computer's processing capacity to produce a 90-degree field of view that had never been seen before. This discovery rekindled my interest in virtual reality and reawakened my enthusiasm for it.

2014

Facebook purchased Oculus VR for two billion dollars. VR took off after this. Thus, it was a seminal point in the history of technology. Project Morpheus, a virtual reality headgear for the PlayStation 4, was recently announced by Sony (PS4). Cardboard is a low-cost, do-it-yourself stereoscopic smartphone viewer introduced by Google.

Samsung revealed its Gear VR virtual reality headgear using a Galaxy smartphone as a viewer. More individuals began experimenting with the potential of virtual reality, such as Cratesmith, an independent developer, who used the Oculus Rift and a Wii balance board to recreate a hoverboard scene from Back to the Future.

2016

The technology for haptic user interfaces is still in its infancy. Many firms were working on virtual reality (VR) products in 2016. There was dynamic binaural audio on the majority of the headsets. Humans can interact with a computer using their touch and movement with haptic interfaces, such as the Gloveone gloves. As a result, most mobile phones were button-operated.

The HTC VIVE SteamVR headset was launched by HTC early this year. The first commercial introduction of headgear with sensor-based tracking lets users roam freely about an area.

2019

According to Forbes, 2018 is the year virtual reality becomes a part of our daily lives.

Oculus Quest, Facebook's standalone headgear, generated $5 Million in content purchases and sparked a lot of attention and excitement. In the immersive environment, the change from tethered to freestanding VR headsets signaled a paradigm shift since independent headsets are far more accessible to the public. For the first time, over one million VR headsets connected to Steam each month, as per Road to VR. On April 12th, Nintendo's Labo: VR kit for the Nintendo Switch was launched.

Applications of Virtual Reality

Many people are familiar with the phrase "virtual reality," but they aren't sure what it means or how it may be used in their everyday lives. Virtual worlds and gaming are obvious uses of virtual reality, but there is a slew of other applications, some of which are more difficult or odd.

Where is Virtual Reality Used?

Below are the applications of virtual reality:

Virtual Reality in Military

The military has used virtual reality for training purposes, involving all three branches (army, navy, and air force).

In war or other risky circumstances, troops need to learn how to respond appropriately. This is very important for teaching soldiers. However, they may do so without risk of being killed or seriously injured thanks to a virtual reality simulation. Reenacting a specific situation, such as a battle with a rival, in a safe and controlled atmosphere. This is more cost-effective and safer than more conventional ways of training.

Military uses of VR are:

- a simulated flight
- Simulation of a battlefield
- Medic education (battlefield)
- Simulating a vehicle

- Virtual training courses

Post-traumatic stress disorder may also be treated using virtual reality. Veterans with PTSD and other mental health issues may get the help they need to cope in a safe setting. As they are exposed to the triggers for their disease, they will progressively adapt to their new environment. This reduces their symptoms and enables them to adjust to new or unexpected conditions, improving their quality of life.

Virtual Reality in Healthcare
Surgery simulation, phobia therapy, robotic surgery, and skill training are some of the uses for virtual reality in healthcare.
Healthcare practitioners may acquire new skills and brush up on old ones in a secure environment is one of the technology's many advantages. Furthermore, this may be done without posing any risk to the patients.

Software for simulating people
As a case in point, HumanSim allows doctors and nurses to engage with each other in an interactive environment.
Only in a 3D environment can they practice their skills by interacting with an actual patient. This is a fully immersive experience that uses a variety of sensors to track the user's emotions.
Testing in a virtual reality setting
When used with other technologies like MRI scans, virtual reality may help physicians arrive at a diagnosis. Ultimately, there will be no need for invasive or surgical operations.
Robotic surgery in a virtual world.
Robotic surgery is an everyday use of this technology.
Surgeons operate on a robot, which a human surgeon manages, reducing the chance of problems and speeding up the healing process. When executing a delicate surgery, the surgeon relies on force feedback from the device, a key element of this technology. Remote telesurgery, in which the surgeon performs the surgery while at a different location from the patient, has also used virtual reality for teaching reasons.

In the virtual reality and healthcare area, you may find information about robotic surgery and other virtual reality and medicine topics. Nevertheless, there's a problem with latency, or the lag time between events, which is a significant worry since even a minor delay might seem strange to the surgeon and cause them to halt the treatment. To avoid this, accurate force feedback is required.

More Examples of VR in Healthcare
This section examines the numerous applications of virtual reality (VR) in healthcare as a series of articles.

- Virtual reality has several advantages in the medical field.
- dental surgery virtual reality in the field of medicine
- Nursing in the age of virtual reality
- Surgery in virtual reality
- Simulated surgery
- Therapies using virtual reality
- Treatment of phobias with virtual reality
- Virtual reality therapy for PTSD
- Autism therapy with virtual reality
- concerns about virtual reality's impact on one's health
- For the handicapped, virtual reality

Virtual Reality in Business
A variety of businesses are embracing virtual reality, including:

- Virtual tours of the workplace
- New hire education and training
- Views of a product from all angles.

Several firms have adopted virtual reality as a low-cost product or service development method. For example, they can test a prototype without producing many copies of this, which may be time-consuming and costly. In addition, it is a valuable tool for spotting design flaws early on when they are easier to fix.

Virtual Reality in Construction
When it comes to the building sector, virtual reality may be a tremendous asset because of the industry's reputation for inefficiency and poor profit margins.

An organization may see the final structure in 3D and interact with it as if it were in the real world using a virtual environment.

What Are the Advantages?

Using a virtual construction environment has several advantages.

It is possible to test many variables without having to construct the structure, which saves time and money while also minimizing the number of faults in the final product.

Viability

Architectural design viability must be extensively examined as a key aspect. For many years, a structure's viability was determined solely by human judgment and scale models. On the other hand, scale models cannot adequately recreate the conditions in which a building must endure. As we know, human judgment may be grossly and sometimes purposely erroneous.

Virtually Investigating the Concept

Before a structure is even constructed, it may be evaluated for feasibility and explored by construction workers and staff. Even minute data, such as whether a worker will be able to fit in a particular place, may be picked up in this way, and the results are astounding.

Constructing a Model

Buildings can be built in virtual reality just as they would be in the real world.

To achieve maximum efficiency and minimal change, an organization may fine-tune its building processes using this method.

Virtual Reality in Programming Languages

Virtual reality needs a strong feeling of realism to be genuinely helpful. In and of itself, this is a significant technological problem, and, as a result, virtual reality is very resource-intensive. Virtual reality takes a vast number of hardware resources because of the high level of realism required. The implementation team's capacity to control everything from hardware performance to intellectual aptitude is significant.

As Moore's law deteriorates, it will become more challenging to meet the primary criterion of processing speed. Creating a believable virtual world necessitates using a powerful graphics processing unit (GPU). The audio output quality must also be exceptionally high, which requires the usage of a high-end sound card. Only a tiny portion of the technical needs are covered here. Aside from the hardware, the individual employing these resources must also have a high level of expertise. Post-graduate study is frequently required to have a thorough understanding of computer science.

As time goes on and the industry grows, these criteria must be dealt with properly, and the barrier to entry must be decreased, much like in software development today.

One approach is to use a virtual reality-specific programming language to achieve this.

Virtual Reality-Specific Programming Languages

DSLs (domain-specific languages) may be customized in various important ways to address a particular issue area. This also holds for virtual reality experiences.

Developers may create less code that is specifically optimized for virtual environments by carefully developing the formal language(s) for virtual reality.

Language for Visual Programming

This is where VSL comes in. VPL Research's Jaron Lanier created it to make virtual reality more accessible. As a "post-symbolic" programming language, VPL is defined as one in which code is "written" in ways other than via the use of alphabetic or numeric characters. Since we're on the subject, most computer programs are written using alphabetic characters, numbers, and punctuation.

Virtual reality in Education and training

Training for real-world tasks has long been an important use case for virtual reality systems.

There are several advantages to using simulations instead of existing systems for training, including lower costs and higher safety.

Commercial simulators were initially used to train pilots during World War II, and they have since become an essential aspect of military training.

In-flight simulators visual and motion feedback are used to enhance the experience of flying while sitting in a closed mechanical system on the ground.

When Edwin Link, a former piano builder, created the Link Company in the late 1920s started building the prototype Link Trainers, the Army Air Corps purchased the "blue box" design in 1934. Motion feedback was employed in the early systems to help pilots get more comfortable with the controls. Sitting in the virtual cockpit, pilots learned how to fly by moving it in reaction to their movements. Cycloramas were painted on the wall outside of simulators for visual input in later editions. Celestial Navigation Trainer, developed by the British government during World War II, was one of the first Link Trainers to employ projected film strips. However, early systems were limited in producing fresh visuals depending on the trainee's movements. Using film and closed-circuit television to improve the visual experience of flying was common to practice for flight instructors by the 1960s.

It was possible to alter the pictures to produce flight trajectories that diverged somewhat from what had been captured; in other cases, numerous cameras were employed to offer various views, or moveable cameras were installed atop scale models to portray the airport for simulated landings.

Sutherland Evans & Sutherland Computer Corporation was created in 1968 by him and his colleague David Evans at the University of Utah. The new firm first concentrated on creating graphical programs, such as flight simulator scene generators. Taking inspiration from the Link flight simulator, Sutherland proposed that such displays include multiple sensory outputs, force-feedback joysticks, muscle sensors, and eye trackers; a user would be fully immersed in the displayed environment and fly through "concepts which never before had any visual representation." In the early 1970s, these systems could render scenes at around 20 frames per second, which is the minimum frame rate required for successful flying instruction. These simulators were developed by General Electric Company for the Apollo program in the 1960s and the US Navy a few years later, respectively.

When these systems were first introduced in the 1970s, they could create a few hundred polygon models using raster graphics (collections of dots) and could represent solid objects with textures to increase the impression of realism (see computer graphics).

Flight simulators for the military began to use head-mounted displays, such as the VITAL helmet from McDonnell Douglas Corporation, in the late 1970s due to its smaller footprint.

The HMD's head tracker tracked a pilot's eye movements to synchronize computer-generated visuals (CGI) with his vision and control of the plane's flying instruments. A new generation of immersive, real-time control systems has been shown for research and training and enhanced performance in flight simulators, human-computer interfaces, and augmented reality. Thomas Furness, an electrical engineer with the US Air Force, has worked on cockpit displays and equipment since the 1960s. A decade later, in 1982, he exhibited the Visually Coupled Airborne Systems Simulator—better known today as the Darth Vader helmet from the blockbuster Star Wars film—which he had been working on since the late 1970s.

From 1986 until 1989, Furness was in charge of the Air Force's Super Cockpit project.

This project's core premise was that human pilots' ability to deal with spatial information was dependent on the data being "portrayed in a fashion that makes use of the human's innate perceptual systems."

For this purpose, Furness built a system that projected computer-generated 3-D maps, forward-looking infrared and radar pictures, and avionics data into an immersive, 3-D virtual world that the pilot could watch and hear in real-time.

It was possible for the pilot to fly the aircraft using gestures, speech, eye movements, and tracking systems built into his helmet. This gave him complete control over the aircraft while immersed in an information-rich virtual environment. As a result, cockpit complexity and the number of rules were decreased due to a more natural perceptual interface.

By establishing a virtual environment where pilots could fly via data, the Super Cockpit fulfilled Licklider's ideal of human-machine coexistence. When British Aerospace (now part of BAE Systems) first started using the HMD in 1987, they utilized it to create the Virtual Cockpit training simulator, which included a head-tracking system and features for monitoring hand and eye movements and voice recognition. Sutherland and Furness extended the concept of simulator technology from real-world visuals to virtual environments that represented abstractions and data. Visual verisimilitude was not as crucial in these systems as immersion and input that was useful to the user.

The ramifications of this strategy for medical and scientific studies were profound.

Frederick Brooks' 1967 the University of North Carolina Project GROPE is significant for its contributions to molecular biology. By building a virtual world of molecular docking forces, Brooks hoped to increase the perception and understanding of the interaction of a drug molecule with its receptor site on a protein. He used "haptic" (tactile) feedback mediated via customized hand-grip devices to organize the virtual molecules into a minimal binding energy arrangement using wire-frame images to represent molecules and physical forces. Scientific researchers experimenting with this technology were like flight students learning to use the instruments in a Link cockpit, "grasping" the physical conditions shown in the virtual environment and hypothesizing novel medications from their experiments.

Brooks' laboratory began using virtual reality in radiology and ultrasound imaging in the late 1980s and early 1990s. Telepresence, the use of robotic equipment controlled remotely via mediated sensory input to complete a job, was used to extend the virtual reality to surgery.

As less invasive surgical techniques such as microsurgery and laparoscopic surgery became more popular in the 1970s and 1980s, they laid the groundwork for the development of virtual surgery. Endoscopic micro cameras to transmit pictures to a group of surgeons viewing one or more displays, typically in different locations, began in the late 1980s.

To build telepresence work stations for surgery in the early 1990s, DARPA financed research. When it came to fine motor control and hand-eye coordination, Sutherland's "window into a virtual world" was on par with that of a surgeon. SRI International built the first telesurgery system in 1993, and the Broussais Hospital in Paris conducted the first robotic surgery in 1998. Visit any of these sites to learn more about a specific use of virtual reality, no matter how well-known they may be. Academic research, engineering, design, business, the arts, and entertainment are just a few areas where virtual reality may be put to use.

In any case, virtual reality generates data that may be utilized to build new models, training techniques, and ways of communicating and collaborating. As far as I can tell, the options are almost limitless. The only stumbling barriers are time, price, and technical limits.

Virtual reality systems, such as the CAVE, are costly and time-consuming to construct. Ergonomics also come into play, focusing on creating systems that are "user-pleasant" and don't lead to difficulties like motion sickness. Virtual reality has a bright future if these issues can be addressed.

Role of Virtual Reality in Metaverse

The Metaverse is one of the most forward-thinking technological concepts to emerge last year. As soon as the proposal was introduced, it was met with both favor and opposition. If you haven't yet taken a position on either side, it's time to discover what the Metaverse is. Is it possible without the use of VR/AR? What are the advantages to you? Let's take it one step at a time.

Virtual reality closes the apparent gaps between digital and physical reality by allowing users to access the Metaverse. Virtual reality enables people to walk inside exhibitions, shops, and educational possibilities. We'll be able to discover new places and things by interacting with virtual representations of people, items, and landscapes. Alternatively, we will enrich our actual environment in unprecedented ways using augmented and mixed reality.

It will be possible for us to bridge the gaps in our connections using haptic feedback technologies and feel the handshakes and embraces of our contacts wherever they are.

Does Metaverse need AR/VR?

Augmented reality and virtual reality are intertwined in the metaverse concept (VR). Using augmented reality, you may place virtual items in the actual environment. To fully engage oneself in a virtual world, virtual reality uses 3D computer modeling, one of the fascinating styles of graphic design.

Virtual reality technology is expected to play an essential role in the Metaverse, even if you don't need to wear a headset. For example, the Facebook metaverse may be accessed through virtual reality headsets, smart glasses with augmented reality, and in restricted ways on desktop and mobile apps in the future. Project Cambria, a high-end virtual and augmented reality headgear, has previously been disclosed by the business. New sensors enable eye contact and facial emotions to be reflected in the virtual avatar, Meta claimed.

Human emotions may be conveyed more effectively in virtual space via avatars' use of body language and improved technology. Statista estimates that the combined AR/VR business will be worth close to $300 billion by 2024, while Morgan Stanley predicts that it will be worth $100 billion by 2030.

Where is the line between VR and Metaverse?
One of the most perplexing elements of the Metaverse is how it varies from our current understanding of virtual reality. Virtual reality (VR) may be a component of the Metaverse, but the Metaverse itself is considerably larger. Social networking, virtual reality, augmented reality, online gaming, and cryptocurrency are all included in the platform. Virtual reality may provide a level of telepresence that is much more immersive than video conferencing. In the Metaverse, we'll be able to consume material in a whole new manner, shifting from 2D to 3D. The Metaverse is predicted to transform the way people interact by bridging the gap between the virtual and actual worlds. It is a shared virtual area.

Even if there are still many unanswered concerns, we may consider the Metaverse to be large-scale and multipurpose, not restricted to the VR/AR experience but fully exposed when these technologies are used. For example, in a remote work setting, it may considerably enhance the degree of communication with a virtual team. Video conversations may be transformed into experiences with a sensation of genuine presence in a virtual conference room using the Metaverse. Compared to today's Internet, which provides a better overall user experience, metaverses have been likened to the next iteration; VR is just one method of accessing it.

Use Cases of VR Technologies for the Metaverse
The purpose of the metaverse designers is to transform the way people interact with the Internet. Therefore, there are many other uses for the Metaverse outside gaming. Since the inception of virtual environments, the video game industry has reaped the most tangible rewards. Game producer Activision Blizzard, for example, has made almost $8 billion in actual money from the virtual world of Warcraft.

The game industry isn't the only one striving to keep up with and gain the newfound popularity. For example, the decentralized service Decentraland recently sold a digital piece of land to a Canadian investment business for 2.5 million dollars using blockchain technology. This area will be utilized for virtual reality fashion shows and the expansion of e-commerce services with fashion labels. Virtual platforms like this may open up new marketing avenues for businesses. We've previously discussed how Metaverse's virtual workplace environment may take on a unique appearance. This technology, as opposed to the more common Zoom and Skype, gives the impression that the whole team is physically there at the same time. Despite the different services described, the Metaverse goes farther, enabling you to alter the backdrop during a conference. It analyzes your motions and facial gestures to create 3D-generated avatars representing you in the virtual conference. Similar use cases are currently available on the market. Virtual reality and mixed reality business called Virtuworx provides customized solutions for virtual meetings, virtual workplaces, and other events. Advertising, tourism, Education, entertainment, shopping, design, engineering, and many more businesses may benefit from the Metaverse. The Metaverse has the potential to extend any action from the physical world.

Chapter 3:
Making Digital Identity in
Metaverse

Definition of Digital Identity
The term **"digital identity"** refers to an account's profile information, including the user's master private key. In Metaverse, each Profile has a DID (Digital Identity, comparable to an alias in Bit Shares) that identifies it. Any digital identity may apply to be an Oracle or an ordinary user and participate in applications utilizing their digital identities. Digital identities can play both these roles.
The following is included in a profile:

- There is no extra storage for personal transaction records, which are kept on the statistical level and contain record information.

- UTXO details are stored on a statistical level. Therefore, no extra storage is needed for this information.

- Users should provide the height interval for a customized description field since it has a lifespan. In order to accommodate varying block heights, this field may be altered.

- When a user enters a string of words into this area, the transaction cost grows exponentially with the number of words.

- More storage is needed.

The Nature of Digital Identity

There is no two Metaverse Digital Identities. It is planned to include an identity module in the protocol, and further applications will be created. A self-sovereign identity means that users are in charge of their identifying data and don't have to depend on a third party or central authority to verify their identity. User claims may be signed and verified with a completely self-sovereign identity, and others who engage with a user will validate their identity. Users will also choose whatever information about themselves is made public.

A person's digital identity may take numerous forms in the virtual world, including a value middleman (institutions and entities). A person may have many digital identities depending on the situation (such as work and individual identities). Still, they are all derived from the user's real-world identity in the end.

After Facebook's recent rebranding announcement, it has prompted many to wonder, "What is the Metaverse?". As with the holodeck in Star Trek: The Next Generation, one might imagine the Metaverse as an immersive digital depiction of a real or imagined setting. Traditional console and PC video games can easily transition to augmented and virtual reality. In many video games, chores and objectives must be completed in a particular order, with minimal room for improvisation. Immersive games like first-person shooters and role-playing games provide greater freedom inside the game world, but your field of vision is constrained. There are no limitations to the possibilities available to you in the Metaverse. There isn't enough computational power to keep everyone interested and running simultaneously, so it won't be whole virtual reality from the start. However, in a nutshell, the Metaverse will be an immersive platform that individuals can interact, connect, and become a part of.

Just like there isn't a single website or nation, there won't be a single Metaverse. Thematic Metaverses are possible. The Metaverses may be linked, and you may move between them. School, college, or university may be a Metaverse. We may even have a Megaverse, which would be a collection of interoperable Metaverses that you could jump between like a web browser. Everybody can take part in the Metaverse from the comfort of their own homes. It's going to be the most integrated and immersive experience we've ever seen on the internet.

Digital identity is at the forefront in the Metaverse, where you'll be able to construct and inhabit a digital version of oneself that can move about and do things. Instead of relying on a humanistic Root of Trust, digital identity depends on a cryptographic Root of Trust. As long as we're dealing with the actual world, I'm comfortable putting my faith in you. These crucial elements are lacking from the internet. At no moment in time do you know if the person you're conversing with is genuine or not? When I see you online, I take a leap of faith and trust that you are who you claim to be. This raises the specter of fraud. Enhancing human trust via digital cryptographic credentials based on leading-edge technology and protocols is the answer to this problem. Adding a layer of protection for our online activities like chat, social media, messaging applications, and everything else we do online is as simple as extending digital cryptographic credential-enhanced human trust.

Since its inception, Metaverse deserves to be treated with the respect it merits. The fact that I'm David Lucatch in the Metaverse doesn't imply you need to know that when you meet my persona. It's enough for you to know that my persona is based on a genuine people identity. A person's identity is not at stake but rather the ability to access the system. Again, it comes down to safeguarding your safety, security, and privacy. To be clear, working for a firm that specializes in this kind of digital identity management. Today it was unable to just go into a business and say, "I forgot my wallet." Sorry. Make a note of my credit card information, expiration date, and security code here. Now, please hand over the TV." However, it seems to be the case on the internet. Assume if someone runs an online store. When he is working with folks who have authenticated digital identities, he knows that he is dealing with actual people—verifying that person is genuine decreases the fraud and identification risks that occur with every online encounter. We're not used to the amount of involvement offered by the Metaverse. What if we started from scratch, knowing that digital identity technologies exist? One of the two worlds we'll inhabit is a digital one in which we may be anybody and even amplify or accelerate our strengths and talents. We've already seen goggles with heads-up displays, as well as glasses with them. Even while the virtual world is still in its infancy, it has already begun to root. Nobody knows what it will look like for the next decade or two. It's likely that the promise of these new experiences and technologies will accelerate faster than any other technology in the previous 50 or 100 years. Because of this, it will be critical for businesses and individuals alike to understand who they are engaging within the Metaverse in the same way they do in the real world.

Operational Flow of Digital Identities

Creation

As long as you have your master private key, you may build a digital identity and link it to your account. This is the case even if a user establishes one. Digital identities that are not linked to any master private keys are considered unauthenticated and cannot be used for any digital identity functions or apps.

If you've already registered assets on the Metaverse blockchain using your master private key, you don't need to attach a digital identity to it. Metaverse will not automatically produce digital identities for every user; users must take the effort to attach their keys to their digital identities. The master private key holder has the authority to bind a DID.

Verification

Profiles may be used to create effective chains of evidence that comprise objective information about a person's online persona. To show that a digital identity belongs to a user, the user must first link the DID to a transaction.

Authorization

It's essential to identify the circumstances in which obtaining prior consent is necessary. Assume that A seeks B's digital identification information (asset information) before delivering any services. There are two possibilities in this situation:

1,000,000 ETP or more of on-chain assets are held by user B. It is possible for B to just share his financial information with A. In contrast to A, B has a large number of off-chain assets. Usually, before B could continue with permission, he would have to transfer his assets to ETP. According to Metaverse's current recommendation, the best way to have one's digital assets registered is to issue their assets on the blockchain and have them authenticated by an Oracle.

Query

DID identifiers may be utilized as the principal entity for over-the-counter trading, as they can generate transactions in trading marketplaces. Digital identities established this notion. Entering a DID into the address bar of trading marketplaces allows us to see the DID's current transaction requests and prior transactions.

Alternatively, the market activity and records of a DID may be utilized as data to construct digital identities.

Avatars represents online identities.

The person is at the core of everything a person does on the internet. Once data is linked to a specific person, it makes sense when used for things like viewing movies on YouTube or searching on Google. Until recently, e-mail addresses or Facebook accounts were used to connect all the dots. Google, Amazon, Facebook, and Apple are the world's most dominant tech corporations for a good reason.

Virtual currencies wallet will also play a role in determining our identity as part of Web 3.0. It's possible to uncover evidence of a person's interest in video games and digital art in their wallet. You may be able to track out the exchanges that they've been utilizing. There are several advantages to using an avatar to symbolize one's identity rather than a wallet. Hence, the development of Crypto Avatars by Polygonal Mind's Garcia and his team of developers. In the Metaverse, these distinct avatars serve as a visual representation of your digital identity in 3D environments.

In order to express oneself, the user selects an avatar that serves as the focal point of attention. Garcia explains that it "adds even another layer of knowledge to their online narrative." A funny or attractive avatar is far simpler to recall than a crypto wallet or username, let's face it. The person is at the core of everything a person does on the internet. Once data is linked to a specific person, it makes sense when used for things like viewing movies on YouTube or searching on Google. Until recently, e-mail addresses or Facebook accounts were used to connect all the dots. Google, Amazon, Facebook, and Apple are the world's most dominant tech corporations for a good reason. Virtual currencies wallet will also play a role in determining our identity as part of Web 3.0. It's possible to uncover evidence of a person's interest in video games and digital art in their wallet. You may be able to track out the exchanges that they've been utilizing. There are several advantages to using an avatar to symbolize one's identity rather than a wallet. Hence, the development of Crypto Avatars by Polygonal Mind's Garcia and his team of developers. In the Metaverse, these distinct avatars serve as a visual representation of your digital identity in 3D environments. In order to express oneself, the user selects an avatar that serves as the focal point of attention. Garcia explains that it "adds even another layer of knowledge to their online narrative." A funny or attractive avatar is far simpler to recall than a crypto wallet or username, let's face it.

What is an Avatar?

Imagine a 3D avatar that not only looks like you but can also be modified in any manner you like. In the world of social media, you're likely to have a photo of yourself or some other personal touch to your profile. This might include everything from the character's appearance, such as their clothes or hairstyle, to more intimate features, such as tattoos.

Consider it in this light. **Avatars** are a crucial component of the Metaverse experience since they represent you in the virtual world. They give a sense of authority over how you present yourself online. However, interoperability is the most important consideration when it comes to avatars. Since they symbolize who you are, Avatars are a crucial part of the Metaverse's interoperability. It's possible to purchase and wear avatar-related items to connect to your own body. When you go between multiple virtual worlds, you can take your assets with you, making for a more seamless transition. You may use your avatar as a virtual wallet.

Avatars may be made to seem as realistic and personable as possible by utilizing 3d model creation services while creating your Metaverse.

Kinds of Avatar in Metaverse

Avatars have recently grown more popular in virtual reality (VR) and sensor-based hardware and software systems. You may build your avatars in either 2D or 3D, and you can also choose between the two options. In most cases, all of this may be categorized as follows:

In a VR avatar, the user views the world through the eyes of an avatar they have created. The avatar's upper torso and arms are visible to those in the real world, but its lower limbs are hidden. Virtual reality applications that don't need complicated leg motions or in-world mobility are likely to have this gameplay style.

There are now full-body avatars, as well. As part of an avatar's kinematic system, all emotions are replicated and re-created. Consequently, the user has more movement inside the virtual environment and may interact with digital objects with all of their limbs. Typically, high-end virtual reality games employ this style, and Facebook's Metaverse is expected to follow suit.

As a result, it's a good idea to use the services of a seasoned metaverse development business when it comes to creating your avatars.

Business Applications of 3D Avatar

Even though we've discussed what an avatar is and how to make one, we haven't yet covered the practical aspects of using one. Virtual meetings, for example, are an intriguing option. Imagine being able to meet with your colleagues in a metaverse where everyone is represented as a 3D avatar instead of utilizing Zoom, Microsoft Teams, or any other video conferencing tool. When the microphone picks up the user speaking, these avatars will be able to mimic the movement of a mouth.

As a part of their first pitch for adopting the Metaverse, both Microsoft and Meta are already promoting this notion as one of the most essential aspects. Additionally, it's worth noting that in the Metaverse, you may relocate your whole work environment, not just conduct meetings. In the Metaverse, we can engage with our colleagues in the same manner as in the real world. These days, with so many firms moving to a partially or entirely remote work style, this is extremely significant. Microsoft intends to make it possible for individuals who already have a compatible VR or AR headset to move about in virtual surroundings, although this is not a must. Accenture, a consulting business, has been utilizing the technique to "onboard" new personnel throughout the epidemic, according to the report. The Hololens is an augmented reality (AR) headgear made by Microsoft's own AR technology division.

But, unlike Facebook's Oculus and Valve's Index VR headsets, it is aimed at corporate users instead of consumers.

What can you do with your Avatar outside of work?

Using your avatar, you may go to any metaverse of your choosing and carry out all of your typical activities as if you were in the real world. Imagine if instead of just playing Fortnite, you and your friends may enter the game and play to see who can be the last one remaining. Epic Games secured $1 billion in financing in April 2021 to "back the long-term goal of the metaverse," according to the firm. Fortnite is being marketed as a "metaverse" that focuses on social interactions rather than interactive entertainment. You've decided to have a night out on the town. It's possible to have a 3D avatar created for any occasion by using a 3D avatar builder. RTFKT, for example, is collaborating with Ready Player Me to create a custom line of virtual footwear and a jacket. In most of the 600+ applications and games supported by the avatar platform, Ready Player Me users may access the assets for free.

Fashion designers are in high demand, but have you ever considered becoming one? Brands like Gucci, which made virtual footwear and sold them to consumers for $9-12 dollars, are among the many fashion houses manufacturing branded clothes for avatars. They recently sold a physical replica of their Dionysus bag for $4,115 on the Roblox gaming platform. You may use a 3D avatar creator to create runway shows and outfits for your virtual models. An example of a celebrity avatar might be Imaan Hammam or Natalia Vodianova. Other players assess his costumes, and the best appearances earn cash that may be used to buy new outfits. The likes of Gucci, Moschino, Off-White, Loewe, and Chloe are available for purchase by gamers.

Generating an Avatar

In the past, having a long-distance meeting had several restrictions. Both telephone and video conferencing can't be used to converse in the same manner as in a shared place. Many of these challenges may be solved by using virtual meeting places provided by Spatial. Using AR and VR devices like the Oculus Quest, mobile platforms like iOS and Android, and an intuitive interactive web browser, Spatial allows you to connect with your team virtually through telepresence. One of Spatial's most important features is the ability to build bespoke avatars that are as lifelike as possible.

As the virtual encounter progresses, the sensation of presence becomes more and more like that of a real one. Other VR systems either provide a limited selection of avatar customization choices or make it difficult and time-consuming to design something realistic. VR avatars from Spatial are not like that. We make it simple and fast.

Best Practices

Virtual meetings should be straightforward to use as a part of a wonderful experience. Having to spend a lot of time getting everything set up is something you want to avoid. In only a few minutes, anybody can create a VR avatar using Spatial. A Spatial account is all you'll need to get started.

1. Lighting must be good, and you have a camera or a simple headshot.
2. There is no limit to what your avatar may be; as long as it has a face and mouth, our AI Avatar Generator will do the same!
3. Change the color of your shirt and arms to match your style!

Getting Started

The first step is to sign up for a Spatial account. If you already have a Google, Microsoft, or Slack account, you may use it to sign up. You can use an email address to sign up for an account. Once you've completed the registration process, you'll be asked to choose an avatar. Your webcam or a snapshot of yourself from a gadget may be used for this. It's essential to take a decent image of your face while creating a virtual reality avatar. With a neutral expression on your face, look squarely into the camera's lens. So, no cheesy grins for the avatar photo. Don't think of the picture you're about to post as a selfie while you do it. Instead, think of it as a headshot as you would take for a driver's license photograph.

We can edit our avatar any time by selecting Edit Profile from the drop-down menu in your account profile. Changes to your subscription, Team, submitted material, and integrations may also be made here.

Lighting and color

Another crucial consideration is the quality of the lighting. Don't forget to take your avatar picture in a well-lit environment. Avatar photos taken in natural light are preferable to those born in artificial light. It's also a good idea to stay away from powerful lights. A 3D bespoke VR avatar that looks like you will be created after Spatial gets a decent photo of the front of your face. The skin tone slider and the shirt color picker are also available from this point on, allowing you to further modify your Avatar's appearance. Simply click Looks Good after generating your Avatar to close the avatar creator. Regenerate Avatar lets you start over with a fresh picture if you don't like the one you currently have. It's that simple to make a virtual reality avatar. There are no specific skills or expensive equipment needed to create a 3D model in a couple of minutes.

Customizing your Avatar

Creating an avatar that resembles them is a favorite pastime for gamers! If we want our avatars to reflect our users' true selves, we need to keep enhancing the mechanisms we employ to create them. For the time being, you may choose between a male or female avatar body and various humanoid faces. If you're a hand talker, you can use hand tracking in your VR headset to fully live your avatar's vibrance. The digits on your keyboard may be used to express various actions or dancing motions, even if you are logged in from the web!

Making Changes to Your Spatial VR Avatar

At any moment, you may modify or update your avatar as well. You may change your appearance at any time. It's as simple as opening your Spatial account in a web browser or using the Spatial app to change your avatar. The profile is located in the upper left corner of the screen while your account is open. Choose the appropriate option from the drop-down menu to adjust your avatar's picture, skin tone, shirt color, or name from this page. Virtual reality (VR) meetings may be improved by using realistic 3D avatars for team members. It seems more like a face-to-face encounter and allows for a more intimate exchange. Creating an authentic avatar using Spatial is as simple as snapping a picture of your face.

Avatar Everywhere

Everyone appears to have an online persona. Everyone appears to be drifting in and out of digital identities, whether it's their Twitter profile picture or playing Fortnite with that great skin you acquired last season. They're all avatars by definition: from 2D profile pictures on Twitter or Discord to 3D representations in VRChat.

Different Avatars

An avatar used to be a more particular phrase that meant your 3D depiction of yourself in an online environment, but that's no longer the case today.

Alteration in the meaning of Avatar

The cultures of virtual and video game worlds differed only in the most minute details, yet there was a distinct difference nonetheless:

Your 3D depiction was often referred to as your "toon" in the gaming community. This indicated a separation from yourself and your virtual self. A game was essentially a vehicle through which your character drove.

Your avatar in open worlds was a representation of yourself. So "self" in this context didn't refer to your physical existence or even your real personality in the same way that "self" refers to your actual self. Even if you were born a man, you might portray yourself as a woman to the world. While your physical self could be extroverted and friendly, your mental self can be chilly and quiet. Identity, personality, and social signaling were all conveyed via the avatar you created for yourself.

Your avatar or profile picture (pdf) was supposed to represent you in 'flat' Internet forums, even if you used various images. When you used it in a conversation or on your Facebook page, you didn't give it much of an identity of its own; it was just your 'badge,' after all.

These phrases typically served as an indicator of cultural disparity between people from different backgrounds. If someone mentioned that they were "playing" in a virtual world, I recall how outraged people would be about it. As in, "I like the alias you're adopting." To say you didn't realize that you weren't playing a game suggested a lack of understanding of the concept of avatar identity.

Similarly, in gaming environments, you'll see tiny schisms in the population. Others saw their avatars as just a way to show off their latest haul of incredible weapons and armor rather than an actual representation of who they were as a person. People who considered their avatars as a way to explore issues like cooperation, identity, lore, and expression took a more "meta" approach.

The Pledge of the 3D Avatar

We are returning to the 3D avatar as a self-portrait, though, for a moment. Considered profound and freeing, this concept was widely accepted. **You have the right to identify with whatever gender you choose (or even any species).** Theoretically, this would promote cultural variety. Whether avatars are 'post-racial' or not, it depends on how individuals express or expose their race.

It is possible to separate your online persona from your real-world identity. In today's internet surroundings, pseudo-anonymity is routinely assumed. In a digital environment, you don't have to worry about being "too young" or "too old" or "less wealthy and handsome" than your avatar to succeed.

Virtually everything you do is transmitted via your avatar, even if you don't interact with it directly. The next step is a little difficult to figure out, and perhaps counterintuitive in some ways. A considerable effort has been spent on this issue by Philip Rosedale, and I recall extensive discussions with him about it back in the day.

It's the theory that other people get extremely delicate and seemingly undetectable signals in addition to voice or text interaction that is 'broadcast' via your avatar. It doesn't make a difference what it takes for you to respond to a message or what direction your avatar is looking in a virtual world; other people can pick up on a wide variety of emotional indications because of this.

Philip's primary goal was to increase the bandwidth and reduce the latency of these transmissions. Facial and body tracking may now transfer social and emotional cues straight from your avatar to your actual body. Even if there is no direct link between your real body and your avatar, other people may tell whether you are upset or preoccupied just by looking at your avatar. This intrigues me more than the direct connection between your physical body and your avatar.

In return, your actual person receives communication from your avatar because the other way around is also the case. Furthermore, the fact that avatars may have a direct effect on our actual selves is mind-boggling. In one idea, mirror neurons were used to suggest that our minds may connect to avatars in the same way we interact with our bodies. As a result of my avatar's weight, my self-esteem will be affected.

Today's Avatar
Several pre-Metaverse developments may be traced back to avatar-based initiatives.

Our understanding of the meaning of the term "self" and the degree to which we attribute "selfness" to our digital identities, as well as their place in broader systems and cultures, have all been subject to many reinterpretations throughout history.

There are a few examples:

- When you see those **"flat" Twitter avatars**, you're getting a lot more than just a pretty picture. We may have entered a new era when symbols on our social media accounts carry more social information than the skins we wear in Fortnite.

These blurry photographs are sending more social cues than my old Pally in WOW, despite their lack of realism.

- **Fortnite's success may be attributed to its creation of a fun gameplay mechanic in disposable skins for players' avatars.** Nevertheless, their financial success was highlighted because they made the game available for free and then made money through skins and other add-ons totaling $9 Billion.

As a result, it was done on purpose for your avatar to have a shorter lifespan. You're participating (and spending money) to get greater levels of ego boosts. It's not a lousy avatar, but it looks like something from Season 2.

A ten-billion-dollar investment is no little sum, but what Epic has done with it is opened the door to new ways of combining IP to tell stories in the Metaverse. Aside from the fact that the appearance of your avatar may be changed, it also enables Fortnite to switch up IP. Superman will be battling with an Ariana Grande avatar.

- **Avatars may be used in various virtual places with the hopes that you'll g et attracted to a particular expression.** You may use them to express yourself in a digital form. There is a sense that Ready Player Me's approach to avatars is almost like a throwback to a previous age of avatars.

It's only one avatar, yet there are many worlds to explore.

- **Artificial Intelligence and blockchain models such as DAOs point to a future in which our personas will frequently act without us,** and I've written about this previously. We may log out, but our virtual selves will continue their work even if we do not (or vote in a DAO or bid on some land while we sleep)

- Rather than relying on humans to interoperate, the **Metaverse's interoperability** will be driven by artificial intelligence. Some of those worlds may have a high degree of detail and seem practically genuine, while others may look more like Minecraft and be voxelized."

How many versions,' then, will we need to maintain? I believe that AI will eventually solve this problem, similar to how style transfer works in machine learning.

- Alternatively, Jin has been experimenting with the concept that avatars may, instead of having a 'core' body, carry a **written description that will be 'interpreted'** by the worlds we explore.

- **There'll be a change in the way economies are organized,** both offline and online, due to blockchain and web3. Economic value is now

250

mostly intangible on the internet. For example, if you publish anything on Facebook, you make revenue (for Facebook and its advertisers). It is hoped that blockchain-based economies would open up the transaction layer, making it more accessible to new ideas. Meanwhile, the creator-based economy will continue to flourish in places like Roblox, where players can already earn money from their inventions.

An even more profound aspect of avatars is that, instead of just "attaching" a wallet or maintaining an inventory, your avatar will function as an economic node in and of itself. In the future, this might lead to totally new kinds of economies that are avatar-based and avatar-centric.

- **How will we know if our avatars aren't real people?** We're going to see a lot of advancements in the area of both realistic AI avatars and ways for validating their identification. If you need a sense of where this is going, check out World coin, a cryptocurrency that stores a picture of your eyeball on the blockchain to verify your identity.

- **Before, I opined that Epic Games' Metahumans would upend whole sectors of the entertainment industry by becoming movie stars.**But this was just one of many projects in which avatars have become media stars of their own. Even when we're not streaming on Twitch or walking down the street, and people with augmented reality glasses can see us, we'll be utilizing our avatars in virtual worlds like these.

Chapter 4:
Metaverse and Cryptocurrency

Cryptocurrency

Cryptocurrency, also referred to as a crypto-currency, is a digitized collection of data that may be used as a means of trade between two parties. Each coin's ownership history is recorded in a digital ledger, a computerized database protected by powerful encryption. There are no commodities backing or convertible into cryptocurrencies; hence they are primarily fiat currencies. In certain cryptosystems, the money is maintained by a " validators " group of people." Tokens are used as collateral in a proof of stake scheme. Members get control over the token in proportion to how much money they put into it. Typically, token stakes get increased token ownership over time via network fees, freshly created tokens, or other compensation mechanisms.

In contrast to traditional forms of cash, cryptocurrencies are digital-only (unlike paper money) and are not backed by any central authority. Rather than relying on a central bank's digital money, cryptocurrencies generally employ decentralized governance (CBDC). It is considered centralized when a cryptocurrency is coined before issuance or issued by a single issuer. Each cryptocurrency uses distributed ledger technology, usually a blockchain, to function as a public financial transaction database when deployed with decentralized governance.

The terminology "cryptocurrency" relates to a digital asset or currency that can only be exchanged online. The terminology "cryptocurrency" relates to the use of encryption to secure and validate transactions. A more equitable future economy, according to proponents of the more than a thousand cryptocurrencies presently in circulation, may be achieved via the use of these digital currencies.

The first decentralized cryptocurrency, Bitcoin, was published as open-source software in 2009.Several different cryptocurrencies have been developed after the introduction of bitcoin.

Basic Technology in Crypto

Blockchain

Transparent, distributed ledger that may track transactions between parties in an efficient, verifiable, and permanent method. A blockchain ensures that every cryptocurrency's coinage is authentic. As its name suggests, the blockchain is a distributed ledger made up of individual documents known as securely linked blocks. A hash reference, a timestamp, and transaction data are generally included in each block. It is impossible to alter data on a blockchain because of its architecture. A peer-to-peer network that follows a protocol for verifying new blocks manages a blockchain for use as a distributed ledger. It is impossible to edit a block's contents retrospectively without altering every block that follows, which needs the agreement of the majority of the network to do so. As a distributed computing system with a high Byzantine Fault Tolerance, blockchains are built to be safe by default. With a blockchain, a decentralized consensus has been established.

Hooking up of Metaverse onto Blockchain/Crypto

Perhaps you imagine a world wide web in virtual reality, but this is not what the Metaverse will look like at all. This is mostly true; however, the blockchain is a key component of the Metaverse that will distinguish it from today's internet.

AOL, Yahoo, Microsoft, and Google were among the first companies to provide a Web 1.0 platform that allowed users to search, explore, and inhabit a network of linked computers and servers. To define Web 2.0, we must go no farther than the centralized gatekeepers of "free" social media sites who monetize user data for advertising purposes.

The Metaverse will be built on the Web 3.0 platform. The economy will be based on user-owned crypto assets and data, supported by decentralized apps built on the blockchain. Blockchain or Decentralized? What's the big deal about that? Crypto-assets? Metaverse technology may be explained by scholars that study social media and media technologies.

Possession of Bits

Transactions are persistently stored on a public ledger, a kind of blockchain technology. Blockchain-based cryptocurrency Bitcoin is the most well-known. Buying bitcoin, for example, records your activity on the Bitcoin blockchain, which is then transmitted to thousands of computers all over the globe as proof of your transaction.

Trying to manipulate or sabotage this distributed recording system is next to impossible. In contrast to conventional banking books, public blockchains, like Bitcoin and Ethereum, are open and accessible to anybody with an internet connection. Unlike Bitcoin, Ethereum's Blockchain may be programmed using smart contracts, which are basically blockchain-based software routines that run automatically when definite conditions are met. A smart contract on the Blockchain may be used to create ownership of digital property, such as a work of art or entertainment, to which no one else can take possession on the Blockchain—even if they save a duplicate of the thing to their computer. Currency, securities, and artwork are all examples of crypto assets.

The antithesis of fungible objects like cash, which are equal in value and may be exchanged for one another, is non-fungible goods. Non-fungible coins on a blockchain include artwork and music (NFTs). You must employ a smart contract that states that you're ready to sell your digital painting for $1 million in ether, the Ethereum blockchain's currency. Art and ether are transferred to each other immediately when I click "yes" on the Blockchain. In the event of a disagreement, any of us could simply link to the public record in the distributed ledger to show that the other person paid the whole amount. There is no need for a bank or third-party escrow. This blockchain crypto-asset crap has nothing to do with what we call the Metaverse. Everything! You may begin by owning virtual products on the Blockchain. If you buy this NFT, you'll be able to use it both in the real world and online.

Another thing to note is that there isn't one organization or corporation behind creating the Metaverse. Virtual worlds built by diverse organizations will interoperate and create the Metaverse in the future. In virtual worlds, individuals will want to carry their belongings with them as they travel from one virtual world to another. As long as two virtual worlds are compatible, the Blockchain can validate your digital commodities in both virtual worlds. A virtual wallet is all that stands in the way of having access to all of your crypto assets in the virtual world.

Crypto Wallet

Is there anything you'd want to store in your digital currency wallet? In the Metaverse, it's a given that you'll want to have Cryptocurrency on hand. Your avatar, avatar attire, avatar motions, virtual decorations, and virtual weaponry will all be stored in your crypto wallet.

When it comes to their crypto wallets, what will individuals do next? Other than that, go shopping. Traditional digital items, including music, movies, games, and software, will be available for purchase. Aside from virtual goods, the Metaverse will allow you to purchase real-world goods as well as examine and "hold" 3D replicas of what you're considering purchasing. Crypto wallets will be able to connect to real-world identities, much like your old leather wallet, and this might make it easier to complete transactions that need legal proof, like purchasing a real-world vehicle or house. Access to age-restricted regions of the Metaverse will be easier with wallets linked to IDs. This means that you won't have to remember the login details for every website and a virtual world you visit - simply connect your wallet with a single click to log in to all of them!

You may be able to transfer your social network data from one virtual world to another if your crypto wallet is connected to your contacts list. Join me for a FILL IN THE BLANK-world pool party!" Reputation ratings might be linked to wallets in the future, determining whether you can broadcast in public and engage with individuals outside your social network. If you behave like a poisonous troll who spreads false information, you risk having your reputation tarnished and the system reducing your sphere of influence. These technologies might encourage good behavior in the Metaverse, but platform developers will prioritize these mechanisms.

Business

Decentralization of Blockchain may eliminate the need for intermediaries in financial transactions; nevertheless, firms still have many options to create income, maybe even more than in the existing economic system. Meta, for example, aims to give enormous platforms for people to interact, collaborate, and have fun. Because money is at stake, businesses will be eager to join in the fun.

Dolce & Gabbana, Coca-Cola, Adidas, and Nike are just a few of the high-profile companies that have jumped on the NFT bandwagon. A connected NFT in the Metaverse might be acquired in the future to purchase a physical world item from a firm.

Buying name-brand clothing to wear to a dance club in the real world may also give you access to the crypto version of the same outfit for your avatar to wear to a virtual Ariana Grande concert, for example." As with the actual costume, you could resell the NFT version for use on someone else's avatar in the same way the physical outfit could. However, although the Metaverse is still in development, foundations like blockchain and crypto assets are being built, paving the way for a virtual future that is expected to arrive in adverse near you soon. Various metaverse business models will likely intersect with the natural world in various ways. It will only grow more complex as augmented reality technologies become more prevalent, bringing together components of virtual reality and reality.

Relationship between Metaverse and Crypto

What if, in 2008, Satoshi Nakamoto had foreseen the future of blockchain technology, where decentralization enabled by Blockchain would be the most significant invention in Metaverse? Had he seen the future of Blockchain with practically unlimited possibilities? Cryptography will play a significant part in the Metaverse. Individuals would have sovereignty over their digital assets if bitcoin was used to decentralize the Metaverse, preventing oligopolistic dominance. Rather than two or more corporations controlling the market as in oligopolistic market structures, Blockchain provides an avenue where every person has a vote in the decision-making and statuses of the digital world based on allocations held.

A virtual environment called the "metaverse" resembles the real world in many ways. How does the experience sound with a virtual environment so intertwined with your real-life and Bitcoin as the key to digital asset ownership, promoting investments? As a result, investments received a considerable boost. MANA, Gala, and Sandbox, three of the most well-known cryptocurrencies, have seen more than 200% gains, putting them on the verge of setting new all-time highs. In the digital world, imagine purchasing USDT (or another cryptocurrency) from a reputable exchange to trade or hold crypto-gaming tokens with similarly significant percentage increases in order to invest, benefit, and have entertainment as the digital world reflects your fantasies and allows you to explore your dreams and wishes in the digital wonderland. How awesome is that?

By using cryptocurrencies, we can provide the digital world the same opportunity that banks have been given via blockchain interventions in the real world. "The role that major cryptocurrencies may play, in my view, is underrated," says Sina Kian, Aleo's vice president of strategy. In a digital universe comparable to the "metaverse," digital currencies may be used as a means of inter-party payment. As previously said, the benefits of the Blockchain are its decentralization, openness, and speed. Blockchain's robust cryptography and encryption technology give you peace of mind while transacting in the digital realm. Since each decision has been made individually, you are not subject to the central authority. There is a functioning replacement for today's 2D Internet known as the Metaverse, which has virtual locations instead of web pages, and everything is secure, lucrative (and completely decentralized) there. With the capacity to execute and confirm many transactions in real-time and the scalability that cryptocurrencies provide due to their decentralized nature, Blockchain and Cryptocurrency have become critical components of Metaverse.

When it comes to the Metaverse, Cryptocurrency is an essential component because it enables people to own their digital assets, and this ownership creates incentives for people to invest in them, according to Sina Kian, Aleo's VP of Strategy and Product Development.

On the other hand, Kian said that the Metaverse's most significant danger is the risk of being taken over by an oligopoly, re-creating the digital monopoly menace. It's "the essential thing that crypto provides is a viable alternative to that society, in which ownership is more decentralized," Kian added.

Global crypto finance firm's co-founder and CEO Phillippe Bekhazi agrees with this assessment and tells GOBankingRates to believe crypto is ready to perform a big part in the Metaverse. New technologies like NFTs and social tokens, such as NFTs and social currency, can be used for several purposes, including incentivizing influencers and their followers to attend virtual concerts.

"I believe that significant cryptocurrencies have an underappreciated role to play. Payments inside a metaverse-like digital environment will benefit from the usage of digital currencies, he said.

It's also possible that crypto traders may use a VR/AR-integrated system to trade Bitcoin and other crypto assets in the future Metaverse. They might then haggle 'in person,' using their digital avatars, over the price at which they wanted to exchange any crypto asset in question. According to other academics, it's not simply AR/VR and cartoon avatars that make up the Metaverse. There are no restrictions to what comprises a metaverse; according to Chris Fortier, Vice President of Product at Rally, the blockchain ecosystem enables creators to issue their own social coins. It can be anything that provides your presence, engagement, and identity in a digital world.

Fortier told GOBankingRates that "crypto has a vital role to play in any metaverse." However, "tokens" represent more than just money in the context of Cryptocurrency.

Cryptocurrency as a Metaverse Pillar

Fiat money is used as a store of value and as a means of exchange in the actual world to facilitate the exchange of goods. On the other hand, how are you going to pay for that Taylor Swift performance in an excellent, immediate way in your virtual world? Simply, the solution is crypto. Cryptocurrency is essential to the operation of the Metaverse, the other reality that is just as real as our own. Faster, more transparent, and more secure transactions have made crypto an absolute requirement rather than a luxury in today's society. For this rapidly evolving hybrid society, bitcoin is the ideal trade means.

It's time to ponder it. Decentralized and transparent transactions like selling your vintage and immediately purchasing a new one, or even getting your hands on that NFT, require decentralization and transparency, where the power to approve and validate your desirable transactions rests with not just one central authority or hub, nor with every participant in the system cumulatively, making it more accountable to the people, readily available, and quick!!" You don't put all of your belief in one entity. You may be sure that your money is safe since cryptocurrencies such as bitcoin use advanced cryptography to encrypt and safeguard your assets on a public record like Blockchain.

Three-dimensional speed is a logical choice for Metaverse's third pillar since it fills the vacuum left by Cryptocurrency's potential for scaling or its capacity to process or complete an increased number of transactions per second! Since crypto can be used across several blockchain systems and provides instant value transfers and digital, irreversible evidence of ownership in the Metaverse, it's a no-brainer. So, if you want to get your feet wet with cryptocurrencies, the best place to start is with a reputable cryptocurrency exchange and trading platform like Coin Switch Kuber. So go ahead and explore the Metaverse, the other reality that may be just as real and comprehensive as our own!

Can Metaverse affect Cryptocurrency?
NFT breakthroughs accelerated, enhancing the potential of blockchain technology. For many people and businesses active in the blockchain industry, Metaverse has brought forth a newfound interest in investing. With Facebook's renaming as Metaverse, the virtual and augmented reality (VR/AR) infrastructure has sparked the curiosity of many people and companies. A worldwide plaza for individuals to be involved in, combining their physical and digital lives into a genuine hybrid experience, is what Metaverse consultancy business founder Igor Tasic believes has the potential to be the ultimate equalizer in the first half of the twenty-first century. When we talk about a "metaverse," we mean a digital concept in the same way physics deals with the physical laws that govern our physical world. In a digital metaverse, people can create an alternate universe in which they can create the person they want to be and carry out real-world activities like shopping, gaming, and more (such as gravity or the properties of waves). You may think of Metaverse as a genuinely hybrid experience, one that may or may not be alive but is unquestionably full of life. I'm glad you've found your way here.
Into the Metaverse: A Guide
As a payment method, cryptocurrencies are already used in certain existing metaverses. As a result, if you plan on making any purchases while in Decentraland, you'll need to bring MANA with you. Many cryptos have fallen from their early November highs, and many are now in the red. Decentraland, Sandbox (SAND), and Enjin (ENJ) are among the few tokens that might show green this week.

A unique digital object with the owner's information encoded into it is a token. In addition to non-fungible tokens, Blockchain and cryptocurrencies play a crucial role in metaverses (NFTs). Many goods may be considered NFTs, including works of art, sports trading cards, and even in-game items.

The gaming business is being transformed by NFTs, which enable players to own and benefit from the objects they acquire or develop in the game, and then take those earnings or assets with them when they exit the game. Previously, the awards you accrued from playing games like Axie Infinity (AXS) had little use outside of the game itself. Players of Axie may now win bitcoin incentives that have real-world worth.

The importance of NFTs in virtual worlds can't be overstated. People in the Metaverse can own land thanks to NFTs. NFT avatars are available for purchase and creation in virtual worlds. They may also design and sell virtual clothing for their avatars as we discussed before.

Where to Start?

Metaverses are a relatively new concept. A wide spectrum of viewpoints emerges on how these digital places will evolve and what function they will play in the future. Meta (Facebook) has a long-term vision, including deploying virtual gym equipment and building virtual business meeting rooms. The field of virtual reality has gone a long way, but there is still more to be accomplished. There is a slew of options open to you as a crypto investor for becoming engaged in virtual worlds. The most straightforward option is to purchase metaverse crypto tokens directly from a cryptocurrency exchange. If you want to invest in a particular planet, you may acquire NFTs or even land. A lot of studies are required, though, if this is your preferred path. To get a sense of what a metaverse is all about, visit an existing one. Decentraland, for example, does not need the use of virtual reality equipment or the expenditure of MANA to be a visitor. It's as simple as logging in and creating an avatar.

Just because Facebook or any other major firm or prominent individual is doing it doesn't mean you should. It is essential to understand these universes and which of them will be around for the long haul. Similarly, purchasing an NFT at random is pointless. You'll have to look at what NFTs match your preferences, which ones you believe may be successful, and how the NFT market operates. These crypto-based metaverses may be less dangerous to invest in since they aren't particular to one virtual world. Many of these crypto-based metaverses are built on ecosystems like Ethereum (ETH) or Solana (SOL). Ethereum and Solana will probably still be there no matter what happens with the Metaverse. Instead of using crypto, you may choose to invest in the shares of a firm active in the Metaverse. There are many ways to become engaged, but Cryptocurrency isn't the only one.

Don't Rush

At that moment, we have no idea how these metaverses will develop. Years of debate about creating metaverses haven't resulted in a lot of action. If this time is different, it's crucial not to be swept up in the excitement. You should only invest money you can afford to lose in bitcoin investing. Do not be motivated by the fear of missing out, since if the Metaverse is worth investing in, it will still be there once you've done your study on it.

Today's Top Metaverse coins

Cryptocurrencies and new technologies are on their way to taking over the banking sector in 2022. It has already taken the crypto market by storm, the term "Metaverse," meaning "A world beyond." The best method to describe it is a digital realm where people may connect, play games, socialize, and transact business with real-life counterparts on the other end. The rise in the number of people selling and purchasing things even though you can't physically visit these assets, metaverse virtual real estate and land is becoming more attractive. As a result, they're prepared to invest millions of dollars and hope to earn a fortune.

Some of the most promising Metaverse currencies to invest in 2022 are listed below:

1. Ethereum (ETH)
2. Axie Infinity
3. The Sandbox
4. Decentraland
5. GALA
6. Enjin
7. High Street (HIGH)
8. Somnium Space
9. Meta Hero
10. Red Fox Labs
11. Star Atlas

A few of them are described below:
Sandbox
It was published on May 15th, 2012, by Pixowl as a sandbox game for iOS and Android devices and Windows PCs. On June 29th, 2015, it was made available on Steam for PC users. The reference for this statement is not available.
A blockchain-based 3D open-world game is named after the brand that Animoca Brands purchased in 2018.

Blockchain Version
Founded by Pixowl, The Sandbox is a virtualization technology where users can create, build, acquire, and digital exchange assets in the form of a game. For a decentralized platform for a healthy gaming community, the Sandbox combines the power of decentralized autonomous organizations (DAO) with non-fungible tokens (NFTs).
As stated in the official Whitepaper, Sandbox aims to effectively incorporate blockchain technology into mainstream gaming. Play-to-earn models are encouraged on the platform, allowing gamers and developers to work together. The SAND utility token, introduced by The Sandbox, uses blockchain technology to simplify transactions on the network.

Founders Of Sandbox
The major motivating factor behind The Sandbox is Pixowl's **Arthur Madrid**, who is also the company's co-founder and CEO. In 2000, he earned his economics degree from the Université Paris Dauphine. He started his work as a consultant at Eurogroup Consulting France but quickly discovered his entrepreneurial drive. He started 1-Click Media in 2001, which Ipercast eventually acquired.
Pixowl's COO, **Sebastien Borget**, is also one of the company's co-founders. He graduated from the Institut national des Télécommunications in 2007 with a degree in computer systems networking and telecommunications. Arthur Madrid started his career as a project manager at 1-Click Media, and he and Sebastien Borget have subsequently formed an entrepreneurial partnership. They started Pixowl together in 2011 and have been working on a variety of projects since.

Uniqueness

The Sandbox integrates blockchain technology into gaming, making it a unique platform. There is a tremendous untapped potential for blockchain adoption in the game sector, Pixowl realized this in 2011. The Sandbox intends to change the industry by providing a platform for players to build and gather blockchain-based goods. As a reason, it has earned itself a distinctive position in the global gaming sector.

The Sandbox establishes a metaverse of players who actively contribute to the platform's growth by concentrating on user-generated content. In addition, the Sandbox encourages decentralized governance by introducing the SAND token, which enables people to submit their thoughts and opinions concerning the progress of the project. Decentralized governance is becoming a need in blockchain-based initiatives because of the advancements in technology.

Numerous big-name gaming companies supported and invested in the startup while just getting off the ground. Brands like Atari, Helix, and Crypto Kitties come to mind.

Sand coins in Regulation

The total number of SAND tokens that may be created is 3,000,000,000. As of March 2021, there are 680,266,194 SAND tokens in circulation, which is 23 percent of the total supply.

A quarter of the entire token supply was earmarked for a corporation reserve. A further 17.18 percent was set aside for the token's seed sale. Of the overall token supply, founders and team members received around a third of it. A little over 12% of the entire supply was reserved for the Binance Launchpad Sale, with the remaining 10% going to advisor incentives.

How is the Sandbox Network Secured?

The Sandbox virtual world is protected by the proof-of-stake (PoS) consensus process since it is based on the Ethereum blockchain. SAND tokens are ERC-20 tokens, which implies that they may be staked and rewarded for doing so.

PoS does not need a large amount of computational or electrical power to validate transactions, unlike the Proof of Work (PoW) consensus technique used by the Bitcoin network. Many different uses may be made of the PoS consensus method without compromising the safety of staked assets. Investors with a large number of SAND tokens are key.

Where can you buy the Sand coins?

SAND token trading is now available on a growing number of platforms, thanks to increased interest from investors and users alike. The trading volume of SAND/BUSD on Binance has thus far totaled $7,015,941 as of March 2021.

Uniswap (V2), Gate.io, and LATOKEN are more methods for purchasing SAND.

Tokens Economy

The token of the Sandbox features five types of Tokens; namely:

- LAND (ERC-721)
- SAND (ERC-20)
- ASSET (ERC-1155)
- GEM (ERC-20)
- CATALYST (ERC-20)

Land in the Sandbox

The Sandbox metaverse's ERC-721 NFT token, LAND in The Sandbox, provides its holder's ownership rights to a 9696-meter plot of virtual land. LAND owners may employ ASSETs to create unique experiences that visitors can enjoy. Only 166,464 pieces of LAND are currently available in The Sandbox. As a result, LAND is one of The Sandbox's most elusive NFTs.

The distribution of land in the world

1. A total of 123,840 LANDS (or 74% of the total) are up for grabs.

2. The Reserve will consist of 25,920 LANDS (or around 16 percent) and be dispersed as incentives to partners, developers, and players.

3. The Sandbox will retain ownership of 16,704 LANDS (about 10%). For special occasions, they will include unique games and ASSETS.

Owners of LANDs have two options for making money from them.

To begin with, they do this by developing gaming experiences on their LAND and charging people in $SAND for the privilege of partaking in such games. If the gaming experience is of the highest quality and/or if players have the opportunity to make some $SAND in the process, this strategy is very beneficial.

For the second time, the LAND may be rented to other Game Creators, artists, or gamers to create their own experience on the LAND that they can exhibit and profit from. LAND owners may reap the benefits of passive income by renting out their land via this strategy.

Estates

Estates are made up of a number of adjoining land lots that are sold together. 3x3, 6x6, 12-inch, and 24-inch sizes are available. An estate can be held by a single individual or a group of people. This means a lot more exposure for owners since gamers who click on The Sandbox map can see them. Estates are generally sought for by large brands and corporations in the Sandbox metaverse that wish to develop a digital presence.

Many different persons own LAND in **a District**, which is why it is referred to as a "District Estate." They are simply a group of LANDs that work together toward a shared goal of self-governance. Even though districts have not yet been published in the current version of the game, they should be accessible when the game is launched to the general public. The Sandbox metaverse's 'districts,' according to the Sandbox developers, will give birth to DAOs. To establish and be a district member, property owners must invest $SAND.

Transaction:

The Sandbox Platform allows artists and gamers to purchase and trade assets using $SAND. Users may only acquire land using $ SAND throughout primary sales and all Sandbox Marketplace transactions, users may only acquire land using $SAND. Uploading assets to the Marketplace costs artists $SAND.

Governance:

A DAO structure will manage the Sandbox, using the governance token $SAND. Holders of tokens have a say in the platform's long-term development. This includes concerns such as how content and game developers are credited for Foundation grant money and how features are prioritized on the platform Roadmap. Additionally, SAND account holders have the option of delegating their voting authority to anybody they want.

Staking:
Holding the token for an extended time might result in passive revenue in the form of $SAND for the user. Artists and other players may only harvest Gems and Catalysts via staking, essential for ASSET production.
Free capture Model:
The Marketplace charges a 5% fee, which will enhance the Sandbox's treasury and Foundation.
Foundation:
The Foundation may be defined as a collection of money utilized to help the economy and its members grow. It is expected that the Foundation would provide awards to eligible artists and games. The Foundation will only award grants in the currency of $SAND.
Price History:
This would be an oversimplification to suggest the $SAND token's early investors have reaped enormous rewards. In August 2020, IEO for the $SAND token was held, and each token sold for only $0.0083. This token's price fell to an all-time low of $0.028 in November 2020. As the token had already obtained a 10x return at launch, IEO investors were primarily responsible for the price drop. The current price of $SAND is $5.91, which is a 72,050 percent return on investment from the coin's debut.

Until the beginning of the 2021 bull market, the token traded at a constant $0.03 to $0.1 per token. The SAND token attained an all-time high of $0.84 in March during the first part of this year's bull cycle, but this pales in contrast to its all-time high of $8.44 in November during the second half of the 2021 bull cycle. Almost all of this price movement is due to a massive injection of institutional money into metaverse enterprises. When Facebook announced that it was renaming itself as "Meta," the crypto markets went into overdrive with excitement over blockchain gaming and metaverse initiatives. We may predict a more substantial upside with the complete launch of the game and public marketplace in late 2022 or early 2023, even if the token is presently witnessing a substantial correction.

The $SAND's total quantity is 3 billion, and the current circulating supply is 919,498,319 (i.e., 30.64 percent of total supply) (i.e., 30.64 percent of total supply). The Sandbox's token unlock timeline implies that 100 percent of the supply will be unlocked by 2024. The project creators have also suggested that their ambition for the Sandbox is to be a completely self-governing community-run DAO; this might imply that the company would progressively be selling all its tokens to the community. This sell-pressure paired with Sandbox's token unlock timeline might suggest that although an upside is inevitable for $SAND, it may not be as stratospheric as compared to its prior pumps.

Conclusions

The Sandbox seems to be the most active metaverse project, with regular updates and events and active partnerships. The lack of decentralization of the server hosting The Sandbox platform is the most concerning aspect, despite it seeming to be all right and good. A single point of failure exists since the game is now hosted on AWS. Due to a recent surge in Ethereum's gas prices, it has become almost impossible for gaming projects like ours to transact on Ethereum's Blockchain. If you're not flush with ETH, that is. On the bright side, the team is exploring adding a second layer to the marketplace. Polygon and Immutable X, two Layer 2 solutions, will dramatically reduce gas prices, making the project more applicable.

Decentraland
Virtual world platform Decentraland is free and open source. Using the MANA cryptocurrency, users may purchase virtual land plots on the site. As of February 2020, it is available to the public and managed by the nonprofit Decentraland Foundation.

History
Ari Meilich and Esteban Ordano founded Decentraland in 2015, and the project has been in progress ever since. Parcels of virtual land were sold for $20 in 2017, and mana tokens were sold for $0.02 at the time. Genesis City, the initial area in the game, has 90,601 individual plots of land. Via 2017, the company raised $26 million in an ICO.
For digital art exhibition at Decentraland, the London-based auction firm Sotheby's produced a digital facsimile of its New Bond Street offices in June 2021. NFT plots sold for between $6000 and $100,000 in April 2021, following a boom in demand for NFTs. For $913,228 per parcel, Republic Realm paid for 259 plots of Decentraland, which is envisioned as a virtual retail area called Metajuku, modeled on the Tokyo shopping district Harajuku.
When events like Facebook's redesign to Meta and positive news releases are beneficial to the currency, it rises to as high as $5.79.
Buying Mana (Decentraland)
MANA, the company's Cryptocurrency, maybe worth considering if you're looking to acquire virtual property, do business with other users, or become involved in the development of the program.
One of the ways Decentraland empowers its residents is via the usage of its Blockchain, which manages and tracks the ownership of digital land.
What is the Difference Between Buying and Trading Mana?
The phrases "trading" and "purchasing" MANA are sometimes used interchangeably; however, there is a significant distinction between the two. Both tasks, of course, require the purchase of MANA tokens, but the execution of each is distinct. It's essential to understand the following fundamental differences:
Buying
1. Buying with the purpose of keeping
2. Most platforms that support MANA may be used to carry out this operation.
3. It's less critical when markets open and close or when prices fluctuate.

You may buy MANA in a matter of minutes. With eToro or similar platforms, you may locate MANA via your preferred investment product and decide how much you want to purchase. That's about all there is to it. Before making a purchase, you're not likely to be analyzing charts or keeping tabs on price movements. As a result, you'll make an investment in MANA depending on your budget or your comfort level and keep it for a reasonable amount of time.

Trading

1. Many transactions may take place in a short time.

2. This is only possible on a limited number of systems.

3. Fees, volatility, and market activity are becoming more significant.

For many individuals, trading is a full-time job, not simply something they do for fun. Good traders may earn a lot of money in the crypto markets as well, particularly with currencies like MANA that are still relatively young and promising. MANA may be quite time-consuming to trade since you must constantly monitor the market and be ready to act at a moment's notice. There are specific traders that make a lot of deals in a short period, and you need to know what you've been doing to prevent being caught in the crosshairs.

What to consider when buying MANA?

Investing in MANA, like any other cryptocurrency, has a degree of risk. Because it's a new currency with a low-price tag, the seas are a bit rougher. The following are some crucial aspects you should keep in mind before making the purchase of MANA:

You have faith in the initiative.

This is an issue that is often overlooked in the bitcoin world. The sudden rise in price takes in many people without considering the project's true purpose or potential. Before investing any money, conduct some research on MANA from this point of view.

Fees for trading

For those who intend to trade rather than just acquire MANA, fees are inevitable. In the long run, even a small percentage may have a significant impact on your bottom line. That's why services like eToro, which have no fees, are so popular.

What shops do you frequent?

Further to the previous point, it is critical to consider where you plan to get your MANA. Ideally, you should only purchase from platforms that have been authorized by the FCA and that have a solid reputation as well as those that are regulated.

With regards to the state of your finances,
Investing in cryptocurrencies might be risky if you're not careful. You should never expect that your investment is going to skyrocket in value. Avoid making an investment that you simply can't afford or need within a short period.

Final Thoughts
Before the end of October 2021, few people had heard about MANA. Until the previous few weeks, the currency and project had been gaining momentum. A combination of FOMO, irrational investors, and widespread media coverage has historically fueled huge price jumps in prior speculative cryptocurrency initiatives. On the other hand, cryptocurrencies linked to digital goods and products have seen a recent uptick in value. When it comes to new and interesting products like NFTs and crypto games, it's crucial to emphasize that they're just that: new. There is still a long voyage to go until Cryptocurrency as a whole is accepted by the general public, but the fire has already been started. Since many individuals throughout the globe already have faith in this niche's future, we'd only encourage you to invest if you're one of them.

Illuvium

Illuvium is a blockchain-based role-playing game set in an open universe. Creatures, known as Illuvials, each with a specific class and affinity, are amassed by players throughout gameplay. Types and affinities have their strengths and limitations, yet they all work harmoniously. Illuvial get stronger as you win fights and accomplish tasks. Illuvial is used by players to compete against each other in order to succeed (ETH). Nfts on Ethereum's Blockchain reflect the Illuvials that players gather and have a real-world value.

Soon, the Illuvium DAO will launch a fantasy role-playing game on the Ethereum blockchain named Illuvium. This "decentralized, NFT collecting and auto battler game based on the Ethereum network" was initially unveiled in January of last year.

Introduction

Recently, the use of blockchain technology in gaming has been on the rise. However, a game with the resources and polish of a blockbuster release is still a way off. Play-to-earn methods and the exploration of the Metaverse will be explored in Illuvium, a high-quality blockchain game. Will the game deliver on its promise of rich gameplay when it launches?

What are ILV and sILV?

There are two Ethereum-based cryptocurrencies for Illuvium's ERC-20 project: ILV (Illuvium) and sILV. Liquidity mining, participation in governance, and incentives are all possible for ILV token holders. A lock-up period applies to ILV prizes, while sILV may be utilized in-game right away.

- The ILV token enables holders to participate in the Illuvium DAO's governance, yield farming, and staking. ILV and sILV prizes are available to token holders who desire to wager their tokens.

- A year-long lock-up period applies to ILV awards if holders opt to accept them. ILV/other coin trading pairings retain strong liquidity thanks to this lock-up period. There is no lock-up time for those who desire to earn sILV; however, sILV can only be used for in-game purchases. Those who stake ILV earn their benefits via various means, including in-game purchases.

For each item in the game, Illuvium employs NFTs, which may also be exchanged on external NFT markets. Purchase ILV and sILV on Binance, and then begin staking to earn ILV on Illuvium's platform. In addition, you may use your partner tokens to participate in their ILV Flash Pools.

272

Working of Illuvium

In 2022, Illuvium will be published as an open-world RPG blockchain game based on Ethereum. It's a fictional environment in which players battle and capture monsters called Illuvial. You may utilize your monsters in fights against other players while completing quests, challenges, or the plot of Illuvium once you've added them to your collection.

Additionally, Illuvium features its own in-game tokens, the ILV, and sILV, as well as Non-Fungible Tokens (NFTs), which represent creatures, aesthetic enhancements, and useful things. Tokens of ILV will be awarded to players who complete challenges, missions, and fights in the game.

Illuvium token

Illuvium (ILV) is an Ethereum-based ERC-20 token with a wide range of applications in the game and broader ecosystem. The ILV pricing is based on a combination of conjecture about the game's performance and its usefulness in staking. Both ILV and sILV versions of the token exist. sILV may be utilized right away in the game, unlike ILV, which must be held for a year before being used. There will never be more than 7 million ILV and sILV in total supply. Staking awards will be handed to the first 3 million holders, bringing the total supply to 10 million. Since many users have already staked their currencies, the circulating supply will be reduced. ILV has three key applications:

- Players are given ILV coins as a reward for their triumphs and achievements in the game.

- ILV holders may stake the Illuvium Vault. ILV or sILV may be used as compensation for stakes.

- Holders may participate in the game's administration (DAO).

Illuvinati's Council is a place where the whole community may work together to enhance the game and modify the government paradigm. ILV and sILV are ERC-20 tokens, which means that users who move them will have to pay Ethereum gas costs. We're still waiting to see how they'll properly integrate ERC-20 transactions into the game while keeping it reasonable, given how pricey they may be at times. Binance and Coinmarketcap have the most up-to-date pricing and an all-time high for Illuvium.

How to buy Illuvium?

Illuvium can be purchased on the following exchanges:

- SushiSwap
- Binance
- Kucoin
- 1inch
- OKEx
- CoinSpot
- Crypto.com

The Binance cryptocurrency exchange is a convenient place to purchase Illuvium.

Binance account registration and KYC/AML processes are required initially.

After registering and logging in, you'll be required to do the following:

1. Select the [Classic] or [Advanced] trading view by hovering your mouse over the [Trade] tab.

2. Search for ILV by hovering over the trading pair and selecting a suitable trading pair.

3. For the sake of illustration, we'll utilize [ILV/BUSD].

With a market order, you may buy ILV quickly and easily. Select an order type and enter the desired purchase amount. The contents of your purchase should be checked before you click [Buy ILV].

How to Stake Illuvium?

There are two ways that ILV investors might profit from their stakes:

- ILV or sILV may be grown by yield farming. Users may earn sILV instead of ILV, redeemable in-game after 12 months.

- Players in Illuvium spend Ethereum on ILV buybacks, which are subsequently returned to stakes. The game's release will include this mechanism.

- Metamask or Binance Chain Wallet is the best option for staking ILV, since they can connect to DApps.

1. The Illuvium Staking DApp requires that you link your wallet to it.

2. [CORE POOLS] will be our next stop.

274

3. It's possible to stake either ILV or ILV/ETH Liquidity Pool (LP) tokens from SushiSwap here. To join a pool, just click [STAKE].
4. There are two types of pools: [FLEXIBLE] and [LOCKED]. Depending on how long you lock your stake in a Locked Pool, your rewards might be doubled (up to a year). Enter the desired stake amount and click [STAKE] to place your bet.
5. You may also use partner tokens to stake in Flash Pools for ILV and sILV prizes.
6. You may accept your prizes in either ILV or sILV when you redeem them. As previously stated, sILV incentives are available immediately, while ILV prizes must wait a year before they may be collected.

Conclusions

Illuvium's ILV coin and Decentralized Finance (DeFi) staking platform has already attracted a lot of attention, momentum, and trading volume since its debut. Since its first debut, the Illuvium pricing has seen steady increases. However, compared to other blockchain games like Axie Infinity, Illuvium seems to be of greater quality in terms of its visual design and user experience. Is it going to be one of the first big-budget AAA experiences in the NFT gaming industry? We'll have to wait until the program's beta testing phase in 2023 to find out.

Chapter 5:
Metaverse And NFT

Virtual reality, once the science fiction domain, has become a scientific fact. Hundreds of millions of individuals across the globe spend a large amount of their time in persistent, networked virtual worlds, such as Fortnite, Roblox, and Animal Crossing. However, the uses of this technology are not limited to video games. As I write this, individuals worldwide are creating and maintaining virtual communities, exchanging virtual goods and services, and squabbling over finite virtual resources. As augmented reality grows more common, we see virtual overlays influencing our perception of the actual world, which we still refer to as the "real" one. As a result, today's virtual worlds tend to be bound to PC or tablet interfaces rather than the indistinguishable other universes depicted in science fiction. These virtual experiences will grow more "real" as virtual reality gear gets more powerful and inexpensive, and the border between our actual and virtual environments will continue to blur.

What Is Metaverse?
The Metaverse may seem like something out of a comic book, but it's a reality that many of us are already familiar with. In a nutshell, the Metaverse is the realm in which your digital self may exist. Your virtual self is known as an avatar, and it can move about and converse with the other avatars in the virtual environment you create. Video games like Fortnite and Roblox have been doing this for years, and now it's much more fun, thanks to virtual reality. Virtual reality isn't likely necessary to become a part of the Metaverse. Virtual reality (VR) will improve your metaverse experience, but you can also control your avatar using a standard computer screen. As a result, it's safe to say that virtual and augmented reality will play a significant role in the Metaverse. Using VR and AR together is likely to make a wide variety of activities far more fun. You attend virtual events with your avatar and engage with others in a VR context. A participatory and widely marketed parallel reality is likely in the works for the Metaverse.

A blockchain-powered metaverse is a virtual world. Virtual and augmented reality (VR and AR) are the visual component suppliers in this scenario, while decentralized media allows constant social interaction and commercial possibilities. These environments are scalable, interoperable, adaptable, and include novel technologies and forms of interaction between users on both the individual and organizational levels. Metaverses have several processes and aspects, including communications, financial transactions, and more. NFTs are also part of the mix. Anyone in the Metaverse may produce, purchase, and view NFTs to amass virtual land, join social networks, establish virtual identities, games, and more, which is why the Metaverse's potential is so great. The metaverse frameworks bring up a wide range of monetization options for both organizations and individuals for real-world and digital assets.

Shift To the Metaverse
The lack of a unified cross-world ecosystem is the most significant impediment to the evolution of virtual reality. Most virtual worlds are geared for specific games, aims, or groups, rather than being open to everyone. A standard interface will eventually be developed to integrate virtual and actual worlds. It's called the "metaverse" because it's a layer of linked virtual worlds that never dies. Exactly how we'll get there is anyone's guess. But there's no denying that virtual and augmented reality — collaborative metaverses — are now becoming a part of life for many people. Smart money is betting big on this sector because of this. At the moment, Facebook is dedicating 20% of its entire staff to developing VR and AR technology. Consequently, the significant majority of enterprises haven't even gotten close to this level of investment. Windows Mixed Reality's ad/short film is designed to let you expand your creativity into the Metaverse.

What Is NFT?
In the digital world, NFTs are digital certificates that may be used to show that you possess something. Many of them have sold for millions of dollars, but the vast majority of them have no evident economic worth and do not fetch exorbitant prices. " One NFT recently sold for more than $500 million. However, it was subsequently found that it had not been sold at that price. A majority of Americans are still baffled.

Shift To NFT

Once a player has purchased an NFT (the blobby creatures known as Axis) in Axie's Metaverse, they may begin playing. Ethereum, the second most popular Cryptocurrency after bitcoin, must be used to purchase a minimum of three Axis at the cost of around $300 each. In other words, if you want to get started, you'll need to pony over a whopping $1,200. Since Axie's acquisition, it has become the world's most valuable collection of NFTs. Things like that pique the interest of wealthy people. Mark Cuban and Reddit co-founder Alexis Ohanian invested in Sky Mavis in May. Play-to-earn (P2E) and GameFi are the focus of Justin Sun, CEO of BitTorrent and creator of the TRON Foundation. A $150 million Series B fundraising round led by Andreessen Horowitz valued Sky Mavis at $3 billion. NFTs in GameFi are significant since they aren't merely digital files that can be seen. There is a lot of activity and social interaction among NFTs. In this manner:

The tenacious Nintendo spin-off series from pre-internet Super Mario Kart may now make you money. Being excellent at it would be an advantage, but not a must. It wouldn't be a chore if you didn't play it constantly. Mario may stay as long as he wants in this thought experiment. Because you own him, you're entitled to be him. It's challenging to replicate your Mario since he's an NFT. He belongs to you and only you. Since you own him, Mario's kart is always quicker and better than the others in the Mushroom Kingdom, such as Luigi, Toad, and Princess Peach. Mariocoins, the virtual currency of the Kingdom of Mario, is your currency of choice.

NFT Mario may cost more than NFT Peach, based on current market conditions. Mario is the quickest player in the Mushroom Kingdom; thus, you'd get more money if you beat him. Even if you quit the game and go back to work, you've still got Mario under your control. Mario will be waiting for you when you go back into the game. Mariocoins are waiting for you. If you choose, you may trade Mario with another player. A well-played version of Mario might be more valuable than the one you purchased at the time. You've shown that Mario may be profitable, perhaps. Playing Mario Kart may attract additional players. Since everyone's talking about Mariocoin on social media, it may have risen in value.

In a word, this is the vision of GameFi proponents. Co-founder Aleksander Leonard Larsen of Axie says players may own the game products and see that they are in short supply. It's more authentic than when you see someone with a Louis Vuitton bag on their arm in public. You have no notion whether or not this is genuine. Just the skepticism you feel is ideally suited to the current state of affairs, as everything is fabricated. The most important benefit of the Blockchain is its ability to build trust. As a result, digital assets are also covered."

Connection Between the Metaverse And NFT

To put it another way, the primary link between the Metaverse and NFTs is how digital assets are valued. To place a price on digital art and property, users will be able to use NFTs to provide evidence of ownership in the Metaverse.

Cryptocurrencies like Bitcoin and Ethereum employ the same blockchain technology as NFTs do, but NFTs are not themselves a kind of money. There is a distinct NFT for each NFT item. It's up to you whatever you want to put on that token: a painting, video game material, music, or anything else. As a result, NFTs have become an excellent tool for artists and creators, in general, to make money from their work. You may purchase and sell NFTs on many different online markets. This is a trend that is sweeping across many other businesses. NFTs are a complicated topic, but this article provides a fundamental understanding of what they are and how they function.

Having discussed NFTs, it is vital to realize that NFTs are likely to be the best money for a metaverse. People will prove their ownership of all types of metaverse items. It's possible to have a virtual deed to a piece of real estate. The NFTs would carry out this act. NFTs might be used as portals to certain metaverse events and benefits. This makes the concept so appealing since it has so many applications and many possibilities.

Blockchain World

Metaverse
The Metaverse is designed to be a completely immersive virtual reality environment. As a result, virtual avatars will take an active role in interacting with the digital world. Users will interact in ways more than just exchanging photographs and papers. The Metaverse has you covered when it comes to pre-screening real estate properties in virtual reality. Tokens from the Metaverse like MANA and GALA have become more popular because of their applications. Tokens in the Metaverse are transactional entities traded in virtual markets.

NFT
Non-Fungible Tokens (also known as NFT) go beyond the simple exchange of digital artwork. Fashion labels and other corporations are already using NFTs to spread the word about their products, so there are plenty of real-world applications for them. When it comes to trading anything from social media postings to celebrity assets, NFTs are the best method to keep the original authorship of the product. As users have begun to "play to earn," NFTs have given gaming platforms a fresh lease of life. Thanks to games, users may now earn NFTs that can be sold at a profit on marketplaces. NFTs and Metaverse are similar enough to be discussed together when it comes to application scenarios. Metaverse currencies may exchange gaming assets in the Metaverse as NFTs.

Is The Metaverse Ready for NFTs?
Metaverse transactions and user engagement have the potential to be fundamentally altered by NFTs. Find out how NFTs can change the world of digital technology.

An Open and Fair Economy
Real-world assets and services may be transferred into a virtual, decentralized environment in the Metaverse. Innovative gaming models using blockchain-based games may bring more real-world assets into the Metaverse.

Players may participate in the Metaverse's financial in-game economy and gain rewards for the value they offer by depending on NFTs. Because participants have complete ownership of their assets rather than being controlled by a single game entity like most conventional games, play-to-earn games are also fair in the Metaverse. As a result, play-to-earn gaming models, such as those used in blockchain games, can both entertain and empower gamers.

Binance NFT's IGO launches provide a range of in-game assets from gaming projects that players may acquire and integrate into various gaming settings if they're wondering how to participate in these in-game financial economies. Among the numerous examples of successful play-to-earn games include AXS, My Neighbor Alice, and many more. Because of this strong demand, all IGO's in-game NFTs were sold out immediately after the release.

Gamers' guilds will also play an essential role in the growth of play-to-earn gaming. Guilds use in-game NFT resources, such as land and assets, as facilitators for players who desire to utilize such resources to generate income in their respective virtual worlds. Guilds take a tiny percentage of what you've made when you play to earn.

Guilds make it easier for everyone to engage in the metaverse economy by lowering the barrier of entry to play-to-earn games. For the most part, guilds act as a jumpstart for the Metaverse's virtual economy by making NFT resources more widely available. A fair and open economy may be achieved by allowing players who lack the initial money to join guilds to obtain a head start.

Yield Guild Games (YGG) is an example of a company that builds a worldwide community of metaverse players that contribute to the virtual worlds to receive in-world benefits and generate money via the rental or sale of YGG-owned assets.

Since users may exchange their NFT assets, like in-game assets and digital real estate, on NFT platforms like Binance NFT, in-world investments can also demand real-world value. Use cases in various metaverse modules determine the economic worth of the in-game NFTs. In this manner, users can create material that appeals to a broad audience and unique digital artwork or specialized NFTs that confer specific skills and appearances in video games.

Metaverses allow for an open and fair economy using the Blockchain's immutability and transparency. It is also important to note that prices are determined by the supply and demand rule, which considers the scarcity and on-chain value of an NFT concerning its application.

Binance Examples of metaverse economic facilitation may be seen in NFT's game drops. New game assets are released every week on IGO, giving players a head start on the NFT gaming scene. A variety of play-to-earn gaming assets may be found in the Mystery Boxes randomly dropped. The Binance NFT secondary market is also a great area to find and trade NFT things in-game. The Binance NFT marketplace provides newcomers with a daily list of recommended NFT collections and creators and a list of top NFT sales, groups, and creators to assist them in navigating the marketplace.

An Extension of Identity, Community and Social Experiences

Metaverse identity, community, and social interactions will be facilitated through NFTs. Some NFT assets may be used to show support for a project or express views on the actual and virtual worlds. As a result, people with similar NFTs might form groups to exchange ideas and generate material. Trending NFT avatars are an excellent illustration of this kind of NFT.

Using NFT avatars as an extension of our real-life identities, we have complete control over creating and maintaining our metaverse personas. A player's actual or imagined self is represented via an NFT avatar. NFT avatars may be access tokens to enter and bounce between metaverse places.

As a result of owning avatar NFTs, you have access to a wide range of exclusive experiences in both the physical and the virtual worlds. NFT avatars are already influencing the Metaverses' experiences and environs via content production and the founding of new startups.

The Bored Ape Yacht Club and the CryptoPunks collections, which provide their owner special privileges and access to gated communities of wealthy users with protected material and even offline private events, are vibrant instances of such avatars that shape one's identity. NFTs' importance as value carriers that connect the digital and physical worlds is highlighted through exclusive parties with NFT-associated admission fees.

Property Ownership: Virtual Real Estate

The Metaverse's virtual lands and places may be reclaimed entirely by their owners via the usage of NFTs. Blockchain technology allows users to verify ownership of the asset and build virtual property in any way they see fit.

Selling a property for profit, renting land for passive income, erecting different buildings like online stores, or holding social gatherings are examples of virtual real estate applications in the Metaverse.

Decentraland recently organized a virtual fashion show in partnership with Adidas, in which designs were auctioned off as non-fungible tokens (NFTs). Artists are also becoming fascinated with virtual real estate since it allows them to play and sell NFT tickets and goods on the Internet.

Opportunities for Businesses

Selling Virtual Products

A virtual product is a product that exists only in digital form. Both real-world products and products that exist solely in the virtual world are possible. Even though these things aren't quite "genuine" in the sense that we usually use the word, real individuals are willing to pay real money for these products anyhow.

Using virtual items may be a no-brainer for many businesses. Buying a virtual high-end Ferrari to get an advantage in a racing simulator is simple to envisage. In a virtual setting, wearing a high-end suit has the same effect as if you were in the actual world.

It's more challenging to see how Taco Bell may benefit from virtual items. Chalupa Supreme's advantages don't appear to transition well into a virtual world. However, they've created and sold virtual things for thousands of dollars in the past month.

The message is clear. There's undoubtedly a method to create and sell your things in virtual settings if you do it in the real world. The worth of these things will only rise as we move toward an immersive multiverse.

Reaching Massive Audiences

The global video game business is more significant than the sports and cinema industries put together worldwide. That's something to ponder for a while. You'd want your goods and brand to be included in a blockbuster movie or on a significant sporting event how much. A Fortnite skin or an Animal Crossing product placement would get your message in front of more people.

283

Despite the fact you may not be able to earn a fortune selling virtual goods right now, you can instantly begin to benefit from enormous increases in brand equity. Whatever your product's use case may be in a virtual environment, you already have a brand that can be applied to virtual clothes, signs, art, and more.

Companies are turning to NFTs and virtual goods to appeal to a younger demographic. Most Fortnite gamers are between the ages of 24 and 35. Two-thirds of Roblox's gamers are under the age of 16. In addition to their sheer size, these target markets are likely to differ significantly from the ones your business is used to targeting. Particularly costly goods may be purchased by virtual customers long before they can be bought in the "real" world by luxury businesses.

Protecting Your IP

When it comes to virtual items, most people's first worry is how to keep a product's worth intact when it's easier to copy or counterfeit. Across the actual world, counterfeiting is an issue in a wide range of businesses, from footwear to fine art. It's much more complex in the virtual world.

In the real world, the materials and quality of a counterfeit Rolex watch distinguish it from a genuine one. There are no noticeable differences in the product files themselves to create "virtually identical" replicas of virtual goods in virtual worlds. How can virtual items' scarcity and exclusivity be preserved and enforced? This is where NFTs come in.

To understand the blockchain, you must conceive of it as a record of ownership for a specific virtual item, such as a virtual product, currency unit, or any other kind of digital asset. Unlike a ledger in your bank account or any record of ownership, there is no owner of a blockchain. It's decentralized, so no one has the power to edit, change, or destroy it.

As a result, if you hold one bitcoin, it is linked to a record on the blockchain. Because no two coins have the same serial number, you can't spend it more than once. When you donate or spend a bitcoin, you're essentially handing someone a unique reference to that bitcoin's blockchain record.

Since NFTs are produced and safeguarded using blockchain technology, they are comparable to cryptocurrency units. The main difference between NFTs and other assets is that an NFT has no inherent "fungible" or "tradeable" value. The worth of a single bitcoin may be compared to the value of other currencies or commodities since each bitcoin is believed to have the same worth. An NFT is worthless on its own. Said, this is a permanent record of ownership for any digital asset, whether it is a piece of 3D digital art (we love David O'Reilly's work!) or a video of LeBron James dunking or a copy of the Kings of Leon CD.

It is possible to prove ownership of a virtual asset via an NFT. By selling an NFT, you can prove that the asset in question belongs to the person who purchased the document. There are no other copies or forgeries of a virtual product protected by an NFT if protected by an NFT.

What's to say that in the virtual worlds of the future, people won't be wandering around in false virtual Yeezys? What's the matter? It doesn't have to be that way, however. It enables virtual worlds to impose regulations on the usage of recognized goods in virtual environments. In the virtual world, IP owners may sell and enforce licenses for the use of their IP. Furthermore, although an NFT is one method of identifying and safeguarding virtual ownership, there are still many others–and likely the final standard–that need to be established.

Additionally, NFTs may be used to safeguard physical objects against counterfeiting and illegal resale, which is a secondary purpose for NFTs. Unauthorized resellers of a company's items on significant marketplaces, for example, are a massive issue for eCommerce organizations nowadays. You may use an NFT-linked virtual depiction of your goods as verified proof of authenticity through approved sales channels to combat this.

HOW THREEKIT CAN HELP

The use cases for virtual goods will become more transparent and helpful as virtual worlds continue to improve and flourish. You need to construct virtual copies of your items to take advantage of current prospects to generate money and expand your brand in the multiverse.

Using Threekit, you may create 3D virtual material that can be used in various environments. In a matter of minutes, you may swiftly create tens of thousands, if not millions, of photorealistic 3D visual assets, then apply layers of crucial digital information to each one before exporting them in the formats you need for virtual presentation.

Using Threekit, you can build 3D models of your whole customizable product catalog, and you can even embed a configurator on your website so that your site visitors may construct their bespoke versions of your virtual items. You might use an NFT to safeguard each bespoke variation of your product and allow just one owner for each one or a certain number of copies.

You are only restricted by your ideas using Threekit's technology. When marketing your wares online, the clock is ticking whether you utilize Threekit or another digitizing your goods. Companies that take action now will reap the most benefits from this massive transformation in defining ownership and using things in the future.

Opportunities for Brands

Because it is a virtual depiction of the actual world, the Metaverse will provide companies with a slew of new options. They had a strategy to deal with the Metaverse's imminent changes. Starting right now, companies may develop virtual representations of their items to help others find them in this new reality.

One day, we'll live in two separate worlds: the offline one that we've always known and a virtual one that we'll be constantly immersed into. To be successful, you'll need to be visible to your target audience in both online and offline environments.

Investing in Metaverse with NFT

Many multi-million-dollar real estate transactions this year have placed the phrase "metaverse" on our lips. Metaverse is a virtual environment where users may interact with avatars of their design and explore it at will. In addition to traditional video games, visitors may engage electronically and participate in various real-time activities. According to industry experts, the Metaverse now offers a one-of-a-kind $1 trillion possibility for income.

We can invest in the Metaverse in a variety of ways. Metaverse tokens like SAND and MANA are two of the most straightforward methods to invest in the Metaverse. One may also purchase non-fungible tickets in the game. The third option is to make a real-world investment in metaverse real estate. If you want to invest in the Metaverse, you can invest in companies like Apple or Facebook. The alternative option is to place your money in a metaverse-based index.

Direct Investment

Step 1: Create a crypto wallet
Every transaction requires a pocket full of cash, precisely like buying tangible goods. Create a crypto wallet and fill it up with virtual cash to invest in the Metaverse.
Meta Mask is the world's most popular cryptocurrency wallet. Topping the list is Coinbase and Binance. The ether (ETH) cryptocurrency is the best way to buy most NFTs since it's based on Ethereum.
Step 2: Open an account on the platform of your choice
To make purchases in a game, you'll need to sign up for an account and link your crypto wallet to it. Axie Infinity has characters and land plots, whereas Decentraland allows you to purchase and trade creative works. Creating an account with OpenSea will enable you to access all of the NFTs in a single location for ease of use.
Step 3: Select the NFT you wish to purchase and make the payment
NFTs do not have a set selling price on any marketplaces, as mentioned earlier. To own the NFT, one must compete with other bidders and win the highest offer. Using the wallet, you generated and stocked with bitcoin in Step 1 enables you to pay for the NFT immediately.
Buying from a significant marketplace (Decentraland, Axie Infinity, Sandbox, etc.) or a secondary market has both advantages and disadvantages to consider (OpenSea, etc.). If you buy an NFT from the primary market, you should expect a more excellent resale value. In the primary market, determining its genuine worth is more complicated. For this reason, comparing NFT prices on the secondary market is more accessible than comparing them one at a time on the primary market.
Indirect Investment
Investing in the Metaverse may also be done in these indirect ways.
Buy metaverse-associated stocks
Metaverse-associated equities are those of companies actively participating in the Metaverse's development. They might be involved in manufacturing virtual reality (VR) goggles, networking technologies, 3D rendering programs, or any other kind of VR technology. Metaverse ETFs or brokerages may be used to buy these equities (Exchange Traded Funds). Apple, Facebook, NVIDIA, Roblox, and Unity are the most widely held stocks.

Invest in Metaverse Index (MVI)
The MVI is a comprehensive measure of the current state of the most popular metaverse tokens. Like stock market indexes, the metaverse index tracks trends in entertainment, business, and gaming that are transitioning into a virtual realm. The current price is $225.86. The MVI significantly reduces the volatility of metaverse tokens, reducing the risk of acquiring them.

The Metaverse is constantly changing, and there are still many new advancements in the works. The physical world is rapidly giving way to the digital one. It's best to do your homework before committing any significant funds, even if the potential is enormous.

Metaverse And Gaming
I believe that a metaverse is the Internet's future and nothing less. Facebook and Microsoft are also making significant investments in technology that some predict will considerably affect how we live our everyday lives. On the other hand, a metaverse is a virtual world where players may interact with each other in real-time. You'll also find it fascinating.

For Mark Zuckerberg, the Metaverse (sometimes spelled "metaverse") is the future of the Internet, but more importantly, the end of our interpersonal relationships on a massive scale. Moreover, he has renamed Facebook Meta and promises to spend $ 50 billion on this new model since he passionately believes in it. He intends to get on board 10,000 engineers in Europe alone. Consequently, we now have virtual places where we may interact with people in the same way we do in real life.

It's not only Meta-Facebook that's interested in this new Grail. Emboldened by its 350 million players, Fortnite's developer, Epic Games, transforms it into a metaverse. Microsoft would also want to remind you that she is working on Mesh, a Teams extension (collaborative communication) near a metaverse. Neither Apple nor Sony are left out of the conversation. As a result of the fact, as per a study by Bloomberg Intelligence, this sector might be worth $2,500 billion by 2030.

Online Video Games

Enormous multiplayer online games like World of Warcraft and persistent worlds like EVE Online have laid the groundwork for the Metaverse. Social relationship games like The Sims, which included an online version, might be argued to be the same. In addition, several tests have previously taken place close to the Metaverse. In 1997, Canal + debuted The Second World, a computer-generated depiction of a parallel Parisian society. Some gamers have engaged in social interactions inside a well-created virtual environment since Second Life first came out in 2003. However, the lack of suitable technology and bandwidth contributed to the popularity of these types of experiences.

Metaverse And Online Video Games

Although the Internet and the Metaverse are pretty different, they have many similarities.

- We assume the role of virtual characters, or "avatars," that we consider the part. We may play the essence of a wizard, a knight, a merchant in an online video game. This will be possible in the Metaverse, whether in our form or character.

- Items that we are willing to pay a premium for. It might be a specific piece of armor or a horse in an online game. For example, a metaverse might have a talent like flying, or it could be an artwork. That we have purchased and that we display in our house.

- It doesn't matter whether it's an actual city or a fictional one; there are locations for pleasure, contests, and so on.

- Homes that you may personalize and use to host people;

- Persistence. No one can stop us from leaving this planet. circumstances have changed as of the last time you looked at them.

How, therefore, can one distinguish between the two? For starters, since there will be no predetermined limit on how many people may participate in a metaverse, it provides a substantial technical problem – and helps us see how much money Meta-Facebook has put into the topic.

Gaming In the Metaverse

Virtual reality has always been an obvious choice for gamers (VR). For example, Minecraft and Second Life combined 3D avatars, world creation, and observation as gameplay in their 2D counterparts. Gaming now has a new home, thanks to firms like Meta and Epic Games, attempting to create an interconnected universe of virtual reality worlds. In a recent poll, 59 percent of industry experts predicted that gaming would continue to be the primary focus of VR spending for the foreseeable future. According to 64 percent of those polled, VR gaming has the most potential to gain from the technology. We'll take a look at what games in the Metaverse would look like, how quickly you might get started, and what to watch out for.

What Is the Metaverse Gaming Environment Like?

The term "metaverse" alludes to a virtual reality (VR) environment in which users may engage with each other and the virtual world around them using cutting-edge technology and software for human-computer interaction (HCI). This is a massive step forward for virtual reality gaming. Immersive video games are now accessible as separate software that may be installed on your PC, VR gear, or mobile devices. You may now experience the game's environment as a three-dimensional VR world that you can explore in 360-degrees and practically "touch" with a realistic sense of perception.

The Metaverse furthers this idea, a term initially used in the science fiction book Snow Crash in 1992. A unified, interoperable experience for users may be created by connecting numerous virtual reality games – or any VR application or area, for that matter. They will be capable of switching between different gaming apps, communicating with the same gamers in other locations, and even transferring their victories without removing their VR headsets from their heads. Gaming in this sense will be defined by the following:

Games-as-platforms

As a result, gamers may expect a more personalized gaming experience. The gaming environment may be used as a platform for various activities, with users able to contribute to the virtual world, generate their material, and establish subgames inside games.

Social gaming

Unlike standard virtual reality, the Metaverse is fundamentally social, a feature that sets it different. Players may invite friends from the real world, communicate with one other, create connections, and so on in multi-player games.

Play to earn

Gaming in the Metaverse will rely heavily on this. Additionally, players can participate in lucrative activities outside of the game's narrative and regulations. They may be able to recoup their investment in the game's virtual currency by selling the things they've acquired.

The possibility of portable game assets

The interoperability of the Metaverse's architecture might allow for asset mobility. For instance, players' weaponry or avatar upgrades may be transferred across games, and NFT regulations regulate their ownership.

Mixed reality experience

AR and MR are used to enhance the natural feel of the Metaverse. Mixed reality gaming in the Metaverse might allow gamers to seamlessly go from AR to MR board games to full-fledged VR worlds.

Several companies are shaping gaming in the Metaverse.

However, it is still in its beginnings; the Metaverse has already garnered significant investment from game businesses, internet heavyweights, and venture capitalists. The Metaverse is, without a doubt, the game industry's future. Companies like Decentraland, Sandbox, Epic Games, and Meta are among the early adopters.

Decentraland

One of the first firms to intentionally develop a metaverse is Decentraland. 3D virtual reality platform, Ethereum-based cryptocurrency, and multiplayer game venues are all included. Additionally, Decentraland has invested in Decentral Games, a game development firm, to expand its gaming capabilities.

Sandbox

You may play, construct, own, and control a virtual place in Sandbox (another metaverse-native video game). User-generated crypto and NFT assets power Sandbox's economy, and it collaborates with worldwide companies to provide memorable and rewarding experiences. More than 20,000 NFTs are available for purchase on the Sandbox marketplace.

Epic Games

Epic Games will build a gaming-centric metaverse, which announced a $1 billion investment. Fortnite, a VR game and place for events, is Epics Games' most well-known product. Many musicians have taken use of the metaverse-like characteristics of Fortnite to host concerts in response to the game's growing popularity.

Meta (Formerly Facebook)

Meta is a relative newcomer to the Metaverse, but it has a long history of VR innovation to its credit. Facebook's Oculus family of devices has established a strong experience world, and these breakthroughs will continue to influence the company's metaverse vision. Developers can build and distribute games in the Metaverse using Meta's Horizon Worlds.

Issues That Will Have to be Considered

In the real world, like in the virtual one, VR and video games have always had to contend with legal and ethical questions. It's vital to keep three things in mind:

Child-appropriate services and controls

When children's avatars are heavily customized, monitoring their activities and distinguishing them from adults might be challenging. Controls must be included in games to ensure that they are acceptable for the age group they are aimed for.

NFT ownership rights

It's still unsure what the rules are regarding the ownership of in-game assets. NFTs won in a game may not be transferred outside of the game. Ownership rights must be clearly stated so that users may engage with, trade, and benefit from NFTs.

Infrastructure shortcomings

There is still a long journey until game metaverse can be fully realized on such a vast scale. It will take a lot of collaboration between tech companies, patent holders, nations, and our technology to create a single set of metaverse regulations.

Considering all of these things, we can say that gaming in the Metaverse is still 5 to 10 years away, but the outlook is incredibly positive.

Cross-over investments between the gaming and metaverse industries.

Even though there has been considerable debate regarding virtual monetization in games, Spencer says the arithmetic is simple enough to sustain additional investments in the Metaverse and gaming.

Gaming is the entertainment industry's most extensive section, with more than 3 billion regular players. ' But it's not going to be the last time that NFTs are used in gaming, according to Sky Mavis of Axie Infinity. Investors are beginning to see the possibilities in the crossover between crypto and gaming. According to the Wall Street Journal, Sky Mavis collected $152 million in October from investors like Andreessen Horowitz and Mark Cuban. However, Spencer believes that the most successful developers will be those developing AAA-quality games that can be played on PC, such as Take-Two Interactive's Grand Theft Auto and EA's FIFA, both available on the PC. Even though they aren't AAA games, Roblox and even Minecraft have seen considerable popularity. GameStop has announced intentions to start its own NFT marketplace in the same way. To carry out the strategy, GME is expected to make many Web3 employees. Gaming income sources are expected to be used by brands as well. If you want to make money, you may do it directly in the game industry." People are accustomed to spending $20, $50, or $100 each skin," Akkineni remarked. The digital counterpart of Gucci's Dionysus bag sold on Roblox for more than the item's IRL retail price, proving that gamers are prepared to pay for their virtual avatars.

Virtual World and NFTs
Today, NFT is a common abbreviation on social media and news. As a result, it should come as no surprise that it has attracted the interest of a diverse group of people. NFT materials, including music, photos, and even films, may now be purchased and sold online via metaverses. As these metaverses have gained popularity, individuals gather in virtual worlds using AR, Augmented reality. People are increasingly using virtual worlds and metaverses to supplement their daily lives. A newcomer to NFTs will be amazed to see how quickly the virtual asset market grows. According to non-findings, fungible's metaverses currently account for 20% of all NFT sales.
It is essential to understand that "metaverse" refers to a distinct digital realm from our own. NFTs are being incorporated into metaverses in a variety of ways now. Virtual reality headsets, computers, and smartphones may all be used to access them. The Black Eye Galaxy is an exciting example of this kind of innovation. Users may digitally explore the cosmos, harvest resources, and begin their civilization using NFTs and virtual environments. Users may earn money by achieving specific goals, such as finding a new planet.

To put it differently, the Metaverse is a collection of computer-generated worlds in which people may connect and engage with one another like that seen in the actual world. This kind of person is usually represented by avatars who create horses, play games, or even collect art. Gaming on the Internet and virtual reality go hand in hand. Gamers have spent millions of dollars every year to purchase the essential equipment for their travels because of these principles. NFTs, on the other hand, have increased the value of the virtual world. NFTs can be traded on various platforms by verifying their ownership.

As previously said, NFTs are a critical component in making the virtual world more engaging and lucrative. In the world of cryptography, an NFT is a digital asset that proves a person's ownership of a particular item. For example, it may be music, gaming, or digital art; it could even be land. Even the real estate market is not insulated from this. On the other hand, Fungible may easily be substituted with this new technology. As a result, no other NFT exists. It is rare because of its originality. In addition, each NFT's underlying information makes it a one-of-a-kind and unique item. NFT is a virtual representation of things like lands in the virtual world. As in early 2021, the values of virtual lands will be comparable to those of fundamental properties.

NFTs and virtual worlds have a revolutionary and disruptive propensity that may be seen in various ways. Axis Infinity just sold virtual land for USD 1.5 million in ether. This is evidence of the collaboration's disruptive tendencies. NFT-based metaverse systems are ready to change virtual reality as we know it. NFT will likely acquire much more momentum in the months to come, given the vast infrastructure it requires and the present attention it's receiving.

NFT that allows you pick your virtual age

Metaverse is a digital environment where users may connect, participate in activities, and host events, all in real-time. Due to the epidemic and the resulting restrictions on physical engagement, these virtual worlds have become more popular. Metaverse Digital assets like music and art may now be owned in a whole new way thanks to NFTs.

AI, VR, and AR are just a few of the cutting-edge technologies used to make virtual reality as lifelike as possible for users. One such effort, Novatar, aims to bring virtual worlds as near as possible to the actual world. The Novatar NFTs can help you age in the virtual world. The Metaverse has developed a method for individuals to experience physiological changes that progress over time.

What Is the Novatar Project?
Using the NFT project Novatar, people may customize their digital identity in the Metaverse and control how old they get in it. Until recently, the sole consideration has been the construction of avatars to promote communication. The aging of avatars is introduced in this project.

If you're looking for an avatar or Novatar that looks like you, you may use the Novatar Project. Or construct a meta-human that is identical to yourself by acquiring comparable features. Your Novatar may also serve as your online persona on other social networks and metaverses.

There will be 25,000 newborn Novatars, each unique skin tone, race, expression, and physical characteristics. Due to the Novatars' blockchain-based nature, the value of each one grows immediately upon issuance. The owner decides when to mint the baby. And they may start aging the baby at a time convenient for them. When the NFT choose to raise their child as an adult, the creators have not yet revealed how much the infant avatar would grow.

How Will Novatar Work?
You'll need to choose a baby avatar that you believe most accurately represents you in the Starting. During conception, each Novatar infant is given nine critical genes that it carries with it until adulthood. There are six distinct variations of each gene in a newborn. When you're born, you'll be given the choice of becoming an adult or remaining a baby for the rest of your life. You have 30 days to make up your mind. The website will include a "growing older" button.

Ten Novatar's 14 genes are necessary, while the other four are optional. Only genes that control skin, hair, eye, and eyebrow color may have 11 variants per gene in adults. This implies that specific genes will be passed on when the infant ages and grows. As they get older, Novatars will show symptoms of maturation, such as the emergence of sexual identity.

You may see the changes in your Novatar's DNA if you opt to raise it to adulthood. They will choose from one of the following occupations when they are adults: Doctor, Blogger; Gamer; Astronaut, and Developer.

According to the developers, each novatar has an 88 percent chance of being born with the "no profession gene," according to the whitepaper. If the gene for professions is discovered, the following disciplines have the following probabilities of being attained:

- It's 3%, doctor.

- blogger: 3% of the total

- 1% of the population is gamers.
- The 1% is for the astronaut.
- 4% percent of the developer

Features of the Novatar Project:
As previously stated, these Novatars may be used to represent you throughout the Metaverse and on all social networking networks. Novatars may be used as access cards to nearly any organized event. As a result, you are welcome to attend these functions in the persona of your Novatar. The main features of the Novatar project are as follows

- No more than 25,000 Novatars will ever be produced.

- Once minted, Novatars will have the appearance of newborn newborns and will begin to age immediately (starting the aging process is user-controlled).

- More genes are created and integrated into the Novatar's look or features as they mature.

- Some very unusual Novatars will be possible because of the many gene pools.

- A Novatar's sexual orientation cannot be pre-determined.

The Novatar team intends to go much farther in this direction. Your Novatars will not only represent you in cyberspace but also in the real world.

Setting the Stage for a Digital Tomorrow
Whenever it ultimately boils down to it, the most exciting aspect about NFTs is not the fact that they're breaking records at auction houses or earning Elon Musk a lot more money. The fascinating thing about NFTs is that they enable ideas like rarity, scarcity, and uniqueness, which were previously impossible in a virtual, digital future. In a few years, this same technology will be a crucial part of your virtual existence, so don't worry about the excitement bubble burst when everyone discovers they've been paying great money for glorified GIFs.

Chapter 6:
Investing in the Metaverse

Snow Crash" was authored by Neal Stephenson in 1992 and was his third book. The Metaverse is the name Stephenson gave to his virtual world. To put it another way: The digital world in which Stephenson's characters live is just as dynamic and full of possibilities for character development as the actual one.

Public enterprises like Meta (previously Facebook) and decentralized autonomous organizations (DAOs) like the Decentraland Foundation are still attempting to make the Metaverse a lucrative reality twenty-eight years after it was first proposed. Gaming, digital collectors, and developers have found new business streams as a result. To be clear, though, the Metaverse is still at an early stage of development, and its value proposition has not yet been demonstrated. Investing in the Metaverse should always be seen as speculative and very dangerous because of the tremendous degree of uncertainty involved.

The Metaverse Market Opportunity

By 2025, virtual games are expected to produce revenues of up to $400 billion, up from an anticipated $180 billion in 2020. The continuing growth of monetization by game creators is a crucial component in this trend. Free-to-play games are becoming more popular among gamers since they allow creators to monetize their virtual worlds by selling users stuff, land, etc.

There was a significant change from closed metaverses (i.e., those controlled by the Web's big players) to open cryptographic ones between web 2.0 and web 3.0. (i.e., democratically owned and managed by users). There is no way for gamers to make money in a Web 2.0 environment. To prevent players from transferring their virtual riches to the real world, game creators prevent them from exchanging stuff with other players.

By removing the capital constraints imposed by Web 2.0 platforms, Web 3.0 open crypto metaverse networks alleviate this issue. These NFTs may be traded in-game with other players and transported to different digital experiences, allowing for the creation of a new Internet economy that can be monetized outside of the virtual environment.

Open ecosystems and the surrender of some of their competitive advantages are consequently a must for established Web 2.0 firms like Facebook. A trillion dollars in advertising, social commerce, digital events, hardware, and developer/creator monetization might be generated in the Metaverse.

Investments in Digital Assets:
A virtual world creates virtual investing possibilities. There has been a meteoric indicator of the strength of digital real estate. Funds obtained by Republic Real Estate to acquire troubled real estate in the actual world are also available to investors looking to buy virtual property. Virtual hotels, shops, and other businesses will be built on plots purchased across numerous "metaverses" to increase their value among bitcoin enthusiasts. NFT art is now one of the year's most popular digital assets. Bain and Co. partner Thomas Olsen recently predicted that all assets would be tokenized in the next 20 or 30 years. Cryptocurrency experimenters are building a digital asset platform that will house "all stocks and all bonds," he claimed.

Online-Only Shopping and Experiences:
As long as businesses have their way, online purchasing will only get complicated. Already, they are raking in millions of dollars from the sale of metaverse-exclusive clothes and accessories. If you spend a lot of time on social media, your online image may become more critical than it is today. So, it's crucial to maintain tabs on how and why avatars of various racial and gender identities are priced online. Unevenness is emerging, and it might have catastrophic consequences.

Metaverse Stocks
Investing in publicly listed firms whose business strategies or profitability are related to the Metaverse is the least volatile alternative for ordinary investors who want to get into the Metaverse. The following are included:

Meta Platforms Inc (NASDAQ: FB)
Previously known as Facebook Inc., Mark Zuckerberg announced the company's renaming to Meta Platforms Inc. in October. Since its introduction, Horizon Worlds, Meta's virtual reality metaverse platform, has been launched. The Oculus Quest 2 VR headset from Meta was one of the most popular Christmas presents. Even if more people buy headsets, it isn't clear whether more people will utilize Horizon Worlds.

Roblox (NYSE: RBLX)

Using Roblox, players can build and share virtual environments with other Roblox members. With 9.5 million creators, 24 million digital experiences, and 49.4 million daily active users – an increase of 35 percent year-over-year – Roblox has been a massive success since its debut in 2006. Despite these figures, the firm has yet to make a profit.

Boeing (NYSE: BA)

Expanding and improving manufacturing capacities are two of Boeing's goals in the Metaverse. In an interview, Boeing's top engineer, Greg Hyslop, told Reuters that the company plans to develop a private digital environment where its human, computer, and robot workers can interact and cooperate without interruption anywhere on the globe.

Microsoft (NASDAQ: MSFT)

Microsoft is looking for a place in the professional sector for its Metaverse. According to the company's schedule, Microsoft Teams Mesh will be available in 2022. People will be able to create their 3D holographic avatars and work together regardless of where they are in the world with the help of this add-on for the popular video conferencing platform. Users will access the previously stated digital world via Microsoft Mesh using a virtual reality headset. Team members see and engage with the user as if they were really in the room with them.

Metaverse real estate

NFTs (non-fungible tokens), digital assets on blockchain networks that may represent a wide variety of unique things, are already being sold on platforms like The Sandbox and Decentraland, even if the Metaverse is still in its infancy. The blockchain network that powers the metaverse platform validates the sale and transfer of ownership when buying a piece of metaverse real estate.

The metaverse real estate NFT owner may rent, sell, or construct on his digital property after he has acquired it. After purchasing 20 virtual plots of land in Decentraland, the Japanese video game company Atari has opened a crypto casino. Gamers may wager and collect their winnings tax-free using the Atari token based on the ERC20 standard. As of 2022, Atari intends to create a virtual hotel complex of its own.

How Can You Invest in the Metaverse?

You might like to keep a closer eye on these options if you're looking for some of the best early stock choices in the Metaverse.

- Metaverse retail, it's possible, you could think. "Will Amazon be the next Amazon?" I don't know. However, there may be money to be

299

made for a firm that provides a tremendous virtual shopping experience for real-world items. It's also worth noting that the Walmart VR shopping video that went popular in 2017 was initially made in 2016!

- Already, fashion and style firms are laying claim to their territories. Nike (NKE) has made several patent applications to make it the dominant player in virtual footwear and clothes in the Metaverse.

- Next-generation VR headsets and other equipment are on the horizon. Oculus Quest, Sony's PSVR, and HP's Reverb are current players with inexpensive, consumer-focused headsets. IT corporations will develop the next generation of metaverse accessories.

- If the Metaverse ever comes to fruition, no matter who is in charge of its creation or what shape it takes, we can all agree that it would need massive amounts of processing power. As a result, companies including Amazon Web Services (AWS) and Microsoft Azure (Azure) may have possibilities.

- Nvidia, for example, is a company that makes the high-performance silicon required to run these servers.

- The conditions of the metaverse state that access will need fast internet connections and zero latency. A metaverse experience may be ruined by sluggishness and poor resolution. In addition to broadband and 5G network providers, content delivery networks will be a significant component of this equation (CDNs). Companies like Akamai Technologies (AKAM) and Fastly (FSLY) run data centers worldwide that store frequently requested material for users. Local consumers may get this material much more quickly than users halfway across the world can if they are linked directly to a provider like Netflix (NFLX) or Amazon. CDNs' revenue exploded during the pandemic as everyone got online, although it may be a blip compared to Metaverse's needs.

Further possibilities may arise as the Metaverse develops. Investment in this sector will need a combination of agility and caution. Numerous businesses will attempt to capitalize on the sudden popularity of the term "metaverse" by tying their brand to this cutting-edge technology. It's just a matter of time until some of these ideas come to fruition.

How to acquire land and other digital goods in the Metaverse

Several metaverse systems have established NFT markets where users may purchase and trade digital land and other valuables. Here's how you can do it.

- To acquire digital real estate in the Metaverse, a user must first choose which platform he intends to utilize. Decentraland and The Sandbox are two popular choices, but there is a slew of more. Before purchasing any territory in the Metaverse, do your study.

- You must build a digital cryptocurrency wallet that connects to the blockchain network, saves crypto, and is compatible with the related blockchain that drives the metaverse platform. The user must do this before using the metaverse platform.

- Once a buyer has picked a metaverse platform, he must log in to the marketplace and link his digital wallet to it. Metaverse platform websites often include marketplaces.

- Real estate purchases in the actual world look a lot like internet real estate purchases right now. A prospective buyer should think about the cost, the location, and the long-term potential of the digital property they're interested in acquiring.

- The buyer must first obtain tokens or money and keep them in his digital wallet to purchase land. To complete the transaction, a particular sort of token or currency is required. In Decentraland, for example, a user must acquire MANA tokens to purchase digital land. To acquire land in The Sandbox, he would need SAND tokens.

- As long as the buyer has previously joined and filled his digital wallet in the metaverse marketplace, placing a bid or purchasing the land outright is all that is required. An NFT (Non-Fungible Token) representing land will be taken from the digital wallet and transferred to the user's wallet.

- The same approach applies to purchasing additional Metaverse NFT things, such as avatar apparel and accessories.

Investment Strategies

What are Investment Strategies?
Long-term, short-term, retirement age, an industry of interest, projected return, level of risk, and other factors all factor into the decision-making process when developing an investment strategy. Investors can tailor their investment strategy to meet their objectives.
Types of Investment Strategies

Investment Strategies

Passive & Active Strategies

Value Investing

Indexing

Contrarian Investing

Growth Investing

Income Investing

Dividend Growth Investing

Passive and Active Strategies
The passive method calls for long-term ownership of equities rather than frequent purchases and sales to keep trading expenses low. Passive techniques are less hazardous since they think they cannot beat the market owing to its volatility. On the other hand, dynamic tactics need a lot of buying and selling. In their eyes, the market is overvalued, and they can earn more returns than ordinary investors do.

Growth Investing (Short-Term and Long-Term Investments)
It's up to investors to decide how long they want to keep their money in the stock market. As long as investors feel a firm will prosper and its stock's intrinsic worth rises, they will put money into it to increase their overall wealth. Growth investing is another term for this kind of investment. On the other hand, investors prefer short-term holdings if they feel a firm will be worth their money in a year or two. It is also up to the investors to decide how long they want to keep their money. For instance, how soon do they need money to purchase a home, send their children to school, or save for retirement?

Value Investing

Companies with high intrinsic value are good candidates for investing since the market undervalues them. With this strategy, investors are betting that when the market goes through its subsequent correction, undervalued firms will have their value corrected, causing their stock prices to soar and providing them with large profits when they decide to sell. Warren Buffet, a well-known investor, employs this tactic.

Income Investing

Instead of investing in companies that enhance the value of your portfolio, this sort of approach focuses on creating a steady flow of cash from your investments. Investing may provide two forms of cash income: dividends and fixed interest from bonds. Such a technique is preferred by investors seeking a consistent stream of returns on their assets.

Dividend Growth Investing

An investor who employs this approach seeks firms with a history of distributing dividends every year. Such dividends are reinvested by investors, who benefit from compounding over time. Firms that account for increasing dividend payouts year after year are more stable and less volatile than others because of their history of paying dividends.

Contrarian Investing

Investors may take advantage of this technique when the market is weak by purchasing shares in their favorite firms. This approach focuses on finding bargains and then reselling them for a profit. Most downturns in the stock market occur during economic uncertainty (such as recessions, wars, and natural disasters). There are times when investors might take advantage of a company's downturn by purchasing its shares. Investors should seek organizations that can provide value and have a strong brand that makes it difficult for their competitors to get an advantage over them.

Indexing

Investors may use this method to invest a modest portfolio in a market index. Mutual funds, ETFs, and the S&P 500 are examples of these.

Investing Tips

Some pointers to keep in mind before making their first investment for those just starting.

Set Goals

Decide how much money you'll need over the next several months or years. Make sure you know what kind of investments are best for you and how much you can anticipate in return before making any decisions.

Research and Trend Analysis
Prepare yourself by doing a thorough study on the stock market and its many instruments (equity, bonds, options, derivatives, mutual funds, etc.). Also, keep an eye on the price and return patterns of the stocks in which you've decided to put your money.

Portfolio Optimization:
Determine which of the several portfolios best suits your needs. An optimal portfolio provides the most potential return with the least possible risk.
Best Advisor/Consultancy:
Make sure you work with a reputable consulting business or broker. They will help you decide where and how to invest to achieve your financial goals.
Risk Tolerance
Be aware of the level of danger you're comfortable with to achieve your goals. Your short- and long-term objectives will play a role here, too. The risk is more considerable if you want a higher return in a shorter period and vice versa.
Diversify Risk
Create a diversified portfolio by combining debt, equity, and derivatives. The two securities should not be fully connected.

Passive and Active Investment Strategies

An Overview
Passive and active investing are two different ways to put your money to work in the market. In terms of benchmarks, both active and passive investing attempt to outperform the S&P 500, but active investment tries to beat the model while passive investing aims to replicate it.
Because investors and wealth managers generally prefer one technique over the other, any conversation regarding active vs. passive investing may rapidly develop into a heated disagreement. The advantages of active investing can't be discounted, even if the passive investment is more popular.

- A portfolio manager or other "active participant" must take an active role in the investment process for it to be considered "active."

- Investing passively means purchasing index funds or other mutual funds rather than individual stocks or bonds.
- Passive investments have attracted more significant investment flows than active investments, notwithstanding the advantages of both.
- An active investment strategy has historically yielded higher returns than passive investing.
- In recent years, active investing has grown more prevalent than at any time in recent memory.

What Is Active Investing?

An investment strategy that includes frequent trading to outperform the market's average returns is active investing. This comes to mind for many people when they think of trading on Wall Street. However, Robinhood and other applications like it allow you to trade from the comfort of your smartphone.

With mutual funds and exchange-traded funds (ETFs), you may perform your own active investing or have it done for you by experts (ETFs). These provide you with a pre-assembled investing portfolio with hundreds of potential assets already selected for you. Investment adviser and senior partner at Dugan Brown, an Ohio financial planning business, Kevin Dugan, argue that this form of investing often requires a high degree of market knowledge and skill to decide the ideal moment to acquire or sell [investments].

A wide variety of data is analyzed by active fund managers for each investment in their portfolios, from quantitative and qualitative data on securities to more extensive market and economic trends. Active fund managers. Managers use this information to take advantage of short-term price movements and keep the fund's asset allocation on track.

Investors' long-term objectives might be jeopardized if their carefully constructed, actively managed portfolios aren't constantly monitored for signs of market instability and short-term losses. This is why most investors, especially when it comes to long-term retirement funds, do not suggest active investment.

Advantages of Active Investing:
Flexibility in volatile markets
According to Brian Stivers, founder, and chief investment officer of Knoxville, Tennessee-based Stivers Financial Services, "the active investor may go to a defensive position or holdings, such as cash or government bonds, to avert catastrophic losses." Investors may also shift their portfolios to more shares in fast-growing economies by reallocating. For short-term gains, they may be able to outperform the S&P 500 and other market indexes that track long-term trends.
Expanded trading options
Trading tactics like hedging with options or shorting stock may help active investors boost their chances of beating market indices by producing windfalls. Using these tactics, the expenses and hazards connected with dynamic investing may be considerably increased. Thus they are better left to specialists and experienced investors.
Tax management
Harvesting of tax losses is what it's called. In the hands of a knowledgeable financial adviser or portfolio manager, active investing may be used to carry out transactions that reduce taxable profits. While tax-loss harvesting is possible with passive investing, the quantity of trading that occurs with active investment techniques may provide more chances and make it simpler to evade the wash-sale rule.

Disadvantages of Active Investing:
Higher fees
Since most stock and ETF purchases are routine, brokerages no longer impose trading fees. Fees may be incurred when using more complex, derivative-based trading techniques. There are additional costs associated with investing in actively managed funds. Actively managed funds have high-cost ratios, averaging 0.71 percent as of 2020 due to the quantity of research and trading needed.
Increased risk
Activist investors have a great chance of making a killing when they get it right. Using borrowed money—or margin—to invest might create catastrophic losses if one of your investments zigs when you zag.

Trend exposure

Knowing whether or not you're at the peak of the trend may be pretty strict regarding trend-based investment. Meme stocks and pandemic-related fitness crazes are two examples of trend-following movements quickly caught up in active trading. Peloton (PTON) was trading at $145 per share on January 4, 2021, when an investor decided they wanted to join in on the at-home training boom and purchased the stock. Home exercises have been a thing of the past once pandemic restrictions were eased in early November 2021.

What Is Passive Investing?

As the name suggests, passive investment is all on long-term asset acquisition. Hands-off investing refers to the process of selecting an asset and holding on to it through the ups and downs, with an end goal in mind, like retirement. Investments in index funds or ETFs, like the S&P 500 or the Nasdaq Composite, are typically passive methods, while active strategies concentrate on individual stocks. Investing in these funds may be done via a traditional brokerage account or through a Robo-advisor.

It's unnecessary to monitor passive investments daily since they are designed to mirror market performance. Especially when it comes to money, this results in cheaper costs and fewer transactions. As a result, it's a favorite of financial consultants when investing for retirement and other financial objectives.

If you're a long-term investor, you'll stick with it. As a result, passive investors can save a lot of money by limiting the number of transactions they make in their portfolios. The plan requires a long-term perspective. In other words, avoid the urge to react or predict the stock market's subsequent moves.

Investing in an index fund that tracks the S&P 500 or the Dow Jones Industrial Average is an excellent example of a passive strategy (DJIA). To keep up with the changing composition of these indexes, the index funds that track them sell the stock that is leaving and purchase the one that is entering the index. Because of this, when a business becomes large enough to be included in a primary index, it's a significant deal: As a result, the stock is guaranteed to be a core position in a large number of substantial mutual funds.

Advantages of Passive Investing:

Lower costs

Individual investors may benefit from decreased trade volumes associated with the passive investment. If that wasn't enough to convince you, passively managed funds have lower cost ratios than most active funds. Passive mutual funds had an average fee ratio of 0.06 percent in 2020; passive ETFs had an average expense ratio of 0.18 percent.

Decreased risk

It is common for passive techniques to invest in hundreds or even thousands of companies and bonds. This makes it simple to diversify your portfolio and reduces the risk that one lousy investment would wipe out your whole holdings. One terrible stock may wipe away considerable profits if you don't have enough diversity for active investing.

Increased transparency

With passive investment, what you see is what you get. An investment fund's name generally includes the index it seeks to monitor, and it will never own assets outside of that index. Contrary to popular belief, actively managed funds are not always as open about their strategies as they claim to be. Managers may even choose to keep some details under wraps to maintain a competitive advantage.

Higher average returns

Passive funds of all sorts nearly consistently outperform active funds in long-term performance. Index funds tracking firms of all sizes beat their functional equivalents during 20 years. Moreover, since 2011, half of the S&P Indices Versus Active (SPIVA) report from S&P Dow Jones Indices has done so, according to the most recent SPIVA report.

Disadvantages of Passive Investing:

It's not flashy

It's hard to beat active investing for adrenaline-pumping thrills that come from seeing a single stock soar in value.

No exit strategy in severe bear markets

Stivers warns against passive investing during market downturns since it is not designed to be exited quickly. There is no certainty that the market will rebound fast following a downturn, even though it has done so historically. As a result, it's critical to revisit your asset allocation frequently. As you reach the conclusion of your investment timeline and have less time to recover from a market decline, you may make your portfolio more conservative this way.

Small returns

As a rule, passive funds cannot outperform the market since their essential assets are locked in to follow the market's fluctuations. Unless the market booms, a passive fund may sometimes outperform the market, but it will never generate the significant returns that active managers want. However, more proactive managers might reap more enormous profits (see the chart below), but these advantages also come with increased risk.

Active vs. Passive Investing Example

A blend including both active and passive approaches is often considered the most effective strategy for investors. There are fee-only financial advisors in Ohio like Dan Johnson. Index funds appear to be the best option for his customers, who wish to escape the significant price volatility in the stock market.

Passive indexing is his preferred method, but as he points out, "Advisors don't have to choose between passive and active management. A portfolio's total risk may be reduced by combining the two."

He explains that he actively searches for ETF investment possibilities in the case of substantial cash reserves right after the market has taken a dip. It's possible for him to actively choose dividend-growing equities for retiring customers while yet adhering to a "buy and hold" philosophy. In return for their stock, firms pay out dividends to their shareholders, who get the money as a reward for their investment.

As a Boston-based financial manager, Andrew Nigrelli agrees. Budgeting is done per his planned targets. It isn't only the diminishing returns but the risk-adjusted returns as well. He prefers long-term passive investment indexing systems over individual companies and strongly encourages passive investing. When calculating a return on an investment, it's crucial to consider the risk involved in achieving that return.

It is possible to safeguard the customer by restricting the amount of money invested in particular industries or even certain firms when rapidly changing circumstances.

Active and passive investment have their place and time in most people's long-term savings plans for essential milestones like retirement. However, much pain both sides inflict on each other, and more advisers end up combining the two approaches.

Active or Passive Investment?

You may ask whether active investing is worth it for the ordinary investor, given that long-term passive investments tend to deliver better returns and cheaper expenses. For some investors, the answer is yes.

Wealth Preservation

Stivers argues active investment techniques might help investors who prioritize asset preservation overgrowth. For example, someone near retirement who lacks time to recover from massive losses or who is focused on establishing a consistent source of income instead of seeing steady long-term financial gains may benefit from an active approach.

Combination Strategies

According to Dugan, many investors might benefit from a mix of both active and passive investments. It is possible for investors who have both active and passive investments to utilize the active portfolios to protect themselves against a decline in the passive portfolio during a bull market. One advantage of a combination strategy is knowing that your passive, long-term plan (like your retirement funds) is on autopilot. In contrast, an active, short-term approach (like a taxable brokerage account) allows you to investigate trends without sacrificing your long-term objectives.

Short-Term and Long-Term Investment

There is no substitute for rapid wealth development in the financial markets. In reality, it's typically a drawn-out process that needs time, dedication, and careful attention on your part. You have two alternatives when it comes to investing your hard-earned money: short-term and long-term. The advantages and disadvantages of each investing strategy are unique.

Market experts recommend doing a thorough study before making any investment. It's possible that what another investor thinks is appropriate may not be in line with your entire investing strategy. As a result, you must consider your long-term financial objectives and risk tolerance.

Short-Term Investment

Investments with a time scale of fewer than five years are referred to as "short-term" because of the ease with which they may be converted to cash. After only three to twelve months, many short-term investments are sold or turned to money. CDs, money market accounts, high-yield savings accounts, government bonds, and Treasury bills are famous examples of short-term investments. Most of the time, these investments are high-quality and easily accessible assets or investment vehicles.

The phrase "short-term investments" may also apply to financial assets held by a firm, which are of a similar kind but have a few extra conditions. These are investments made by a firm that is anticipated to be turned into cash within a year and they are kept separate from other assets and included in the section for current assets on the company's financial statements.

- Marketable securities and transitory investments are other terms for short-term financial assets, which may often be converted to cash within five years.
- If a corporation expects to sell its short-term assets within a year, they're considered short-term investments, too.
- Treasury bills and short-term assets like certificates of deposit (CDs) are typical examples of short-term investments.
- A lower return rate is expected from short-term investments because of their high liquidity, which allows for swift withdrawals in an emergency.
- The quarterly income statement reflects any changes in the value of a company's short-term assets.

How Short-Term Investment Works
For businesses and individual or institutional investors, a short-term investment's primary purpose is capital preservation while simultaneously yielding a return comparable to a Treasury bill index fund or another comparative benchmark.
A short-term investments account will be listed on a company's balance sheet. Consequently, the corporation can afford to invest surplus funds in stocks, bonds, and similar instruments to earn more income than would be available from a standard savings account.
Two essential prerequisites exist for a corporation to categorize an investment as short-term. To begin, it should be easy to trade, such as stock on a well-known market or a Treasury bond. Second, the company's management must intend to sell the security within a short period, such as a year. Investments having a maturity of one year or less, such as Treasury bills and commercial paper, are also considered "short-term paper" or marketable debt instruments.

Equity securities that may be sold on the open market include ordinary and preferred stock shares. To be called liquid, marketable debt assets, such as corporate bonds, must have short maturity dates and be regularly traded. Examples of Short-Term Investment

Money market accounts
These FDIC-insured accounts provide higher returns than savings accounts, but only if you put a certain amount of money into them. Make sure you understand the difference between FDIC-insured money market accounts and mutual funds.
Treasuries:
Notes, bills, and Treasury Inflation-Protected Securities are examples of government-issued bonds (TIPS).
Bond funds:
These funds, offered by professional asset managers or investment firms, are superior for a shorter period since they give greater returns than average for the risk. Remember to budget for them.
Municipal bonds:
Non-federal government entities that issue these bonds may provide greater yields and tax benefits since they are frequently excluded from income taxes.

Long-Term Investment
A company's assets, such as stocks, bonds, real estate, and cash, are included on the asset side of the balance sheet as long-term investments. It is essential to distinguish between short-term and long-term investments. Investments in the short term are often sold. However, long-term investments may never be sold.
To be a long-term investor, you must be ready to take on some risk in exchange for the possibility of more significant gains, as well as the ability to be patient over an extended period. It also implies that you have the financial resources to keep a fixed sum of money for a lengthy period.

- If a corporation intends to hold on to a long-term investment like stocks, bonds, or real estate for a year or more, it is a long-term investment.

- The account is included on the company's balance sheet as an asset.

- Generally speaking, long-term investors are more ready to take on more risks in exchange for more significant gains.

- On the other hand, short-term investments are supposed to be sold within a year.

How Long-Term Investment Works

It's a systematic long-term investment strategy where one firm invests a substantial amount of money in another company but does not own a majority stake in it. The acquisition cost would be considered an investment in the long run.

Investments made by holding companies or other businesses are classified as either short-term or long-term. This classification has a significant impact on the assets' balance sheet value. If the value of a short-term investment decreases, a loss is recorded.

It isn't until after the object has been sold that the rise in value becomes apparent. As a result, the net income recorded on the income statement is directly impacted by the investment categorization on the balance sheet, whether long-term or short-term.

Examples of Long-Term Investment

Stocks

- There is a tangible representation of a portion of a company's worth in the form of stock options. Investors are invited to participate in a company's Initial Public Offering (IPO). After the initial public offering (IPO), the company's stock is traded on the stock market.

- It is the most refined technique to get the most money from the stock market. Stock investments are the best of all investing options when it comes to long-term returns. Stock trading has brought simpler in the digital era.

- Investing in stocks requires extensive knowledge of the market. If you want to succeed in the stock market, you'll need to keep tabs on the latest trends.

- Choose a reputable financial partner if you wish to invest in stocks and securities and create an online Demat Account and a trading account online. If you can find them, search for unmatched advantages like brokerage cashback, free AMC periods for Demat Account, and zero-cost Demat Account creation. In addition to maintaining a single

Demat account for all of your investments, you need also make sure that you are receiving the most critical market information to maximize your profit potential.

Equity mutual funds
Investments for the long-term are an excellent way to generate more money. Investment in small and midcap equities mutual funds may help you reach your financial objectives over the long run.
Short- or Long-Term Investment?

- A clear winner cannot be found. Both investments have pros and cons. To reach your financial objectives in a short period, short-term investments are ideal. On the other hand, long-term investments are an option for investors willing to take on more risk in exchange for better returns.

- Short-term investments are a good option if you're looking to protect your money and are OK with minimal returns. However, if you want to see your money grow, you should look at long-term investing options.

Risk Tolerance in the Metaverse Investing

Doing business in the Metaverse will have its challenges, to be sure. In the Metaverse's early years, up to 2035, this will be especially true for forays into new business categories or investments in new channels.
Unpredictable user engagement
While 2D applications and desktop participation may be possible in the Metaverse, virtual reality (VR) will be the primary mode of interaction. Despite this, the number of VR headset shipments continues to be modest compared to the entire global population and social media users. A person's tastes and health circumstances may impact responding to virtual reality (VR). Businesses may find it challenging to attract a global audience.

Shifting value of crypto

Blockchain will be used in many metaverse commercial transactions, whether in cryptocurrencies or non-fungible tokens (NFTs). Even while crypto values are known to fluctuate considerably from day to day, the Metaverse as a whole may suffer from this. NFTs may not be as dependable as real-world transactions when making large-scale investments. If, for example, a customer pays for an NFT, they may be unable to change the work lawfully. This may put customers off.

Portability to the physical world

Businesses operating in the Metaverse face this danger. Consequently, they might find themselves in an area where they are only accessible to a tiny percentage of the world's population.

If metaverse native enterprises fail to be sustainable in the long run, we might be looking at a situation similar to the dot-com boom of the 1990s.

Decentralized therefore deregulated

Most observers, analysts, and developers agree that a genuinely decentralized metaverse is impossible. No one will control it, and it will be completely open and democratic. However, this also implies that it will be challenging to manage the Metaverse. Even if the regulatory agencies had adequately stringent laws, it would be impossible to enforce because of its decentralized design. SMEs, in particular, would be put in danger if there was no regulation.

Chapter 7:

The Metaverse and its Implications on our Digital Future

It might be possible that the 21st century will be remembered for building and growing the virtual world or Metaverse since the past century was known for mass industry and internet rise. More immersive, dynamic, and team-based than the internet has ever been, this new technology is set to revolutionize how we work and communicate. Although many businesses participating in this arena has excellent promises, it has become evident that blockchain technology will underlie the Metaverse and help build a sustainable environment for all stakeholders. Traditional professions and hobbies will not be unaffected by the Metaverse, but society and the way people interact with one another will be profoundly altered. Internet and Work from Home (WFH) technological assistance were essential in keeping businesses viable during COVID-19's global epidemic and allowing them to grow at a fast pace. After the epidemic, several industries, such as education, saw major transformations, becoming more reliant on new technologies.

Wearable virtual reality technology introduced by the Metaverse can significantly reshape these industries. From the relief of their own homes, individuals may enter a new virtual world via the usage of these wearables. In the coming times, people will not have to carry long distances, breathe in pollution. This means that children could grasp the knowledge at their own tempo and broaden their horizons beyond what is now available with regular school curricula. In the virtual world, habits such as watching movies or socializing with friends after work will be possible without the inconveniences of the real world. In other words, the Metaverse opens up an infinite number of options.

As part of a recent announcement by technology startup Together Labs, the VCORE token, an ERC-20 token that rewards gamers, producers, and earners throughout the Metaverse, will be accessible to anyone outside of the United States and Canada. As soon as 2022, VCORE's users will have access to a new sort of economy that will allow everyone to participate in the Metaverse development. However, like with any ecosystem, the Metaverse's ability to operate will rely on how simple individuals can trade in the environment. Here, cryptocurrencies come in and have already started the ball rolling by facilitating real-world and digital transactions via numerous initiatives. The ability to effortlessly convert fiat monies to cryptocurrencies will make it much easier for users to move between the real world and the Metaverse. Customers will use crypto tokens issued by organizations supporting these virtual connections to buy digital avatars and virtual land and arrange parties for loved ones.

Artists will perform in the Metaverse, get paid in cryptocurrencies, and use those funds to buy items in the real world. The emergence of the Metaverse might lead to a fast increase in the global economy as more value is discovered. According to vampire CEO Dominic Ryder, Metaverse is the next logical step in the evolution of how humans engage with technology. Sandboxes and other choices are available (for creative minds and gamers that want to build experiences). There is also a Decentraland, which is becoming a center for many kinds of activities. Other models and platforms that are similarly successful in the digital arena include Axie Infinity and Starl. Because so many people have been forced to work remotely and digitally due to the epidemic, I feel this trend is now in overdrive. According to Ryder's prediction, people will start spending more time outside of work in the Metaverse. With digital commodities like Non-Fungible Tokens (NFTs) resembling popular art and digital artefacts already in existence, the Metaverse has already begun taking shape. It's only a matter of time until other major businesses like Meta Platforms Inc. join this domain and firmly announce that it may be a new reality. An exponential extension of the Metaverse's borders might open up enormous new markets for consumers and investors alike.

To better represent Meta's goal of "putting the metaverse into life and helping individuals connect, build communities, and develop enterprises," the firm announced in October that it would change its name to Meta. There was no shortage of conjecture and discussion in the event of the global most valuable firms making such a significant turn.

Moving towards greater adoption

Virtual reality has been in the works for a long time, much as artificial intelligence has been developing for a long time. In the mid-1800s, stereoscopes enabled 3D encounters with drawings and images. In the 1960s, Hollywood experimented with immersive cinema experiences, such as the Sensorama, to see what might happen. The Air Force's budget supported the development of 3D flight simulators in the 1970s. The "Eyephone," an early pair of VR goggles produced and marketed in the late 1980s, may be humorous in its naming.

Recent research suggests that since 2000, interest in and technological capability for these immersive experiences has increased. I believe this to be the case. In a year, Fortnite gained 100 million new players, pushing the total number of registered players to 350 million. Second Life, a virtual environment founded in 2002, only had 1 million registered users after four years. When Second Life launched in 2006, it had a user base of only 0.08 percent of the internet's total population. By 2020, Fortnite's user base is expected to be at least 8 percent. As a tourist attraction, Fortnite would be one of the most visited places on Earth. To put things in perspective, 145 million people visited China in 2019, while roughly 80 million people visited the United States. Even so, players of Fortnite don't have to leave their homes to go on a trip.

Do people Adapt to this technology?

Without sounding like a visionary, I believe the epidemic only expedited what may have already been underway in our organizational reality: a change from single-location corporate campuses to more regionally spread teams and organizations.

There is no way everyone will work remotely. Still, as technology becomes better at enabling dispersed work and social experiences and becomes more accessible, a significant number of individuals are likely to work from where they are most productive. This group of employees is more like to devote more time to any technology that allows them to achieve their ideal work environment. With these skills and knowledge, those who remain in the main office will also be able to adapt.

A Better Understanding

It is important for leaders to grasp the digital platforms on which metaverses are created to comprehend how they will impact the future of work in the digital age. A "walled garden" architecture means that Facebook intends to own and profit from all user data created by its Metaverse. Metaverses that are open, decentralized, and designed to respect the privacy and liberties of people who use and inhabit the technology are already being built. It's imperative that businesses are ready for the emergence of positions that don't exist yet.

The contrast between "open" and "closed" is crucial to comprehend how the internet is growing, thereby affecting the fundamental nature of employment. Because of the emergence of new employment categories necessitated by the coming together of metaverses, digital platforms, cryptocurrency, data analytics, and decentralized and open apps, the internet will undergo a transformation. The fact that many metaverses will be open and decentralized implies that every firm will have to comprehend how their present business models, even if they are digital, will be challenged. In-game digital stuff and real-world commodities like music, art, and apparel may all be tokenized on the DAT platform from Reality Gaming Group. Companies will have to reconsider how they provide value to consumers in a future where intellectual property ownership is dispersed among members of metaverse communities as a consequence of this.

A new Architecture of Work

Prior to that, executives must work with their teams to create a shared vision for the organization's future. This is an in-depth knowledge of digital platform logic and design and how digital systems combine into a coherent and scalable enterprise-wide architecture. Architects with extensive expertise in blockchain, artificial intelligence, computer vision, data analytics, quantum computing, and high-speed networks will be needed to drive digital transformation initiatives in organizations.

The nature of metaverses is that the volume and quality of personal data gathered and analyzed will increase exponentially. To support strategic-level decision-making, organizations will need metaverse analysts who can apply artificial intelligence and deep analytical tools. Metaverse marketing and branding, business development, and innovation professionals will need to engage with these architects to revamp their company's product and service offerings as well as virtual reality consumer experiences, as well as find new markets and business models.

Facebook's own research shows that consumers are hesitant about merging their social media presence with their professional life in such an invasive way. As a result, organizations will have to show that their data is safe from the next generation of quantum computers by understanding the importance of health and safety in immersive digital environments. They'll also need to incorporate metaverse expertise into their governance structure to prevent employees from being subjected to oppressive management methods such as excessive surveillance and dehumanizing control.

Using Metaverse technology, individuals will communicate and work online in new and exciting ways. Workers who spend too much time in virtual worlds will experience burnout if leaders don't take steps to prevent this picture of the future of work from becoming a reality. Rather than focusing on the home-workplace divide, hybrid working will focus on creating a balance between the virtual and real worlds. Healthy metaverse working practices will need new hybrid policies from human resources. Customers and workers alike will benefit from the potential of metaverses, which may be used as tremendous creative canvases for organizations.

Companies that can attract a new generation of brilliant transdisciplinary metaverse experts by concentrating on the human element as much as the technological and developing purposeful innovation cultures based on a more humanized and aware approach to work will thrive in the future.

Anti-abuse efforts

Individuals' emotional and physical health are adversely affected by this abuse, and it has the potential to push people away from online platforms. Because of the Metaverse's immersive and lasting character, it is reasonable to assume that online abuse will be much more of a concern in these locations. Because virtual reality can blur the distinction between what's real and what isn't, research shows that virtual reality abuse is "much more devastating than in other digital environments." It took three punches to the face of a researcher's avatar for her to recoil into a kneeling posture in her office, her mind and body recognizing the blows as genuine. She was plagued by "intrusive thoughts" for weeks following due to post-traumatic stress disorder.

Keeping hatred and abuse out of sophisticated virtual worlds will be one of the major problems for corporations in the years to come, given how poorly they've done so far. This, however, must be a key concern. These virtual worlds must be built to keep people secure and stop the violence that is prevalent on social media. However, until firms can properly regulate abuse on a large scale, the Metaverse will be another digital area where hatred may flourish unless it can generate exciting new avenues for people to interact and find a community.

In order to ensure compatibility
Sir Tim Berners-Lee developed the website to be a place where anybody could come and share their thoughts and ideas. "This is for everyone," he said on Twitter during the 2012 Olympic Opening Ceremony.
No one firm should have exclusive control over the Metaverse, which should be developed as an open field rather than a walled garden. There will be several metaverses, not just one. So that we don't end up with distinct digital bounds but instead may wander smoothly between virtual places with the same avatars and other digital assets. We need common standards and interoperability. We have the Metaverse Interoperability Community at W3C (web standards organization) and other interoperability initiatives creating the foundations for this. These and other organizations' activities will significantly affect the Metaverse's eventual form. There is still a considerable distance to go before this becomes a reality, but the digital future might be much more interesting if it does.

Enabling access
Beyond the thrill of a potential future, there is the fact that over one-third of the globe is still without a basic internet connection, and even fewer have the significant connection necessary to make most of the internet access. So, we must not ignore the critical imperative to link individuals still unable to access online.

A select few will only utilize the Metaverse in the future; it will not be the main mode of communication for most people. Because of the exorbitant prices of technology and the bandwidth needed to utilize it, most of the world's population cannot afford it. In nations where the UN Broadband Commission's "1 for 2" cost requirement for basic internet access has not yet been met, more than a billion people are still without it.

To ensure that the online we have is accessible and powerful for everyone, we must first and foremost work on that. That implies an all-out campaign to link the globe and acknowledge and ensure internet access as a human right. Because if we don't, we'll have a generation of young people exploring the Metaverse before millions of others have ever seen a website.

Metaverse jobs exists in future

Do you recall how things ended in 2016? There were those who believed that Pokémon GO represented the beginning of a new era in augmented reality. This hasn't come to fruition. When it comes to Facebook and Meta, we have a similar argument today about how much money they're pouring into the creation of a completely immersive digital environment for us all to inhabit.

Workers now have a plethora of easy alternatives to conventional jobs because of the advent of emerging technology. While Zoom has revolutionized the remote and hybrid workplace, the emergence of the Metaverse has the potential to be the last game-changing innovation. Wearing goggles and entering a new virtual world isn't simply a fun and entertaining notion; the Metaverse has a profound relationship to virtual reality and game-based learning. Globally, the economies of popular virtual worlds such as Fortnite, Roblox, and Minecraft are comparable to those of tiny nations. These virtual worlds and the Metaverse will play what role?

It's hard to avoid the feeling that our Tech Overlords' intent to have a functional Metaverse is a self-fulfilling prophesy when many people invest in it. Because I'm an expert on the future of work, I've looked at this potential and asked myself, "what kinds of occupations may the Metaverse create?"

The following are some first ideas.

- Metaverse Research Scientist
- Metaverse Planner
- Ecosystem Developer
- Metaverse Safety Manager
- Metaverse Hardware Builder
- Metaverse Storyteller
- World Builder
- Ad-Blocking Expert
- Metaverse Cyber-Security
- Unpaid Intern

The Future of Work and Society in the Metaverse
In the world of technology, fad terms come and go. Some of them, though, choose to remain. The Metaverse is the new term, and it's here to stay. What is the Metaverse, exactly? It describes (paywall) a future where our daily activities go beyond the confines of a single reality and into the realms of augmented and virtual reality. Virtual reality, augmented reality, and other cutting-edge digital simulations have all been incorporated into this concept throughout time. When Mark Zuckerberg outlined his vision for Facebook's long-term strategy earlier this year, it was a bold one. He envisioned the social network becoming a supplier of next-level digital and virtual experiences rather than just a linked family of social applications. Ball, a venture investor, wrote an article in January 2020 that attempted to define the Metaverse. Interoperability, which would allow users to utilize their characters and things from one platform or Metaverse to another, was also mentioned in this list of features, which included both the real and virtual worlds. The Metaverse is the sci-fi idea that is closest to fulfillment, considering how many components of its consumers may already experience today if there is one thing that is true.

So, what can we expect from our future if the Metaverse takes over as the norm? Cryptocurrency and digital money are anticipated to become the primary means of transacting in the Metaverse, which has its economy. The number of digital currencies is expected to grow as new ones are created regularly. Either way, these digital currencies will be essential for cross-border trade, and they'll be backed and disseminated by cutting-edge technology like blockchain.

Companies like Epic, the maker of the popular Fortnite video game, are among the early adopters of this new economy. The game has radically reimagined virtual gaming by building a compelling, genuine environment. The concerts that the game held, like those with Travis Scott and, more recently, Ariana Grande, were among the largest measures that the game took to ignite the Metaverse. As the borderline between the digital and the real become more blurred, other businesses will be quick to follow suit.

It's secure to say that the Metaverse will have an effect on how individuals do their jobs, if not entirely rewrite them. Even before Covid-19, it was clear that this epidemic would be a major challenge for the business world, moving work and workers to remote cooperation and driving individuals to integrate their actual and virtual identities. Platforms like Zoom and Slack, which allow remote and time-diverse cooperation, have risen even more suddenly in recent years, and they've proven crucial in the struggle for high levels of engagement and productivity in challenging times. Some things will never change, and one of those things is the fact that individuals have realized that working remotely opens the door to new prospects for cooperation, development, and success, even if it all sounded daunting at the beginning of the worldwide epidemic. For both workers and employers, Metaverse's work environment of the future is highly automated, streamlined, and user-friendly.

The world of business will never be the same again. It is just a matter of time until internet shopping and delivery become the new norm after the epidemic. Before making a purchase, customers won't have to visit actual shops to test new items in person. Users will be able to learn more about companies and products from the comfort of their own homes with the help of virtual reality and augmented reality experiences. It will also allow for more engaging in-store experiences, thanks to the Metaverse. Whether a product is in stock or not, customers will be able to test it out in the shop using VR and AR headsets. Those possibilities are no longer speculative - they've been for some time now. For the most part, we aren't even aware of the Metaverse's existence until we use apps like Snapchat. The future is already here, even if people aren't aware of it yet, as seen by bespoke filters that enable marketers to engage with customers on a deeper level and a Snapchat survey that suggests users want to see more interactive content like this. The Metaverse is just one of many buzzwords in the IT industry, but unlike many others, it has roots in society. The Metaverse is no longer a sci-fi future, thanks to Covid-19, which is accelerating large-scale digitalization and making people throughout the globe immerse themselves in the digital world. The likelihood of this possibility coming to fruition is higher than any other.

Race of Tech Companies to build the Metaverse
CEO of Microsoft has said that the business is focusing on creating the "corporate metaverse." According to Nadella, "We're leading in a new layer of infrastructure stack—the corporate metaverse"—with the digital and physical worlds merging. In April, a $1 billion investment round for Epic Games' metaverse plans was disclosed. Work and the workplace will undergo a fundamental shift as a result of tech corporations' ferocity in populating this new digital frontier. Rather than using Zoom calls, the Metaverse lets you communicate with your colleagues in a virtual world that is almost as immersive as the real thing. It's possible to buy a home, play video games, communicate with pals, go to concerts, and shop for things.

According to Zoom CEO Eric Yuan, virtual reality will play a huge part in the future of work, incredibly remote employment. So far, multiplayer video games have mostly served as the primary entry point into the Metaverse. Last year's virtual Travis Scott concert, which was attended by more than 12 million people and remained the most explicit demonstration of the Metaverse's possibilities, gave many Fortnite players their first glimpse of the proto-metaverse.

Facebook CEO Mark Zuckerberg noted in a Facebook post that "in the future, working together will be one of the key ways people utilize the metaverse." In a virtual conference on the future of work, Yuan remarked, "We're not there yet," because "the headgear is too heavy, and there's no eye contact." PwC technology head Scott Likens says that the main barrier to the broad adoption of virtual Reality in the workplace is a perception that it's just for gaming and a worry that it's too complicated.

Business Profit

Digital transformation may be facilitated through immersive technology, as shown at the Global HR Summit in 2016.

For the three-day conference, 50 presenters wore Oculus Quest headsets, and virtual participants may either bring their own headsets or use their laptops to participate in the immersive environment. It was noticed that shipping headsets to all 50 presenters were much less expensive than flying speakers out, providing lodging, and other conference-related fees. A shared, virtual economy necessitates new approaches to marketing for businesses.

Companies will have to do metaverse market research to learn more about their new clients. Cathy Hackl, a digital futurist and speaker with experience in AR/VR and the Metaverse, says that although there will be commercials in the Metaverse, businesses may genuinely be part of developing the Metaverse itself.

Four Dominating Metaverse Projects in the Future

Since Facebook's announcement that it would create the Metaverse and change its name to Meta Platform Inc., Metaverse has gained significant notoriety. The Sandbox is one of several beginnings in the crypto community working on expanding the concept of the "metaverse" (SAND).

Since Mark Zuckerberg renamed his firm Meta, the value of the crypto SAND has risen precipitously in tandem with the stratospheric surge in popularity of the Metaverse. As a prelude to that, a significant cryptocurrency-gaming metaverse initiative is worth noting. The following are four well-known metaverse initiatives scheduled to begin in 2021:

A Sandbox for Experimentation (SAND)

The Sandbox, conceived initially as a mobile game for the year 2021, is now a more sophisticated Ethereum-based game. In the Sandbox, users may explore a virtual metaverse populated with non-fungible tokens (NFT), user-created environments, and more. Ethereum (ETH) and The Sandbox (SAND) tokens are also used for transactions in The Sandbox. The usage of ETH and SAND will support the in-game economy.

As a bonus, users of The Sandbox game may design their avatar and digital persona. The Metaverse's central notion includes this idea. It is also possible for gamers to manage their NFT, SAND token, and other blockchain assets directly from their wallet. Players may even design their own virtual games and objects using the VoxEdit and Game Maker tools to convert them to NFTs. As a result, players of The Sandbox may barter for and sell these products to get some extra cash.

The Decentraland region (MANA)

As the name implies, Decentraland is a three-dimensional virtual space. Virtual parcels of land may be grown, events like music concerts can be staged, and social activities can also be held there. The primary token of Decentraland is MANA, which is based on Ethereum's ERC-20 protocol. There are many unique goods in Decentraland, and they are all assigned digital identities and a limited supply through the blockchain. One of the most well-known initiatives before the metaverse craze of late 2021 was Decentraland. Esteban Ordano and Ari Meilich launched Decentraland in 2016 and worked on the project ever since. Sharing high-priced NFT products between the two allowed them to create a wider virtual environment in 3D.

We are developing the Metaverse using Decentraland. This is because Decentraland already has a propensity to lead to the virtual world than others, including Facebook. With a 3D UI, digital economy, social components, and a variety of in-game events, Decentraland was built from scratch. The LAND that Decentraland is famous for is a kind of virtual property.

Cylinder of the Engine (ENJ)

This Engine, unlike MANA and SAND, focuses more on producing NFT goods for usage in the game. In light of the fact that NFT assets are by far the most significant aspect of the Metaverse, this project has successfully developed an SDK to make the creation of Ethereum-based NFTs easier for the general public.

Printing NFT on the Engine means that users don't have to spend time searching for a buyer for their NFTs. The NFT of Enjin may be traded for ENJ, the primary currency of Enj. Because of this, a switch from NFT to ENJ provides immediate liquidity. The Engine can become the essential aspect of the metaverse business because of these benefits.

Bloktopia (BLOCK)

Bloktopia offers a VR metaverse game with a 21-story building named Reblok, similar to The Sandbox and Decentraland. In other words, there will be a total of 21 million Bitcoins in circulation. In Bloktopia, you'll find an event center, a place to meet, work, socialize, and so on. It is possible to rent out each Reblock floor. This is where Bloktopia differs. Bloktopia is based on the Polygon network (MATIC) to support its four most critical points: learn. The first of the four primary factors mentioned above is learning. There will be a place where people can learn about blockchain and help the Metaverse. This project offers an interactive approach to studying cryptography.

BLOK native tokens, Reblok virtual real estate, and Adblok, a place for advertisements, are all used in the second model, called "earn." Players in Bloktopia will be rewarded with BLOCK tokens and goodies. Bloktopia's Metaverse allows gamers to interact online while playing the third game. Other users' games and material are also available for users to enjoy. Last but not least, it has been made. Bloktopia has supplied tools for players to develop their own digital environment and advertising space as a promotional tool.

Conclusion

Metaverse is three-dimensional if you have a two-dimensional Internet experience; that is, if you can scroll and browse across the Internet on a single screen, then Metaverse. To put it another way, this implies that you'll be able to use linked glasses or headphones to move around it as well as scroll and browse through it. The fact that Metaverse does not exist now makes it more difficult to grasp. Many people are intrigued about it and want to know how it will influence their internet use. There are a lot of firms talking about it, and people want to know more about it. I don't know whether there will be a single Metaverse or several Metaverses at this point. On the other hand, Metaverse is the next step in the evolution of cyberspace. It is most likely to be ready by augmented or virtual reality technology. As a result, Meta (Facebook) has said that Metaverse would be available for business and social situations. Microsoft's efforts are geared toward the virtual office environment.

The whole notion is fresh, and a sci-fi author included it in his story that talked about humans being represented by numerous avatars that allowed them to speak with others. Additionally, I've run across several folks who are trying to explain the Metaverse to me. Instead of giving you my definition, I'm here to describe a few aspects and what you may anticipate from the Metaverse. Take a quick look at this. The likelihood of other civilizations in the cosmos may be a response to the question, "Why has no civilization contacted us?" As a result of civilizations taking sanctuary in virtual worlds after they have advanced enough. According to what I've read, the actual world is too hostile and vast to be investigated. Our culture may be just beginning to follow this trend if that is the case. Building our Metaverse is still in its infancy.

Real-world multiverses include our own and any number of other universes, whether or not they are in some way related to our own. We might think of a metaverse in virtual reality as a collection of distinct worlds formed by different applications, games, or simulations. Metaverse is a virtual universe that is constantly evolving and expanding. Using this approach, you can accomplish almost whatever you want. When you do this, you're behaving as if you're immersed in a virtual world. There's no limit to what you can do with the virtual environment. In Cape Town, South Africa, you may pretend to be a New Yorker even when you're really in Cape Town. You may pretend to be a pilot and fly jets across the globe while working as a banker at the back of a counter in real life. The Metaverse, on the other hand, will enable you to create the world you've always wanted to live in and experience it in a virtual setting. Almost everything is possible in your freshly constructed fantasy universe. And how does Meta intend to do this? Utilizing virtual and augmented reality technologies. As a result, Meta will be subsidizing the fee so that many individuals may join the Metaverse. Thus far, the Metaverse seems to be a fascinating piece of technology from what we've learned. Metaverse is much more than simply a collection of different gaming realms. It's a hybrid of virtual, augmented, and real-world elements. To put it another way, the Greek word meta, which means beyond, is the root of the term "metaverse."

Nevertheless, as with any modern technology, there are pluses and minuses. To begin with, let's look at the positives.

Potential Positives of the Metaverse

We'll start with "Experience" since it's the first thing that comes to mind when discussing the Metaverse.

Experience

In the Metaverse, you have the freedom to be anybody or anything you wish. All of your desires and aspirations may come true. You're taken to a new degree of immersion in this environment. Among other options, you may play the part of the finest chef in the world in the morning and then go to the Bahamas for some surfing in the afternoon. As if you were there, you may do all these things from the comfort of your own home. As a result, we arrive at our second "Expression."

Expression

We use DPs, or cover photos, for all of our social media accounts. When someone visits our profile, this is the first thing they see. The Metaverse, on the other hand, gives you a full-fledged Avatar rather than merely a DP. It is a 3D representation of oneself. However, you are able to design and change it to suit your needs. You may get taller, gain weight, and wear whatever kind of clothing you like. Anything goes when it comes to who you can be in this world. Avatars, it's been said, won't only look like cartoons; they'll be more like real-life photographs of you. As a result, the experience will be more authentic. As a result, you won't feel confined to the physique you were born with. This is a whole other level of communicating with others regarding what you have to say.

Now we're getting to "Teleportation," an intriguing benefit of the Metaverse. It is possible to make persons born with severe impairments normal again. These folks have the power to develop the person they've always wanted to be.

Teleportation

You may construct your own house, office, and more in the Metaverse and invite others to visit. Teleportation in the Metaverse is considerably more exciting if you like video calls. Consider creating a virtual home or workplace where you can invite people to join you. Their near-live avatars will allow them to join, and you may converse as if you were all in the same room. As a result, teleportation in the Metaverse is simply a single click away. You really shouldn't need to do anything more than setting up the place and distributing the URL to your friends. That's how easy and quick it is.

Knowledge and Study

Library borrowing was the primary method of gathering information and learning new things prior to the Internet age. That's where Google came in. With the click of a button, you can find everything you need using the Google search function. The Metaverse may overtake Google. You may learn about items in the Metaverse by examining and touching them. And this information will be given to you more graphically and engagingly. Alternatively, you might go off on a trip of your own to learn about the world around you.

You'll be able to do more in less time if you learn quicker. Aside from this, Metaverse's "Fast and Improved Productivity" is yet another beneficial feature.

Fast and Improved Productivity

In the Metaverse, productivity will increase as well as speed up. There is no restriction to where you may work, thanks to the latest technology. You may choose to be in a quiet spot if you like the sound of nothingness. It's also possible that you like listening to music when you're at your desk? Create the atmosphere you choose.

To put it differently, you have absolute control over the conditions in which you do your best. As an added benefit, the Metaverse is advertised as having a more rapid input mechanism. Instead of writing with a pen or typing on a keyboard, you may just think about what you want to say and then speak it out loud. That one is in the works, but we still have a long way to go before we can get there.

Safer Environment

A significant environmental issue is the release of Carbon Dioxide by businesses and cars. Fortunately, with the Metaverse, this will all change. For starters, you'll use fewer physical automobiles, which means fewer emissions of greenhouse gas carbon dioxide. In addition, the Metaverse's virtual teleportation capability means that you won't even need a vehicle there. Consequently, fewer automobiles, aircraft, and trucks may be required. As a result, will there be fewer industrial enterprises and a reduction in carbon dioxide emissions? Possibly. Digital items will be increasingly popular as more people enter the Metaverse, increasing the number of people who spend money on the Metaverse.

New Economy

The Horizon marketplace is being designed by Meta in the Metaverse. You don't need to know how to code to sell on this marketplace. You may charge consumers to test out your virtual goods and services, like as clothing or a whole new virtual experience. It's not going to be an issue. Imagination and coding abilities are all you need. A new group of people will be able to profit from the Metaverse. Your firm may go to the Metaverse and meet a lot of potential clients. The Metaverse concept is, to put it mildly, a lot of fun. Digital items may be sold in order to generate revenue. It allows you to connect with anybody, create and experience anything, and earn money. It's like you're in a whole other world. However, it has its own drawbacks, and we'll begin with "Addiction."

Potential Negatives of the Metaverse
Addiction

That time spent playing games, watching movies, making TikTok videos and even streaming films is already a topic of discussion. A whole lot more so when you consider the concept of Metaverse.

Think about it: Who would want to swiftly depart a setting that they've worked so hard to create? In other words, they're living the life of their dreams, looking great, traveling the world, and doing anything they want. It's all too simple to get disengaged from the actual world and begin to favor the virtual one over your own. Even adults may fall prey to this, and we may end up needing a slew of restrictions to keep it under control.

Inferiority Complex and Depression

Already, we notice how social media images engender dissatisfaction with certain aspects of the human body. The number of youngsters worldwide who have had cosmetic surgery to improve their appearance has increased over the last several years. Nonetheless, what happens if you live in a dream world where you build the ideal body then return to reality to discover that your body is still you?

It's as easy as realizing you're not who you imagined yourself to be in the Metaverse when you exit the Metaverse. Your height and weight aren't what you want them to be in real life. With time, despair will set in, and you'll find yourself spending more time in the Metaverse than you'd want to in the actual world. I'm not implying that this is a certainty, but there is a possibility. Imagine yourself in the shoes of a person with a life-threatening illness. Until he returns to the real world, the Metaverse seems to be ideal, but what happens when he exits the virtual world?

Data Security

Is there a drawback to this world's openness and sharing of information? I mean, if you want to join the Metaverse, you'll have to share a lot of details with Meta. How you act and what you're interested in on a much broader scale are examples of this. Meta has a poor track record of data management, as seen by its past. To put it mildly, giving up all of this information is a bad decision. It's also possible that someone else may get access to your private information in the event of a data breach.

Denying Reality

In the Metaverse, you may build your reality, but who decides what is genuine and what isn't? In other words, it's not because something isn't really that someone might choose to delete it from the Metaverse because they don't like it. Let's imagine you don't like folks from a certain tribe, and you may elect to exclude them from your Metaverse. It's entirely up to you whether or not you want to include elements like homeless people or hospitals in your design. What I'm trying to say is that in the Metaverse, people have the ability to create other realities without regard to truth. What's the issue here? They'll have to cope with these issues as soon as they exit the virtual world. Even in the virtual world, they can't remain there forever.

Moderation

Who is going to keep this virtual world safe from racism and other forms of bigotry? Do you know how the moderation is going to be done? In other words, if managing social media sites is already hard, imagine how much more unpleasant it would be to oversee a whole world constructed by several individuals. The question is whether or not Meta will be able to monitor all of its users to ensure that they aren't spreading hateful or racist content. Even if Meta has the resources to do this, it will still be very tough. And if the virtual world is not adequately moderated, it may quickly devolve into anarchy. Because, you know, not everyone will be there only to spread good feelings. We are still human beings and must eat, drink, and sleep. Even if we build a beautiful world in the Metaverse, we'll still have to return to reality and experience it for ourselves. This is a great idea, and it might be the future of social media, in which you can engage more genuinely with other people. Every aspect of your life is up to you; there is no limit to what you may achieve. Social media may lead to addiction, harassment, mental health difficulties, and even security concerns. When it comes to this virtual world, the speed of the 5G connection is a major factor.

Final Thoughts

The term "metaverse" refers to merging the virtual and real worlds. Real-world constraints might be solved by this technology. Stephenson's initial Metaverse vision was exhilarating, but it also carries a lot of potential for damage in the real world and online, notably in terms of crime, addiction, and the deterioration of democratic institutions. There is now heightened friction between governments and large firms when it comes to internet damages, privacy, freedom of expression, etc. As a result, I urge everyone to think carefully about the kind of Metaverse they want to build, as well as who will be in charge of regulating and owning it.

Thank you for reading this book. If you enjoyed it please write a brief review. Your feedback is important to me and will help other readers decide whether to read the book too.

Easy Blockchain Academy